FOURTH IFIP INTERNATIONAL CONFERENCE ON THEORETICAL COMPUTER SCIENCE- TCS 2006

FOURTH IFIP INTERNATIONAL CONFERENCE ON THEORETICAL COMPUTER SCIENCE- TCS 2006

IFIP 19th World Computer Congress, TC-1, Foundations of Computer Science, August 23-24, 2006, Santiago, Chile

Edited by

Gonzalo Navarro
Universidad de Chile, Chile

Leopoldo Bertossi
Carleton University, Canada

Yoshiharu Kohayakawa
Universidade de Sao Paulo, Brazil

Fourth IFIP International Conference on Theoretical Computer Science- TCS 2006

Edited by G. Navarro, L. Bertossi, and Y. Kohayakawa

p. cm. (IFIP International Federation for Information Processing, a Springer Series in Computer Science)

ISSN: 1571-5736 / 1861-2288 (Internet)
ISBN: 10: 1-4899-9050-X
ISBN: 13: 978-1-4899-9050-1
ISBN: 10: 0-387-34735-6 (eBook)
Printed on acid-free paper

9 8 7 6 5 4 3 2 1
springer.com

Preface

The papers contained in this volume were presented at the fourth edition of the IFIP International Conference on Theoretical Computer Science (IFIP TCS), held August 23–24, 2006 in Santiago, Chile. They were selected from 44 papers submitted from 17 countries in response to the call for papers. A total of 16 submissions were accepted as full papers, yielding an acceptance rate of about 36%. Papers solicited for IFIP TCS 2006 were meant to constitute original contributions in two general areas: Algorithms, Complexity and Models of Computation; and Logic, Semantics, Specification and Verification.

The conference also included six invited presentations: Marcelo Arenas (Pontificia Universidad Católica de Chile, Chile), Jozef Gruska (Masaryk University, Czech Republic), Claudio Gutiérrez (Universidad de Chile, Chile), Marcos Kiwi (Universidad de Chile, Chile), Nicola Santoro (Carleton University, Canada), and Mihalis Yannakakis (Columbia University, USA). The abstracts of those presentations are included in this volume. In addition, Jozef Gruska and Nicola Santoro accepted our invitation to write full papers related to their talks. Those two surveys are included in the present volume as well.

TCS is a biannual conference. The first edition was held in Sendai (Japan, 2000), followed by Montreal (Canada, 2002) and Toulouse (France, 2004). TCS is organized by IFIP TC1 (Technical Committee 1: Foundations of Computer Science). TCS 2006 was part of the 19th IFIP World Computer Congress (WCC 2006), constituting the TC1 Track of WCC 2006, and it was sponsored by TC1 and the Center for Web Research (CWR), at the Department of Computer Science of the University of Chile.

We thank the local WCC organizers and TC1 for their support in the organization of IFIP TCS. We also thank the members of the Program Committee and the additional reviewers for providing timely and detailed reviews. Finally, we thank TC1 for inviting us to chair this edition of TCS.

Santiago, Chile

Gonzalo Navarro, TC1 Track Chair & PC Cochair
Leopoldo Bertossi, PC Cochair
Yoshiharu Kohayakawa, PC Cochair

TCS 2006 Organization

Technical Committee 1 (TC1) Chair

Mike Hinchey — NASA, USA

WCC 2006 TC1 Track Chair

Gonzalo Navarro — Center for Web Research
Department of Computer Science
Universidad de Chile, Chile

Program Committee Chairs

Gonzalo Navarro — Center for Web Research
Department of Computer Science
Universidad de Chile, Chile

Leopoldo Bertossi — School of Computer Science
Carleton University, Canada

Yoshiharu Kohayakawa — Department of Computer Science
Institute of Mathematics and Statistics
Universidade de São Paulo, Brazil

External Reviewers

Eugene Asarin
Marie-Pierre Béal
Liming Cai
Ivana Černá
Florian Diedrich
Olga Gerber
Stefan Göller
Serge Grigorieff
David Ilcinkas
Elham Kashefi
Markus Lohrey
Anil Maheshwari
Marc Moreno Maza
Michele Mosca
Pedro Ortega
José Miguel Piquer
Philipp Rohde
Alan Schmitt
Peter Selinger
Imrich Vrtó
Ingo Battenfeld
Flavia Bonomo
Roberto Caldelli
Luc Devroye
Mitre Dourado
Mihaela Gheorghiu
Cristina Gomes Fernandes
Arie Gurfinkel
Philippe Jorrand
Werner Kuich
Sylvain Lombardy
Arnaldo Mandel
Robert W. McGrail
Thomas Noll
Holger Petersen
Iván Rapaport
Mauro San Martín
Stefan Schwoon
Ralf Thöle
Steven (Qiang) Wang

WCC 2006 Local Organization

Mauricio Solar Universidad de Santiago, Chile

Contents

Part I Invited Talks

Part II Invited Papers

Part III Contributed Papers

Contents

Part I Invited Talks

Part II [illegible]

Part III Contributed Papers

Part I

Invited Talks

Locality of Queries and Transformations
(Invited Talk)

Marcelo Arenas *

Center for Web Research &
Computer Science Department, Pontificia Universidad Católica de Chile,
Escuela de Ingeniería - DCC143, Casilla 306, Santiago 22, Chile.
marenas@ing.puc.cl

Abstract

Locality notions in logic say that the truth value of a formula can be determined locally, by looking at the isomorphism type of a small neighborhood of its free variables. Such notions have proved to be useful in many applications especially in computer science. They all, however, refer to isomorphism of neighborhoods, which most local logics cannot test. A more relaxed notion of locality says that the truth value of a formula is determined by what the logic itself can say about that small neighborhood. Or, since most logics are characterized by games, the truth value of a formula is determined by the type, with respect to a game, of that small neighborhood. Such game-based notions of locality can often be applied when traditional isomorphism-based locality cannot.

In the first part of this talk, we show some recent results on game-based notions of locality. We look at two, progressively more complicated locality notions, and we show that the overall picture is much more complicated than in the case of isomorphism-based notions of locality.

In the second part of this talk, we concentrate on the locality of transformations, rather than queries definable by formulas. In particular, we show how the game-based notions of locality can be used in data exchange settings to prove inexpressibility results.

* Partially supported by FONDECYT grant 1050701 and the Millennium Nucleus Center for Web Research, Grant P04-067-F, Mideplan, Chile.

Please use the following format when citing this chapter:

Arenas, M., 2006, in International Federation for Information Processing, Volume 209, Fourth IFIP International Conference on Theoretical Computer Science-TCS 2006, eds. Navarro, G., Bertossi, L., Kohayakwa, Y., (Boston: Springer), p. 3.

From Informatics to Quantum Informatics
(Invited Talk)

Jozef Gruska*

Faculty of Informatics, Masaryk University, Brno, Czech Republic.
gruska@fi.muni.cz

Abstract

During the recent years, exploration of the quantum information processing and communication science and technology got a significant momentum, and it has turned out quite clearly that paradigms, concepts, models, tools, methods and outcomes of informatics play by that a very important role. They not only help to solve problems quantum information processing and communication encounters, but they bring into these investigations a new quality to such an extend that one can now acknowledge an emergence of a quantum informatics as of an important area of fundamental science with contributions not only to quantum physics, but also to (classical) informatics.

The main goal of the talk will be to demonstrate the emergence of quantum informatics, as of a very fundamental, deep and broad science, its outcomes and especially its main new fascinating challenges, from informatics and physics point of view. Especially challenges in the search for new primitives, computation modes, new quality concerning efficiency and feasibility of computation and communication, new quality concerning quantum cryptographic protocols in a broad sense and also in a very new and promising area of quantum formal systems for programming, semantics, reasoning and verification.

The talk is targeted to informaticians that are pedestrians in quantum world, but would like to see what are new driving forces in informatics, where they drive us and how.

* Support of the grants GAČR 201/04/1153 and MSM0021622419 is acknowledged.

Please use the following format when citing this chapter:

Gruska, J., 2006, in International Federation for Information Processing, Volume 209, Fourth IFIP International Conference on Theoretical Computer Science-TCS 2006, eds. Navarro, G., Bertossi, L., Kohayakwa, Y., (Boston: Springer), p. 5.

From Informatics to Quantum Informatics

(Invited Talk)

[illegible] Gruska

[illegible]

[illegible]

RDF as a Data Model
(Invited Talk)

Claudio Gutiérrez *

Center for Web Research, Computer Science Department, Universidad de Chile, Blanco Encalada 2120, 3er piso, Santiago, Chile. cgutierr@dcc.uchile.cl

Abstract

The Resource Description Framework (RDF) is the W3C recommendation language for representing metadata about Web resources. It is the basic data layer of the Semantic Web. The original design was influenced by the Web, library, XML and Knowledge representation communities. The driving idea was a language to represent information in a minimally constraining and flexible way. It turns out that the impact of the proposal goes far beyond the initial goal, particularly as a model for representing information with a graph-like structure.

In the first half of the talk we will review RDF as a database model, that is, from a data management perspective. We will compare it with two data models developed by the database community which have strong similarities with RDF, namely, the semistructured and the graph data models. We will focus the comparison on data structures and query languages.

In the second half of the talk, we will discuss some of the challenges posed by RDF to the Computer Science Theory Community:

1. RDF as data model: Database or knowledge base?
2. Abstract model for RDF: What is a good foundation?
3. Concrete –real life– RDF data: What are the interesting fragments?
4. Theoretical novelties of the RDF data model: Are there any?
5. RDF Query Language: Can the database experience be of any help?
6. Infrastructure for large-scale evaluation of data management methodologies and tools for RDF: Waiting for something?
7. Storing, Indexing, Integrity Constraints, Visualization et al.: Theory is required.

---

* The speaker acknowledges the support of Millennium Nucleus Center for Web Research, Grant P04-067-F, Mideplan, Chile.

Please use the following format when citing this chapter:

Gutiérrez, C., 2006, in International Federation for Information Processing, Volume 209, Fourth IFIP International Conference on Theoretical Computer Science-TCS 2006, eds. Navarro, G., Bertossi, L., Kohayakwa, Y., (Boston: Springer), p. 7.

Adversarial Queueing Theory Revisited
(Invited Talk)

Marcos Kiwi*

Depto. Ing. Matemática & Ctr. Modelamiento Matemático UMI 2807,
Universidad de Chile. Blanco Encalada 2120, piso 5, Santiago, Chile.
www.dim.uchile.cl/~mkiwi.

Abstract

We survey over a decade of work on a classical Queueing Theory problem; the long–term equilibrium of routing networks. However, we do so from the perspective of Adversarial Queueing Theory where no probabilistic assumptions about traffic patterns are made. Instead, one considers a scenario where an adversary controls service requests and tries to congest the network. Under mild restrictions on the adversary, one can often still guarantee the network's stability. We illustrate other applications of an adversarial perspective to standard algorithmic problems. We conclude with a discussion of new potential domains of applicability of such an adversarial view of common computational tasks.

Background

In 1996 Borodin et al. [9] proposed a robust model of queueing theory in network traffic. The gist of their proposal is to replace stochastic assumptions about the packet traffic by restrictions on the packet arrival rate, which otherwise can be under the control of an adversary. Thus, they gave rise to what is currently termed Adversarial Queueing Theory (AQT). In it, the time–evolution of the routing network is viewed as a game between an adversary and a packet scheduling protocol.

The AQT framework originally focussed on the issue of stability of queueing policies and network topologies. Characterizations and efficient algorithms were developed for deciding stability of a collection of networks for specific families of scheduling policies. Generalizations of the AQT framework were proposed. End–to–end packet delay issues were addressed. Time–dependent network topology variants were considered, etc.

We survey a decade of results in AQT. We point to other work where a similar adversarial approach has been successfully developed. We conclude with a discussions of other computational domains where a similar adversarial approach might be fruitfully applied.

* Gratefully acknowledges the support of CONICYT via FONDAP in Applied Mathematics and Anillo en Redes.

Please use the following format when citing this chapter:

Kiwi, M., 2006, in International Federation for Information Processing, Volume 209, Fourth IFIP International Conference on Theoretical Computer Science-TCS 2006, eds. Navarro, G., Bertossi, L., Kohayakwa, Y., (Boston: Springer), pp. 9–10.

Distributed Algorithms for Autonomous Mobile Robots
(Invited Talk)

Nicola Santoro

School of Computer Science, Carleton University, santoro@scs.carleton.ca

Abstract

The distributed coordination and control of a team of autonomous mobile robots is a problem widely studied in a variety of fields, such as engineering, artificial intelligence, artificial life, robotics. Generally, in these areas, the problem is studied mostly from an empirical point of view. Recently, a significant research effort has been and continues to be spent on understanding the fundamental algorithmic limitations on what a set of autonomous mobile robots can achieve. In particular, the focus is to identify the minimal robot capabilities (sensorial, motorial, computational) that allow a problem to be solvable and a task to be performed. In this talk we describe the current investigations on the interplay between robots capabilities, computability, and algorithmic solutions of coordination problems by autonomous mobile robots.

Please use the following format when citing this chapter:

Santoro, N., 2006, in International Federation for Information Processing, Volume 209, Fourth IFIP International Conference on Theoretical Computer Science-TCS 2006, eds. Navarro, G., Bertossi, L., Kohayakwa, Y., (Boston: Springer), p. 11.

Recursion and Probability
(Invited Talk)

Mihalis Yannakakis *

Department of Computer Science, Columbia University,
455 Computer Science Building, 1214 Amsterdam Avenue, Mail Code 0401
New York, NY 10027. mihalis@cs.columbia.edu

Abstract

We discuss recent work on the algorithmic analysis of systems involving recursion and probability. Recursive Markov chains extend ordinary finite state Markov chains with the ability to invoke other Markov chains in a potentially recursive manner. They offer a natural abstract model of probabilistic programs with procedures, and generalize other classical well-studied stochastic models, eg. Multi-type Branching Processes and Stochastic Context-free Grammars. Recursive Markov Decision Processes and Recursive Stochastic Games similarly extend ordinary finite Markov decision processes and stochastic games, and they are natural models for recursive systems involving both probabilistic and nonprobabilistic actions. In a series of recent papers with Kousha Etessami (U. of Edinburgh), we have introduced these models and studied central algorithmic problems regarding questions of termination, reachability, and analysis of the properties of their executions. In this talk we will present some of the basic theory and algorithms.

* Research partially supported by NSF Grant CCF-4-30946.

Please use the following format when citing this chapter:

Yannakakis, M., 2006, in International Federation for Information Processing, Volume 209, Fourth IFIP International Conference on Theoretical Computer Science-TCS 2006, eds. Navarro, G., Bertossi, L., Kohayakwa, Y., (Boston: Springer), p. 13.

Recursion and Probability
(Invited Talk)

Mihalis Yannakakis*

Department of Computer Science, Columbia University
455 Computer Science Building, 1214 Amsterdam Avenue, Mail Code 0401
New York, NY 10027, mihalis@cs.columbia.edu

Abstract.

We discuss recent work on the algorithmic analysis of systems involving recursion and probability. Recursive Markov chains extend ordinary finite state Markov chains with the ability to invoke other Markov chains in a potentially recursive manner. They offer a natural abstract model for probabilistic programs with procedures, and generalize other classical well-studied stochastic models, eg. Multi-type Branching Processes and Stochastic Context-free Grammars. Recursive Markov Decision Processes and Recursive Stochastic Games similarly extend ordinary finite Markov decision processes and stochastic games, and they are natural models for recursive systems involving both probabilistic and nonprobabilistic actions. In a series of recent papers with Kousha Etessami (U. of Edinburgh), we have introduced these models and studied central algorithmic problems regarding questions of termination, reachability, and analysis of the properties of their executions. In this talk we will present some of the basic theory and algorithms.

* Research partially supported by NSF Grant CCF-04-30946.

Please use the following format when citing this chapter:

Yannakakis, M., 2006, in International Federation for Information Processing, Volume 209, Fourth IFIP International Conference on Theoretical Computer Science-TCS 2006, eds. Navarro, G., Bertossi, L., Kohayakawa, Y., (Boston: Springer), p. 13.

Part II

Invited Papers

From Informatics to Quantum Informatics

Jozef Gruska*

Faculty of Informatics, Masaryk University, Brno, Czech Republic
gruska@fi.muni.cz

Abstract. Quantum phenomena exhibit a variety of weird, counter-intuitive, puzzling, mysterious and even entertaining effects. Quantum information processing tries to make an effective use of these phenomena to design new quantum information processing and communication technology and also to get a better understanding of quantum and information processing worlds.
During the recent years, exploration of the quantum information processing and communication science and technology got a significant momentum, and it has turned out quite clearly that paradigms, concepts, models, tools, methods and outcomes of informatics play by that a very important role. They not only help to solve problems quantum information processing and communication encounter, but they bring into these investigations a new quality, and to such an extend, that one can now acknowledge an emergence of a quantum informatics as of an important new area of fundamental science with contributions not only to quantum physics, but also to (classical) informatics itself.
The main goal of this paper is to demonstrate the emergence of quantum informatics, as of a very fundamental, deep and broad science, its outcomes and especially its main new fascinating challenges, from informatics and physics point of view. Especially challenges in the search for new primitives, computation modes, new quality concerning efficiency and feasibility of computation and communication, new quality concerning quantum cryptographic protocols in a broad sense, and also in a very new and promising area of quantum formal systems for programming, semantics, reasoning and verification.
The paper is targeted towards informaticians that are pedestrians in the mysterious quantum world, but would like to see what are new driving forces in informatics, where they drive us, why and how. In the paper, oriented towards broad audience, main mysteries, puzzles and specific features of quantum world are dealt with as well as basic models, laws, limitations, results and the state-of-the-art of quantum information processing and communication.

1 Introduction

In quantum computing we witness a merge of two arguably the most important areas of science of 20th century: quantum physics and informatics. It would

* Support of the grants GAČR 201/04/1153 and MSM0021622419 is acknowledged.

Please use the following format when citing this chapter:

Gruska, J., 2006, in International Federation for Information Processing, Volume 209, Fourth IFIP International Conference on Theoretical Computer Science-TCS 2006, eds. Navarro, G., Bertossi, L., Kohayakwa, Y., (Boston: Springer), pp. 17–46.

glement will have also large practical impacts. For example, to increase quality of measurements (see Childs et al. 1999).

To summarize, quantum entanglement is now considered as a new very important resource for quantum information processing and communication, a resource that has, in addition, the following potentials (see also Gruska 1999-2005, 2003):

- To provide a new gold mine for science and technology;
- To give an edge to quantum versus classical information processing and communication.
- To help to understand better various important physical phenomena.

Surely, the most puzzling and powerful consequence of the existence of entangled quantum states is non-locality their measurements exhibit. Namely, if a set of particles is in an entangled state and one of the particles is measured, then this measurement immediately influences/determines results of subsequent measurements of other particles. There are therefore non-local correlations between results of the measurements of particles in an entangled state.

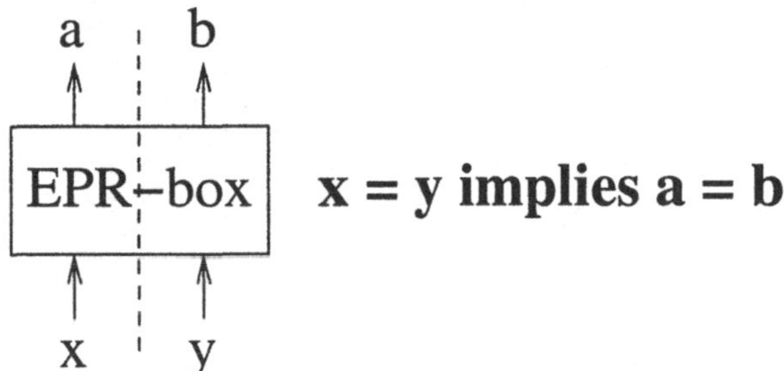

Fig. 1. EPR-box

Quantum nonlocality, exhibited by the measurement of so-called EPR-state $\frac{1}{\sqrt{2}}(|00\rangle + |11\rangle)$, can be modelled by so-called EPR-box shown in Figure 1. There are two parties involved, A and B, much separated by space, that do not communicate with each other, and an imaginary box with two input-output ports, each for one of the parties. If the party A puts in its input port a, it gets out, immediately, an output x, and if the party B puts in an input b it gets out, as the output, immediately, a y. The key property of the EPR-box is that if $a = b$, then $x = y$, no matter in which order the parties put their inputs in and how much time is between their entries. No-scommunication (no-signaling) condition meanes that output of Alice (Bob) does not depend on the input of Bob (Alice). Nonlocality exhibited in the EPR-box can be manifested by the measurement of entangled states, namely of the EPR-state. However, non-locality exhibited in so called PR-box, shown in Figure 2, where inputs and outputs are always in the relation $x \cdot y = (a \oplus b)$, seems to be beyond

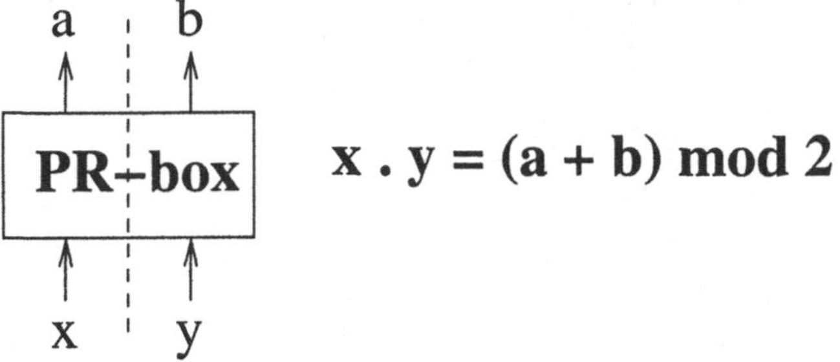

Fig. 2. PR-box

Quantum superposition, that stands for the fact that any quantum state is a weighted superposition (with complex numbers as weights - probability amplitudes specifying probabilities of the transfer from a given state to particular state of the basis) of the states of a basis, is another very special quantum phenomenon. One of the implications of that is *quantum parallelism* that allows, for example, on a single state of n quantum bits to perform, in a single step, an action that corresponds, in some sense, to 2^n computation steps in the classical world. For example, one can get, in one step, into amplitudes of a quantum n-qubit state, all values of a function $f : \{0, \dots, 2^n - 1\} \rightarrow \{0, \dots, 2^n - 1\}$.[6] There is a certain catch in this result/fact, because there is no way to get faithfully out all these values from the resulting quantum state. However, in some important cases, as it is in Shor's algorithm for factorization of integers n, this does not really matter, because what one needs to compute is only a single value, a period of a properly chosen function $f(x) = a^x \bmod n$, and in such a case such a massive quantum parallelism is indeed useful.

A mysterious fact is why we do not observe superposition and entanglement between objects of the classical world if our world is actually fully quantum.[7]

[6] With more technical details, it works as follows: If $f : \{0, 1, \dots, 2^n - 1\} \leftrightarrow \{0, 1, \dots, 2^n - 1\}$, then the mapping $f' : (x, 0) \Longrightarrow (x, f(x))$ is one-to-one and therefore there is a unitary transformation U_f such that for any $x \in \{0, 1, \dots, 2^n - 1\}$.

$$U_f(|x\rangle|0\rangle) \Longrightarrow |x\rangle|f(x)\rangle$$

The state $|\psi\rangle = \frac{1}{\sqrt{2^n}} \sum_{i=0}^{2^n-1} |i\rangle|0\rangle$ can be obtained in a single step, using Hadamard transform, from the basis state $|0^{(n)}\rangle$ and with a *single application* of the mapping U_f, on the state $|\psi\rangle$ we get

$$U_f|\psi\rangle = \frac{1}{\sqrt{2^n}} \sum_{i=0}^{2^n-1} |i\rangle|f(i)\rangle$$

Hence, in a single computation step, 2^n values of f are computed! We have therefore a really massive parallelism.

[7] Of interest in this context are two well known citations: *There is no quantum world. There is only an abstract quantum physical description. It is wrong to think that the*

F[illegible] 3[illegible]

Quantum superposition[illegible] stands for the fact that [illegible] quantum state is [illegible] weighted superposition [illegible] with complex numbers as weights [illegible] probability amplitudes specifying probabilities of the transfer from a given state to particular state of the basis [illegible] the very special quantum phenomenon[illegible] is quantum parallelism that allows, for example, [illegible] state of a quantum [illegible] in a single step, an action that [illegible] in some sense [illegible] in the classical world. For example, [illegible] the [illegible] amplitudes of a quantum [illegible] state [illegible] of a function [illegible]

[illegible] this result [illegible] because there is no way to get [illegible] from the resulting quantum state. However, in some important cases, [illegible] Shor's algorithm [illegible] factorization of integers, this [illegible] because [illegible] needs to [illegible] only a single [illegible] of a [illegible] function [illegible] mod [illegible] such a massive [illegible] parallelism [illegible] used.

[illegible] fact is [illegible] superposition [illegible] between [illegible] of the classical [illegible] quantum[illegible]

[6] With [illegible] details [illegible] as follows [illegible] $\{0, 1, \ldots, 2^n - 1\}$ [illegible] $(x, 0) \to (x, f(x))$ [illegible]

$$U_f|x, 0\rangle \to |x, f(x)\rangle$$

[illegible] the state [illegible] and with [illegible] of the mapping [illegible]

$$[illegible] \sum [illegible]$$

Hence in a single [illegible] step [illegible] are computed. We have therefore a really massive parallelism.

[illegible] interest in this context [illegible] There is no quantum world. There is only an abstract quantum [illegible] It is wrong to think that the

2 Basics of quantum information processing and communication

Quantum physics deals with fundamentals entities of physics — particles, like (a) protons, electrons and neutrons (from which matter is built); (b) photons (which carry electromagnetic radiation); (c) various "elementary particles" which mediate other interactions of physics. We call all of them *particles* in spite of the fact that some of their properties are totally unlike the properties of what we call particles in our ordinary world. (Actually, it is not clear in which sense these "particles" can be said to have properties at all.)

It is also clear that quantum physics is an elegant and conceptually simple theory that describes with surprising precision a large spectrum of the phenomena of Nature. Predictions made on the base of quantum physics have been experimentally verified to 14 orders of precision. No conflict between predictions of the theory and experiments is known. Without quantum physics we cannot explain properties of superfluids, functioning of laser, color of stars, ...

Quantum physics is of special interest for informatics for several reasons. One of them is similarity, in a sense, and close relation between these two areas of science. Indeed, the goal of physics can be seen as to study elements, processes, laws and limitations of the physical world. Goal of informatics can then be seen as to study elements, processes, laws and limitations of the information world. Of large importance is therefore to explore which of these two worlds, physical and information, is more basic, if any, and what are the main relations between the basic concepts, principles, laws and limitations of these two worlds.

Quantum physics can be also seen as an excellent theory to predict probabilities of quantum events. Such predictions are to a large extend based on three simple principles:

- P1 To each transfer, from a quantum state ϕ to a state ψ, a complex number $\langle\psi|\phi\rangle$ is associated, which is called the *probability amplitude* of the transfer, and $|\langle\psi|\phi\rangle|^2$ is then the *probability* of such a transfer.
- P2 If a transfer from a quantum state ϕ to a quantum state ψ can be decomposed into two subsequent transfers $\psi \leftarrow \phi' \leftarrow \phi$, then the resulting amplitude of the transfer form ϕ to ψ is the *product* of the amplitudes of subsequent subtransfers: $\langle\psi|\phi\rangle = \langle\psi|\phi'\rangle\langle\phi'|\phi\rangle$
- P3 If the transfer from a state ϕ to a state ψ has two independent alternatives, then the resulting amplitude is the sum of the amplitudes of two subtransfers, which can be zero if $\alpha = -\beta$. (This has surprising consequences. It may happen that there are two ways, each with positive probability $k = |\alpha|^2$, how to get from a state $|\phi\rangle$ to a state $|\psi\rangle$, but if both options are possible, then such a transfer has zero probability.)

To the physical concept of *quantum system*, the mathematical concept of the *Hilbert space* is usually associated, and to the physical concept of a (pure) state of a closed (that is not interacting with environment) quantum system, the mathematical concept of a vector/state of a Hilbert space corresponds.

A *quantum bit*, called usually *qubit*, is then a quantum state in H_2, $|\phi\rangle = \alpha|0\rangle + \beta|1\rangle$, where $\alpha, \beta \in \mathbf{C}$ are such that $|\alpha|^2 + |\beta|^2 = 1$ ($\{|0\rangle, |1\rangle\}$ is the *standard basis* of H_2).

Important operations on one qubit are Hadamard transform, represented by the matrix

$$H = \frac{1}{\sqrt{2}}\begin{pmatrix} 1 & 1 \\ 1 & -1 \end{pmatrix}^{11} \text{ and Pauli matrices } \sigma_x = \begin{pmatrix} 0 & 1 \\ 1 & 0 \end{pmatrix} \text{ and } \sigma_z = \begin{pmatrix} 1 & 0 \\ 0 & -1 \end{pmatrix}.$$

Now we can say that the essence of the difference between the *classical computers* and *quantum computers* is in the way information is stored and processed. In *classical computers*, information is represented on *macroscopic level*, by *bits*, which can take on one of two values, 0 or 1. In *quantum computers*, information is represented on *microscopic level*, using *qubits*, which can take on any from uncountable many values $\alpha|0\rangle + \beta|1\rangle$, where α, β are arbitrary complex numbers such that $|\alpha|^2 + |\beta|^2 = 1$.

Very important is also difference between the ways compound classical and compound quantum systems are created. In the classical case, any state of a composed system is composed of the states of subsystems. This is not so in the quantum case.

If a Hilbert space $\mathcal{H}$ ($\mathcal{H}'$) corresponds to a quantum system $\mathcal{S}$ ($\mathcal{S}'$), and $\{\alpha_i\}_i$ ($\{\beta_j\}_j$) is a basis of $\mathcal{H}$ ($\mathcal{H}'$), then the tensor product of $\mathcal{H}$ and $\mathcal{H}'$, notation $\mathcal{H} \otimes \mathcal{H}'$, corresponds to the quantum system composed of $\mathcal{S}$ and $\mathcal{S}'$ and this Hilbert space has a (standard) basis consisting of all tensor products of states $|\alpha_i\rangle$ and $|\beta_j\rangle$.

For example, Hilbert space $\mathcal{H}_4$ can be seen as the tensor product of two one-qubit Hilbert spaces, $\mathcal{H}_2 \otimes \mathcal{H}_2$, and therefore one of its (standard) basis consists of the states $|0\rangle \otimes |0\rangle$, $|0\rangle \otimes |1\rangle$, $|1\rangle \otimes |0\rangle$, $|1\rangle \otimes |1\rangle$ These states are usually denoted shortly as:

$$|00\rangle, \quad |01\rangle, \quad |10\rangle, \quad |11\rangle.$$

Another important orthogonal basis in $\mathcal{H}_4$ consists of the following four so-called Bell states:

$$|\Phi^+\rangle = \frac{1}{\sqrt{2}}(|00\rangle + |11\rangle, \quad |\Phi^-\rangle = \frac{1}{\sqrt{2}}(|00\rangle - |11\rangle),$$

$$|\Psi^+\rangle = \frac{1}{\sqrt{2}}(|01\rangle + |10\rangle, \quad |\Psi^-\rangle = \frac{1}{\sqrt{2}}(|01\rangle - |10\rangle).$$

Similarly, the (standard) basis states of an n-qubit Hilbert space $\mathcal{H}_{2^n}$ are the states

$$|i_1 i_2 \dots i_n\rangle = |i_1\rangle \otimes \dots \otimes |i_n\rangle,$$

where $i_k \in \{0, 1\}$ for all k.

[11] Hadamard operation transforms the standard basis $\{|0\rangle, |1\rangle\}$ into the dual basis, consisting of the vectors $\{|0'\rangle = \frac{1}{\sqrt{2}}(|0\rangle + |1\rangle), |1'\rangle = \frac{1}{\sqrt{2}}(|0\rangle - |1\rangle)\}$

We can now also say that important properties of the classical information are: (a) transmission of information in time and space is very easy (b) making unlimited number of copies of information is very easy. On the other side, important properties of the quantum information are: (a) transmission of the quantum information in time and space is very difficult; (b) there is no way to make faithful copies of unknown quantum information. (c) attempts to measure the quantum information destroy it, in general.

3 Outcomes and challenges of quantum computation

Quantum polynomial time algorithms of Shor, in 1994, that could be used to break important classical cryptosystems, were so far main apt killers for quantum information processing. A natural quantum version of the Fourier transform has been the main tool[13] and the quantum Fourier transform has been also used later to design various other quantum algorithms that are more efficient than the most efficient classical algorithms for the same algorithmic problems. Main generalized result is that there are quantum polynomial time algorithms for so called Hidden Subgroup Problem for Abelian groups.[14] Perhaps the most important open problem in the design of quantum algorithms is to determine whether the Hidden Subgroup Problem is always solvable in polynomial time also for non-Abelian groups. Would this be true, it would imply, for example, that there is a quantum polynomial time algorithm also for the graph isomorphism problem.

Even of large impact on the design of efficient quantum algorithms have had the discovery of Grover (1996). who has shown that one can find in an unordered database of N elements a unique element satisfying a given condition P in $\sqrt{N}$ quantum steps. His idea was generalized and applied in numerous ways and resulted also into so-called probability amplification technique. Recently, quantum random walks got a momentum as a way to design quantum algorithms (see Aharonov et al., 2001). Of interest are also non-traditional modes of quantum computation as adiabatic (see Farhi et al., 2000). Several ingenious techniques have also been developed to prove lower bounds: for example, the polynomial method (Beals et al., 1998), the quantum adversary method (Ambainis, 2000) and its various variants. They have been used to show a variety of impressive lower bound results (see Gruska, 1999-2005, for an overview).

[13] Also other quantum generalizations of transforms known from signal processing and applied mathematics have turned out to be useful for the design of quantum algorithms.

[14] The Hidden Subgroup Problem is the following one: Given is an (efficiently computable) function $f : G \rightarrow R$, where G is a finite group and R a finite set and a *promise* that there exists a subgroup $G_0 \leq G$ such that f is constant on any left cosset and distinct on different cossets of G_0. The task is to find a generating set for G_0 (in polynomial time (in $\lg |G|$) in the number of calls to the oracle for f and in the overall polynomial time).

We can now say, that important properties of the classical information are (a) transmission of information in time and space is very easy (b) making unlimited number of copies of information is very easy. On the other side, important properties of the quantum information are (a) transmission of the quantum information in time and space is very difficult; (b) there is no way to make faithful copies of unknown quantum information; (c) attempts to measure the quantum information alter it irreversibly in general.

[illegible] Potentials and challenges of quantum computation

Quantum polynomial time algorithms of Shor in 1994, that could be used to break (most of) current classical cryptosystems, were so far main [illegible] killers for quantum information processing. A natural quantum version of the Fourier transform has been the main tool used. The quantum Fourier transform has been also used later to design various other quantum algorithms that are more efficient than the best ones known classically, [illegible] for the computational [illegible] problems. Most generalized results [illegible] that there are quantum polynomial time algorithms to solve the Hidden Subgroup Problem for Abelian groups.[14] It seems that the most important open problem in the design of quantum algorithms is to determine whether the Hidden Subgroup Problem is solvable in polynomial time also for non-Abelian groups. Would this be true, it would imply, for example, that there is a quantum polynomial time algorithm also for the graph isomorphism problem.

Even more important [illegible] in the design of efficient quantum algorithms has had the discovery of Grover (1996) who has shown that one can find in an unordered database of N elements an element satisfying a given condition in $O(\sqrt{N})$ quantum steps. This idea was generalized and applied in many ways and resulted [illegible] amplitude amplification technique. [illegible] quantum random walks [illegible] of quantum algorithms [illegible] (see [illegible] et al. 2001) [illegible] new [illegible] non-trivial [illegible] (Farhi et al., 2000) [illegible] quantum [illegible] (see [illegible] 2001, [illegible]).

[13] Of other [illegible], [illegible] transforms [illegible] digital signal processing [illegible] have been shown to be useful for the design of quantum algorithms.

[14] The Hidden Subgroup Problem is the following one: Given is an (efficiently computable) function $f : G \to X$, G is a finitely generated group and X a finite set and a promise that there exists a subgroup H such that f is constant on any left coset and distinct on different cosets of H. The task is to find a generating set for G in polynomial time (in $\lg |G|$) in the number of calls to the oracle for f and in the overall polynomial time).

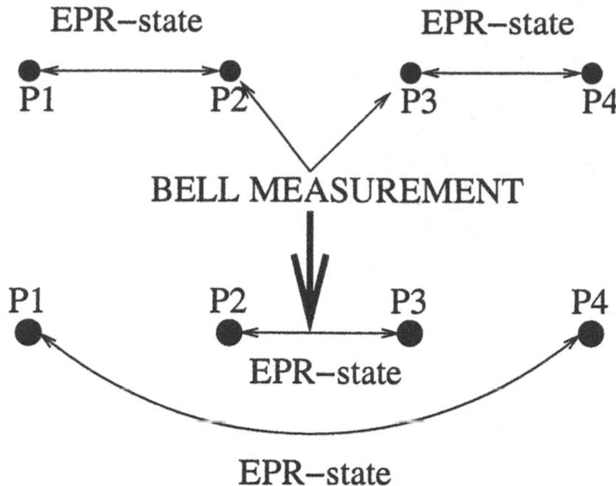

Fig. 3. Entanglement swapping

following three operations: CNOT, Hadamard and $\sigma_z^{1/4} = \begin{pmatrix} 1 & 0 \\ 0 & e^{\frac{\pi}{4}i} \end{pmatrix}$. For computational purposes with classical input and output, universal is also the set of only two simple gates: the Toffoli gate and the Hadamard gate (Shi, 2002). This actually means that in order to get universality for quantum computation one has to add the Hadamard gate to the Toffoli gate that is universal for classical reversible computation. (Hadamard gate can actually create a perfectly random bit.) It is also known that any n-qubit unitary operation can be implemented by a circuit consisting of $\mathcal{O}(4^n)$ gates CNOT and one-qubit gates (see Vartianen et al., 2003). One of the recent surprising results in QIPC is that universal, from the computational point of view, are also circuits with gates performing only measurements and that what is needed for that are measurement-gates from only a very small set of gates. Measurement gates can be specified by Hermitian operators and measurements then correspond to the orthogonal basis created by the orthogonal set of eigenvectors of these Hermitian matrices. Actually, universal is a set of only four different Hermitian operators (measurements, see Perdrix, 2004). Measurement-based computations are probabilistic, up to a Pauli matrix, but this is only a small handicap. Another surprising model of universal computation are so-called one-way computers at which computation starts with a special entangled, so-called cluster state, but then only one qubit measurements are performed (Raussendorf and Briegel, 2000). All these results indicate that search for primitives in quantum computation is likely still to be full of surprises and options, what is actually not so strange because Nature offers so many way quantum information processing processes can be exhibited.

CNOT gate has to be able to make entangled two particles that have never before interacted, see Figure 3.

Fig. 3. Entanglement swapping

[illegible]

[illegible]

Another very basic model of quantum computation are quantum finite automata. Actually, there are several versions of them. Three very basic problems for models of quantum automata to explore are: (a) What is the class of languages accepted by a given model? (b) Which accepting probabilities can be achieved with a given model of automata? (c) How does the size of automata of the model (the number of states) compares to the size of equivalent minimal deterministic finite automata?

Comparing with classical finite automata, quantum finite automata have special strength, due to the power of quantum superposition (parallelism), but also a special weakness, due to the requirement that they have to be reversible. (It is important to notice that negative impacts of reversibility can be, to a large extent, compensated by a suitable distribution of suitable measurements.) For some models, quantum finite automata accept a smaller class of languages as regular languages and for some other models they accept exactly the class of regular languages. Of large importance is what kind of measurements are performed and which measurement policy is used. For example, a measurement is performed after each computation step or only at the end of computation - two extreme options. It has also be shown that in some cases quantum finite automata can be exponentially more succinct than classical deterministic finite automata. However, in some cases the opposite situation occurs. The very basic models of quantum finite automata, so called one-way (or real time) quantum automata, are defined similarly as probabilistic automata, only instead of probabilities, probability amplitudes are used and there is one additional requirement, namely that the overall evolution has to be unitary. More peculiar are quantum two-way automata. In the most basic model, they are a natural generalization of the classical two-way probabilistic finite automata. Quantum two-way automata can accept, with high probability, even some non-regular or non-context-free languages. In another model, quantum two way automata work almost as classical ones, they only have an additional quantum memory and at each step they either perform a usual classical move and a unitary operation on the state of their quantum memory, or a measurement on quantum memory is performed that then specifies, in a random way, the next move. Such automata have been shown to be much more powerful than classical probabilistic two-way finite automata (Ambainis and Watrous, 1999), even in the case quantum memory is restricted to one qubit (for an overview of concepts and results concerning quantum finite automata, see Gruska (2000).

The very basic model of quantum Turing machines, originally due to Deutsch (1985), is again a modification of that of a probabilistic Turing machine - probabilities are only replaced by probability amplitudes. However, a non-trivial additional requirement is that the overall evolution of a quantum Turing machine has to be unitary. A state of such a quantum Turing machines can be seen as a weighted superposition of many configurations of a classical Turing machines. This model has been used to define basic quantum complexity classes and to develop quantum structural complexity. Such a model has classical inputs and outputs, only its evolution is quantum. Two new quite different models

and quantum complexity theory in particular, is to help to resolve this puzzle. In behind is actually question whether our world is polynomial or exponential, as pointed out by Aaronson (2005). The fact that such a basic question is unresolved makes also of large importance the task to study more elementary models as are that of quantum circuits, quantum programmable circuits and quantum finite automata.

Main new challenges of quantum complexity theory can be seen as follows (see also Gruska (2005): (a) To help to determine whether we can build (and how) powerful quantum computers. (b) To help to determine whether we can effectively factorize large integers using a quantum computer. (c) To use complexity theory paradigms to classify quantum states (d) To use complexity theory (computational and communication) to study quantum entanglement and nonlocality. (e) To use complexity theory to determine power of decoherence and to find ways to fight decoherence. (f) To use complexity theory to formulate laws and limitations of physics. (g) To study feasibility in physics on a more abstract level. (h) To study various quantum theory interpretations from a new and more abstract (complexity) point of view. (e) To develop a more firm basis for quantum mechanics. (f) To develop new tests of quantum mechanics.

4 Outcomes and challenges of quantum communication

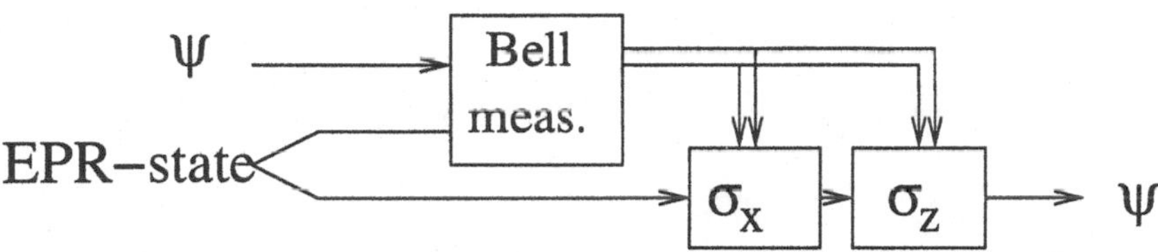

Fig. 4. Quantum teleportation

Quantum teleportation was the first and is still the most amazing new feature of quantum communication. The basic idea is very simple: if two parties, say Alice and Bob, share two particles, say A and B, in the EPR-state and Alice gets a new particle P in an unknown state $|\psi\rangle = \alpha|0\rangle + \beta|1\rangle$, then by performing the Bell measurement (that is the measurement using the Bell states), on her two particles, Bob's particle gets with the same probability into one of the four states $|\psi\rangle$, $\sigma_x|\psi\rangle$, $\sigma_z|\psi$ and $\sigma_x\sigma_z|\psi\rangle$, and Alice gets information (say, in the form of two bits) which of these four cases took place. If Alice sends this information to Bob, through a classical public channel, for example by email. Bob can then make his particle B to get into (still unknown for him) state $|\phi\rangle$ by performing on his particle one of the operations σ_x, σ_z or $\sigma_x\sigma_z$, because $\sigma_x^2 = \sigma_z^2 = I$. This way Alice can teleport, not knowing what, to not knowing where.

is perhaps the most counterintuitive way to generate entangled states. To decide whether a given mixed state is entangled is another important problem and many methods to do that were developed. Problem how many pure and maximally entangled states one can get from a given set of mixed states is also pretty good understand and many methods to do that were explored. The same is true for entanglement concentration problem: to get some maximally entangled pure states from a set of less entangled pure states. Discovery of bound entangled states - those mixed entangled states from which one cannot get pure entanglement - has been a big surprise and so were discovery of various properties of such states and of various ways how bound entangled states can be useful. Study of entanglement monotones, invariants and measures[17] is another important area of research with many interesting and important results. The fact that entanglement can be used as a catalyst that can help, without being destroyed, to transform one quantum state to another using local quantum operations and classical communication (LOCC) has been another surprising discovery. laws and limitations of entanglement sharing and also quantitative and qualitative classification of multipartite states is another big challenge. On a more applied level, a big challenge is still to understand how important is entanglement for quantum computation. Another big challenge is to get a proper understanding how frequent is entanglement and how robust such a concept can be (for example that in some vicinity of some entangled states all states are entangled). For a review of results in all these areas see Gruska (2003).

Concerning quantum channels perhaps the main issue is to study various types of channels and various capacities. Entanglement plays by that a very important role. An important task was to find nice formulas to express different capacities and to find relations between different capacities, see Nielsen and Chuang (2000) and Gruska (1999-2005).

5 Outcomes and challenges of quantum cryptography

So called BB84 quantum protocol, due to Bennett and Brassard (1984), for generation of classical shared and perfectly secret keys, and numerous proofs, using a variety of techniques, under more and more realistic conditions (concerning perfection of the photon sources, quality of channels and perfection of the receivers), that BB84 protocol is unconditionally secure, have been the first highlights of quantum cryptography. The first experiment, due to Bennett and Brassard (1989), demonstrated feasibility of such a protocol for the distance of 32 cm. This has been increased, step by step to 120-150 km what used to be seen as limit set up by photon loses and detectors loses. Zhang et al., (2005) claim to increase maximal distance to 260km exploiting entanglement swapping

[17] An important measure is so called entanglement of formation E_f (how many maximally entangled states are needed to create a given state) is one of such measures and the additivity problem for this measure - that is if always $E_f(\rho_1 \otimes \rho_2) = E_f(\rho_1) + E_f(\rho_2)$) - is a very important open problem.

[illegible] to generate entangled states. To [illegible] entangled is another important problem and many methods to do that were developed. Problem how many pure and maximally entangled states one can get from a given set of mixed states is also [illegible] methods to do that were explored. The same [illegible] entangled [illegible] pure states. [illegible] entangled states [illegible] from which one cannot get pure [illegible] bound [illegible] research with [illegible] and important [illegible] that can help, without [illegible] using local quantum [illegible] has been another surprising [illegible] sharing, and also quantitatively [illegible] states is another big challenge. [illegible] important [illegible] another big challenge is to get a proper [illegible] and how much such a concept [illegible] entangled states all states [illegible] review [illegible] (2009).

[illegible] entangled [illegible] Nielsen and [illegible] (2002).

6 Outcomes and challenges of quantum cryptography

[illegible] and Brassard (1984) [illegible] [illegible] and much [illegible] and numerous protocols [illegible] quality of [illegible] correction [illegible] the first [illegible] The first [illegible] to Bennett and [illegible] distance of [illegible] to 120-150 km [illegible] loss and detectors losses, Zhao et al. (2006) [illegible] ment [illegible]

[illegible] issue [illegible] of [illegible] how many max- [illegible] entangled states are needed [illegible] such measures [illegible] and the additivity problem for these measures [illegible] always $E_f(\rho \otimes \sigma) = E_f(\rho) + E_f(\sigma)$, [illegible] is a very important open problem.

one can get the qubit back perfectly, only two classical bits are sufficient (and necessary) - see Mosca et al. (2000).

6 Outcomes and challenges of quantum formal systems

In the classical informatics, the development of high level formal systems, based on the concepts and tools of logic and formal semantics, to precisely specify and reason about computation, cooperation and communication processes in general, and about algorithms, protocols and concurrent systems in particular, has turned out of large importance for design and analysis of provably correct software for computation and communication systems. At the same time, this line of research in the classical informatics has brought theoretically surprisingly deep and practically very important and useful insights and outcomes concerning the laws and limitations of very large information processing, cooperation and communication systems.

Classical complexity theory research community, with emphasis on lower bounds, clearly underestimated, for a long time, an importance of this area of research. However, step by step, this, logic and formal semantics and abstraction based, area of research started actually to dominate in broadly understood theoretical computer science and there are good reasons to believe that it can be so, and even more, also in the area of the classical/quantum computing. Moreover, there is also a good chance that also this area of research can bring new view points and tools to deal with quantum mechanics in general, and with quantum information processing and communication in particular, and to put new lights on these areas.

There are two main reasons why quantum (quantum/classical) programming theory is much needed and has a chance to be insightful and useful. At first, any formal description of algorithms, protocols and processes, that make use of quantum phenomena has to to take into account both quantum and classical computation, cooperation and communication components and assemble them in such a way that they coexist, communicate and cooperate. (For example, preparation of quantum states is an (always inevitable) example of classical/quantum interaction and quantum measurement (and control actions that depend on its random outcome) is an (always inevitable) example of a classical/quantum/classical interaction. One can also say that classical/quantum interaction and cooperation is inherent in the classical/quantum information processing and communication. Fortunately, concepts and tools developed in the classical programming theory have been so abstract and powerful that they are now quite easy to adjust to cover classical-quantum case in a homogeneous way. Secondly, concepts and tools developed in the classical programming theory are so abstract and powerful that they allow to generalize naturally current (von Neumann) quantum mechanical framework that was created to deal just with "minimal view of quantum mechanics". This more general framework, that

one can [illegible] back [illegible] only two classical bits are sufficient (and [illegible] Moore et al. (2000)).

6 Outcomes and challenges of quantum informal systems

[illegible] for [illegible] analyses of provably correct [illegible] for [illegible] and communications [illegible]. At the same time, this line of research in the classical information [illegible] brought theoretically surprisingly deep and practically very important and useful insights and outcomes concerning the laws and limitations of [illegible] information [illegible] and communication systems.

[illegible] believe that [illegible] quantum computing. [illegible] research [illegible] in general, and with [illegible] in particular [illegible] and [illegible] put [illegible]

[illegible] classical [illegible] them [illegible] and [illegible] classical [illegible] the class [illegible] with [illegible] process [illegible] classical programming [illegible] and powerful [illegible] are now quite [illegible] classical [illegible] have [illegible] level [illegible] classical programming [illegible] allow to generalize naturally [illegible] to deal just with [illegible] new [illegible]

can be realized in a fault-tolerant way. All that has been achieved by a clever generalizations of the ideas known from the classical linear codes. Second major breakthrough came with the discovery of threshold theorems that say that if elementary gates and channels have certain reliability,'then, using so-called concatenated codes, arbitrarily long, in time and space, reliable quantum information processing and communication is possible. Each such threshold theorem establishes some bounds and any improvement of upper and lower bounds on such thresholds is currently an important task and challenge that could help to see realistically what needs to be achieved and where we are currently concerning the development of elements for QIPC. Concerning fighting the decoherence, the main current challenges are: (a) to develop error models for specific QIPC technologies and for them also quantum error correcting codes; (b) to develop error detecting and preventing codes; (c) to generalize the concept of errors (see, for example, the concept of *nice error bases*, see, for example, Klappenecker and Rotteller (2000); (d) to explore various ideas of so called error-free subspaces.

8 Outcomes and challenges in beating quantum limitations and barriers

We will discuss here only three limitations: the one established by no-cloning theorem and its variations (no-deletion theorem and so on), and so called Turing barrier and **BQP**-barrier.

Buzek and Hillery (1996) were first to show that one can determine a reachable upper bound on the best way how to do cloning on qubits in an approximate way. Their results have been generalized in various ways to cover Hilbert space of larger dimension and other mathematically well defined operation that cannot be realized perfectly physically.

Finally, let us discuss Turing barrier or better Church-Turing barrier. Turing thesis, or Church-Turing thesis, can be formulated as follows: Every function that can be computed by what we would naturally regard as an algorithm is a computable function, and vice versa. So called Turing principle, formulated by Deutsch, reads as follows: Every finitely realizable physical system can be perfectly simulated by a universal computing machine operating by finite means. It is important to realize that Church-Turing thesis can be seen as one of the guiding principles for mathematic, physics and informatics and that since its very beginning Church-Turing thesis is under permanent attack from both mathematical and physical sciences. In mathematics and computing, all these attack used to be based on uncritical use of infinity, continua and density. It is also important to realize that recognition of physical aspects of the Church-Turing thesis has had important impacts also for physics. Turing barrier puts important restriction when searching for new physical theories

It is interesting and important to ask and answer the question what is the sense of trying to beat such a barrier that seems to be unbeatable. To that one can say the following: (a) It is interesting and intellectually usually very

can be realized [illegible] that has been achieved by a clever general [illegible] classical [illegible] codes. Second [illegible] for [illegible] threshold theorems that say that if elementary [illegible] certain reliability, then using so-called [illegible] quantum infor[illegible] threshold theorem [illegible] bounds on [illegible] to [illegible] the main [illegible] to develop [illegible] error-correcting [illegible] the concept of errors (see, for example, the [illegible] Klappenecker and [illegible] (2007); (d) [illegible]

[illegible] Outcomes and challenges in [illegible] quantum [illegible]

[illegible] only three [illegible] the [illegible] and so-called Turing [illegible]

[illegible] complete [illegible] quantum [illegible] physically.

[illegible] Church–Turing thesis [illegible] follows: Every function that can be computed [illegible] computation is a [illegible] Deutsch [illegible] used [illegible] of the Church–Turing thesis [illegible] important [illegible]

[illegible] what is the [illegible] of trying to beat such a barrier that seems to be unbeatable. [illegible] one can see the following: (a) It is interesting and fundamentally [illegible]

relativistic Turing machine that models the above relativistic computer and that recognizes exactly Δ_2 set of Arithmetical Hierarchy.

BQP-barrier says that effectively computable are problems that are in **BQP**. The question whether we can beat this barrier seems to be more intriguing and it does not have (yet) such a statue of unbeatability as other barriers. Actually, previous versions of this barrier, that included complexity classes **P** and **BPP**, seem to be beaten, though we are not sure, yet.[24]

There are still many mysteries concerning the class **BQP**. Not only we do not know whether **NP** $\subseteq$ **BQP**, but we even do not know whether **NP** $\subseteq$ **BQP** would imply **P**=**NP**.

Related to that is the **NP**-barrier that says that not all **NP**-complete problems can be solved in polynomial time using the resources of the physical world.

There have been many attempts to beat **NP**-barrier and they are to large extend well summarized and analyzed by Aaronson (2005a). He discuss such ideas as quantum adiabatic computing, variations on quantum mechanics (non-linearity, hidden variable theories), analog computing, but also more esoteric ones as relativity computing[25], time travel computing, quantum field, string and gravity theories, and even *anthropic computing*[26] Main conclusions are: (a) searches for overcoming **NP** barriers are important, they can bring a better understanding of the physical worlds; (b) none of the well specified attempts is successful - they usually forget to count all resources needed and/or all physics known.

In connection with **NP**-barrier, of interest and importance is the question, see Aaronson (2005) whether we should not take "**NP**-hardness assumption" saying that **NP**-*complete problems are intractable in the physical world* as a new principle of physics (as, for example, Second Law of Thermodynamic is). This principle starts to be used. Perhaps main problem with it is that why **NP**, why not **BQP** or **#P** or **PSPACE**.

On a more philosophical level, all above considerations lead to two basic questions: Is universe computable? Is it efficiently computable? It is nowadays clear that the assumption of the founders of the Hilbert space quantum mechanics that any state and observable are in principle implementable is wrong. That would allow to compute uncomputable functions. Less clear is what to consider as feasible.

[24] In this connection it is perhaps worth to observe that, on one side, likely nobody believes that classes **P** and **BPP** are identical, and, on the other side, Impagliazo and Widgerson (1997) gave quite convincing evidence that they are.

[25] The idea behind relativity computing can be informally described as that one makes a computer to deal with an intractable problem, then boards a spaceship and accelerates it to nearly speed of light. After returning to Earth, answer will wait for him (though all his friends would be long dead).

[26] They are models of computing in which the probability of one's own existence might depend on a computer's output.

References

1. S. Aaronson. Multilinear formulas and skepticism of quantum computing. quant-ph/0311039, 2003.
2. S. Aaronson. Is quantum mechanics an island in Theoryspace? quant-ph/0401062, 2004.
3. S. Aaronson. Are quantum states exponentially long vectors? quant-ph/0507242, 2005.
4. S. Aaronson. NP-complete problems and physical reality. quant-ph/0502072, 2005a.
5. S. Abramsky and B. Coecke. A categorical semantics of quantum protocols. quant-ph/0402130, 2004.
6. D. Aharonov, A. Ambainis, J. Kempe, and U. Vazirani. Quantum walks on graphs. Proc. of 33th STOC, 50-59, 2000.
7. A. Ambainis. Quantum lower bounds by quantum arguments. quant-ph/0002066, 2000.
8. A. Ambainis. Quantum walks and and their algorithmic applications. quant-ph/0403120, 2004.
9. A. Ambainis and J. Watrous. Two-way finite automata with quantum and classical states. quant-ph/9911009, 1999.
10. Ch. H. Bennett Logical reversibility of computation. *IBM Journal of Research and Development*, 17:525–532, 1973.
11. Ch. H. Bennett and G. Brassard. The dawn of a new era for quantum cryptography. The experimental prototype is working! *SIGACT News*, 20(4):78–82, 1989.
12. Ch. H. Bennett and G. Brassard. Quantum cryptography: public key distribution and coin tossing. In *Proceedings of IEEE Conference on Computers, Systems and Signal processing, Bangalore (India)*, pages 175–179, 1984.
13. Ch. H. Bennett, G. Brassard, C. Crépeau, R. Jozsa, A. Peres, and W. K. Wootters Teleporting an unknown quantum state via dual classical and Einstein-Podolsky-Rosen channels. *Physical Review Letters*, 70:1895–1899, 1993.
14. G. Brassard, A. Broadlent, and A. Tapp. Quantum telepathy. quant-ph/0306042, 2003.
15. B. Brezger, L. Hackermüller, S. Uttenthaler, J. Petschinka, M. Arndt, and A. Zeilinger. Matter-wave interferometer for large molecules. quant-ph/0202158, 2002.
16. H. Buhrman, R. Cleve, and A. Wigderson. Quantum versus classical communication complexity. In *Proceedings of 30th STOC*, pages 63–68, 1998.
17. V. Bužek and M. Hillery. Quantum copying: beyond the no-cloning theorem. *Physical Review A*, 54:1844–1852, 1996.
18. N. Cerf, N. Gisin, S. Masar, and S. Popescu. Quantum entanglement can be simulated without communication. *Physical Review Letter*, 94:220403, 2005.
19. A. M. Childs, J. Preskill, and J. Renes. Quantum information and precision measurement. quant-ph/9904021, 1999.
20. B. S. Cirel'son. Quantum generalization's of Bell's inequality. *Letters in Mathematical Physics*, 4(2):93–100, 1980.
21. B. Coecke. Kindergarten quantum mechanics. quant-ph/0510032, 2005.
22. R. de Wolf. Lower bounds on metric rigidity via a quantum measurement. quant-ph/0505188, 2005.

47. G. Mitchison and R. Jozsa. Counterfactual computations. quant-ph/9907007, 1999.
48. M. Mosca, A. Tapp, and R. de Wolf. Private quantum channels and the cost of randomizing quantum information. quant-ph/0003101, 2000.
49. M. A. Nielsen and I. I. Chuang. *Quantum information processing.* Cambridge University Press, 2000.
50. M. A. Nielsen and I. L. Chuang. Programmable quantum gate arrays. quant-ph/9703032, 1997.
51. S. Perdrix. State transfer instead of teleportation in measurement-based quantum computation. quant-ph/0402204, 2004.
52. S. Perdrix and P. Jorrand. Classically controlled quantum computing. quant-ph/0407008, 20004a.
53. S. Perdrix and Ph. Jorrand. Measurement-based quantum Turing machines and questions of universalities. quant-ph/0402156, 2004.
54. S. Popescu and D. Rohrlich. Causality and non-locality as axioms for quantum mechanics. quant-ph/9709026, 1997.
55. R. Raussendorf and H. J. Briegel. Quantum computing by measurements only. *Phys. Rev. Lett, 86*, 2004.
56. R. Raz. Exponential separation of quantum and classical communication complexity. In *Proceedings of* 31*st ACM STOC*, pages 358–367, 1999.
57. V. Scarani. Feats, features and failures of the PR-box. quant-ph/0603017, 2006.
58. V. Scarani, W. Tittel, H. Zbinden, and N. Gisin. The speed of quantum information and the preference frame: analysis of experimental data. quant-ph/0007008, 2000.
59. B. Schumacher and R. F. Werner. Reversible quantum cellular automata. quant-ph/0405184, 2004.
60. Y. Shi. Both Toffoli and controlled-NOT need little help to do universal computation. quant-ph/0205115, 2002.
61. P. W. Shor. Algorithms for quantum computation: discrete log and factoring. In *Proceedings of 36th IEEE FOCS*, pages 124–134, 1994.
62. P. W. Shor Scheme for reducing decoherence in quantum computer memory. *Physical Review A*, 52:2493–2496, 1995.
63. P. W. Shor Fault-tolerant quantum computation. In *Proceedings of 37th IEEE FOCS*, pages 56–65, 1996.
64. T. Short, N. Gisin, and S. Popescu. The physics of no-bit commitment generalized quantum non-locality versus oblivious transfer. quant-ph/0504134, 2005.
65. R. Somma, H. Barnum, and G. Ortiz. Efficient solvability of hamiltonians and limits on the power of some quantum computational models. quant-ph/0601030, 2006.
66. W. van Dam. Implausible consequences of superstrong nonlocality. quant-ph/0501159, 2005.
67. J. van Leeuwen and J. Wiedermann. *Mathematics unlimited, 2001 and beyond*, chapter The Turing machine paradigm in contemporary computing, pages 1139–1156. Springer Verlag, 2001.
68. J. J. Vartiainen, M. Möttönen, and M. M. Salomaa. Efficient decomposition of quantum gates. quant-ph/0312218, 2003.
69. F. Vatan and C. Williams. Optimal realization of a general two-qubit quantum gate. quant-ph/0308006, 2003.
70. F. Vatan and C. Williams. Realization of a general three-qubit quantum gate. quant-ph/0401178, 2004.

47. [illegible] quant-ph/0002/06[illegible]
48. [illegible] quantum channels and the cost of [illegible] quantum information [illegible] 2006.
49. [illegible] Nielsen and I. L. Chuang. [illegible] Cambridge [illegible]
50. [illegible]
51. [illegible]
52. [illegible]
53. [illegible] Perdrix and [illegible] measurement-based quantum Turing machines and [illegible] quant-ph/0402156, 200[illegible]
54. S. Perdrix and [illegible] Causality and non-locality [illegible] for quantum mechanics [illegible]
55. R. Raussendorf and H. J. Briegel. [illegible] quantum computing [illegible] measurements only. *Phys. Rev. Lett.* 86 [illegible]
56. [illegible] quantum and classical [illegible] STOC [illegible]
57. [illegible]
58. [illegible] The speed of [illegible] quant-ph/0007008 [illegible]
59. [illegible] quant-ph/0[illegible]
60. [illegible]
61. [illegible]
62. [illegible]
63. [illegible]
64. [illegible] quantum [illegible]
65. [illegible]
66. [illegible] quant-ph/0[illegible]
67. [illegible] Springer [illegible]
68. [illegible] Efficient decomposition of quantum [illegible] 2004.
69. F. Vatan [illegible] two-qubit quantum gates [illegible]
70. F. Vatan [illegible] three-qubit quantum gate. quant-ph/0[illegible] 2004.

Distributed Algorithms for Autonomous Mobile Robots

Giuseppe Prencipe[1] and Nicola Santoro[2]

[1] Dipartimento di Informatica, Università di Pisa, prencipe@di.unipi.it
[2] School of Computer Science, Carleton University, santoro@scs.carleton.ca

Abstract. The distributed coordination and control of a team of autonomous mobile robots is a problem widely studied in a variety of fields, such as engineering, artificial intelligence, artificial life, robotics. Generally, in these areas, the problem is studied mostly from an empirical point of view. Recently, a significant research effort has been and continues to be spent on understanding the fundamental algorithmic limitations on what a set of autonomous mobile robots can achieve. In particular, the focus is to identify the minimal robot capabilities (sensorial, motorial, computational) that allow a problem to be solvable and a task to be performed. In this paper we describe the current investigations on the interplay between robots capabilities, computability, and algorithmic solutions of coordination problems by autonomous mobile robots.

1 Introduction

In this paper we describe the current investigations on the algorithmic limitations of what autonomous mobile robots can do with respect to basic coordination problems.

The current trend in robotic research, both from engineering and behavioral viewpoints, has been to move away from the design and deployment of few, rather complex, usually expensive, application-specific robots. In fact, the interest has shifted towards the design and use of a large number of "generic" robots which are very simple, with very limited capabilities and, thus, relatively inexpensive, but capable, together, of performing rather complex tasks. The advantages of such an approach are clear and many, including: reduced costs (due to simpler engineering and construction costs, faster computation, development and deployment time, etc); ease of system expandability (just add a few more robots) which in turns allows for incremental and on-demand deployment (use only as few robots as you need and when you need them); simple and affordable fault-tolerance capabilities (replace just the faulty robots); re-usability of the robots in different applications (reprogram the system to perform a different task). Moreover, tasks that could not be performed at all by a single agent become manageable when many simple units are used instead [19, 34].

One of the first studies conducted in this direction in the AI community is that of Matarić [30]. The main idea in Matarić's work is that "interactions

Please use the following format when citing this chapter:

Prencipe, G., Santoro, N., 2006, in International Federation for Information Processing, Volume 209, Fourth IFIP International Conference on Theoretical Computer Science-TCS 2006, eds. Navarro, G., Bertossi, L., Kohayakwa, Y., (Boston: Springer), pp. 47–62.

Distributed Algorithms for Autonomous Mobile Robots

[illegible] and Nicola Santoro[2]

[illegible]

[illegible]

1 Introduction

[illegible]

[illegible]

[illegible], G., Santoro, N., 2006, in International Federation for Information Processing, Volume 209, Fourth IFIP International Conference on Theoretical Computer Science-TCS 2006, eds. Navarro, G., [illegible], L., Kohayakawa, Y., (Boston: Springer), pp. 47–62.

2 Modeling Autonomous Mobile Robots

In the general model, the computational universe is a 2-dimensional plane populated by a set of n autonomous mobile robots, denoted by $r_1, \ldots, r_n$, that are modeled as devices with computational capabilities which are able to freely move on a two-dimensional plane.

2.1 The robots and their behavior

A robot is a computational unit capable of sensing the positions of other robots in its surrounding, performing local computations on the sensed data, and moving towards the computed destination. The local computation is done according to a deterministic algorithm that takes in input the sensed data (i.e., the robots' positions), and returns a destination point towards which the executing robot moves. All the robots execute the same algorithm. The local view of each robot includes a unit of length, an origin, and a Cartesian coordinate system defined by the *directions* of two coordinate axes, identified as the x and y axis, together with their *orientations*, identified as the positive and negative sides of the axes.

Each robot repeatedly cycles through four *states*: (i) initially it is inactive – *Wait*, (ii) it observes the positions of the other robots in its area of visibility – *Look*, (iii) it computes its next destination point by executing the algorithm (the same for all robots) – *Compute*, and (iv) it moves towards the point it just computed – *Move*. After the *Move* it goes back to the *Wait* state.

The sequence: *Wait* - *Look* - *Compute* - *Move* form a *computation cycle* (or briefly *cycle*) of a robot. The operations performed by each robot r in each state will be now described in more details.

1. **Wait.** The robot is idle. A robot cannot stay indefinitely idle. Initially, all robots are in *Wait*.
2. **Look.** The robot observes the world by activating its sensors which will return a *snapshot* of the positions of all other robots within the visibility range with respect to its local coordinate system. Each robot is viewed as a point, hence its position in the plane is given by its coordinates, and the result of the snapshot (hence, of the observation) is just a set of coordinates in its local coordinate system: this set forms the *view of the world* of r.
3. **Compute.** The robot performs a *local computation* according to a deterministic algorithm $\mathcal{A}$ (we also say that the robot *executes* $\mathcal{A}$). The algorithm is the same for all robots, and the result of the *Compute* state is a *destination point*.
4. **Move.** If the destination point is the current location of r, r performs a *null movement* (i.e., it does not move); otherwise it moves towards the computed destination but it can stop anytime during its movement[1].

[1] e.g. because of limits to the robot's motorial capabilities.

1. Since the time that passes after a robot starts observing the positions of all others and before it starts moving is arbitrary, but finite, the actual move of a robot may be based on a situation that was observed arbitrarily far in the past, and therefore it may be totally different from the current situation.
2. Since movements can take a finite but unpredictable amount of time, and different robots might be in different states of their cycles at a given time instant, it is possible that a robot can be seen *while* it is moving by other robots that are observing[2].

These consequences render difficult the design of an algorithm to control and coordinate the robots. For example, when a robot starts a *Move*, it is possible that the movement it performs is not "coherent" with the current configuration (i.e., the configuration it observed at the time of the *Look* and the configuration at the time of the *Move* can differ), since, during the *Compute*, other robots can have moved.

Restricted Setting: Semi-synchronous Robots A computational setting that has been extensively investigated is one in which the cycles of all the robots are synchronized and their actions are atomic.

In particular, there is a global clock tick reaching all robots simultaneously, and a robot's cycle is an instantaneous event that starts at a clock tick and ends by the next.

The only unpredictability (hence the name *semi-synchronous*) is given by the fact that at each clock tick, every robot is either *active* or *inactive*, and only active robots perform their cycle. The unpredictability is restricted by the fact that at least one robot is active at every time instant, and every robot becomes active at infinitely many unpredictable time instants. A very special case is when every robot is active at every clock tick; in this case the robots are *fully synchronized.*

In this setting, at any given time, all active robots are executing the same cycle state; thus no robot will look while another is moving. In other words, a robot observes other robots only when they are stationary. This implies that the computation is always performed based on accurate information about the current configuration.

Furthermore, since no robot can be seen *while* it is moving, the movement can be considered *instantaneous.*

An additional consequence of atomicity and synchronization is that, for them to hold, the maximum distance that a robot can move in one cycle is bounded.

2.3 Capabilities

Different settings arise from different assumptions that are made on the robots' capabilities, and on the amount of information that they share and use during the accomplishment of the assigned task. In particular,

---

[2] Note that this does not mean that the observing robot can distinguish a moving robot from a non moving one.

leader election) can be reformulated as geometric problems in our model (e.g., forming an asymmetric pattern).

3.1 Pattern formation

The PATTERN FORMATION problem is one of the most important coordination problem and has been extensively investigated in the literature (e.g., see [8, 38, 39, 41]). The problem is practically important, because, if the robots can form a given pattern, they can agree on their respective roles in a subsequent, coordinated action. The geometric pattern to be formed is a set of points (given by their Cartesian coordinates) in the plane, and it is initially known by all the robots in the system.

The robots are said to *form the pattern* if, at the end of the computation, the positions of the robots coincide, in everybody's local view, with the points of the pattern. The formed pattern may be *translated*, *rotated*, *scaled*, and *flipped* into its mirror position with respect to the initial pattern. Initially the robots are in arbitrary positions, with the only requirement that no two robots are in the same position, and that, of course, the number of points prescribed in the pattern and the number of robots are the same.

The basic research questions are which patterns can be formed, and how they can be formed. Many proposed procedures do not terminate and never form the desired pattern: the robots just converge towards it; such procedures are said to *converge*.

Arbitrary Pattern In this section, we review our results on the formation of an arbitrary pattern. The problem has been investigated by Flocchini *et al* [21, 23] and Oasa *et al.* [33] in the general setting, and by Suzuki and Yamashita [39] in the semi-synchronous setting; both investigations consider robots with unlimited visibility.

In the *general setting* with *unlimited visibility*:

- With total agreement *oblivious* robots can form any arbitrary given pattern [21].
- With partial agreement, *oblivious* robots can form any arbitrary given pattern if n is odd. If n is even, *oblivious* robots can form only symmetric patterns that have at least one axis of symmetry not passing through any vertex of the pattern [23].
- With no agreement at all, *oblivious* robots cannot form an arbitrary given pattern [21].

In the *semi-synchronous setting* with *unlimited visibility*, let m be the size of the largest subset of robots having an equivalent initial view.

- Robots with *unbounded memory* can form [39]
  1. any pattern if $m = 1$;
  2. only patterns whose vertices can be partitioned into n/m regular m-gons all having the same center, if $m \geq 2$.

– In the *semi-synchronous setting* with *unlimited visibility*: *oblivious* robots can converge towards an n-gon [16, 37, 7].

Line Formation Let us now consider another simple pattern for the robots: a line. That is, the robots are required to place themselves on a line, whose position is not prescribed in advance; we just defined the LINE FORMATION problem. Note that, if $n = 2$, a line is always formed. Despite the simplicity of its formulation, this problem has some subtleties that render its solution not so easy. In fact, the solvability of this problem heavily depends on the amount of agreement the robots have on their local coordinate systems.

Clearly, if the robots can rely on *total agreement*, then the problem is easily solved: after lexicographically ordering the robots' positions (e.g., left-right, top-down), the first and the last robot in the ordering define the line to be formed. Then, all robots move sequentially (in order to avoid collisions) to this line (see Figure 2.a).

If the robots have *partial agreement*, for instance on the direction and orientation of y, the robots can not rely on an unique total ordering of the robots' positions. In this case the robots can place themselves on the axis that is median between the two vertical axes tangent to the observed configuration (see Figure 2.b). The robots on the tangent axes are the last to move.

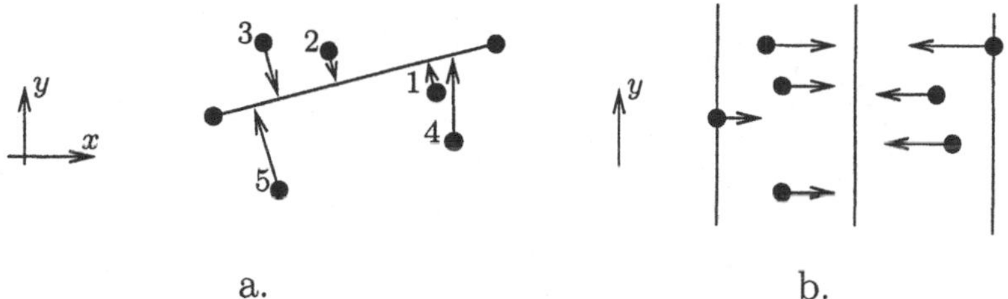

Fig. 2. Line formation with (a) total and (b) partial agreement.

In a recent study [15], the LINE FORMATION problem has been tackled by studying an apparently totally different problem: the *spreading*. In this problem, the robots, that at the beginning are arbitrarily placed on the plane, are required to evenly spread within the perimeter of a given region. In their work, the authors focus on the one-dimensional case: in this case, the robots have to form a line, and place themselves uniformly on it. A very interesting aspect of the study, is that [15] addresses the issue of *local algorithms*: each robots decides where to move based on the positions of its close neighbors. In particular, in the case of the line, the protocol, called *Spread*, is quite simple: each robot r observes its left and right neighbor. If r does not see any robot, it simply does not move; otherwise, it moves to the median point between its two neighbors. The authors prove its convergence in the semi-synchronous setting.

The *multiplicity detection* assumption is crucial to prove the correctness of these algorithms. In fact, the main idea is first to create a unique point p on the plane with two robots on it, and then to move all other robots on this point, taking care in not having other points with multiplicity greater than one while the robots move towards p.

In contrast, the multiplicity detection is not used in the solution described in [9]; however, it is assumed that the robots can rely on an unlimited amount of memory: the robots are said to be *non-oblivious.* In other words, the robots have the capability to store the results of all computations since the beginning, and freely access to these data and use them for future computations.

- In the *general setting*, $n \geq 3$ robots *with unbounded memory* can gather in finite time [9].

Another study [13] has been devoted to study the behavior of a particular simple solution to the problem: the robots use the center of gravity as gathering destination. The authors prove that this simple algorithm represent a convergence solution to the problem in the semi-synchronous setting. In [12] the same algorithm has been proven to be a convergence solution to the problem in the asynchronous setting.

Let us then consider the case of *limited* visibility. With limited visibility, an obvious necessary condition to solve the problem, is that at the beginning of the computation the *visibility graph* (having the robots as nodes and an edge (r_i, r_j) if r_i and r_j are within viewing distance) is connected [2, 22]. In [2] the proposed protocol works in the semi-synchronous setting; however, it is a *convergence* solution to the problem: the robots do not gather in finite time. In fact, the authors design a protocol that guarantees only that the robots converge towards the gathering point. In contrast, in [22], the authors present an algorithm that let the robots to gather in a finite number of cycles. However, the robots can rely on the presence of a common coordinate system: that is, they share a compass.

- In the semi-synchronous setting there exists an *oblivious* procedure that lets robots *converge* towards (but not necessarily reach) a point for any n [2].
- In the *general setting oblivious* robots with agreement on the coordinate system (e.g., with a compass) can gather in finite time [22, 24].

The GATHERING problem has been also investigated in the context of robots *failures.* In this context, the goal is for the non-faulty robots to gather regardless of the action taken by the faulty ones. Two types of robot faults were investigated by Peleg *et al.* [1]: *crash* failure, in which the robot stops any activity and will no longer execute any computational cycle; and the *byzantine* failure, in which the robot acts arbitrarily and possibly maliciously.

- In the semi-synchronous setting, gathering with at most one *crash* failure is possible [1].
- In the semi-synchronous setting, gathering with at most one *byzantine* failure is *impossible* [1].

Fig. 3. Trace of the vehicles while forming and keeping a wedge shaped formation.

to gain a better understanding of the power of distributed control from an algorithmic point of view.

The area offers many open problems. The operating capabilities of our robots are quite limited. It would be interesting to look at models where the robots have more complex capabilities, e.g.: the robots have some kind of direct communication capabilities; the robots are distinct and externally identifiable; etc. Little is known about the solvability of other problems like *spreading* and *exploration* (used to build maps of unknown terrains), about the physical aspects of the models (giving physical dimension to the robots, bumping, energy saving issues, etc.), and about the relationships between geometric problems and classical distributed computations.

In the area of reliability and fault-tolerance, lightly faulty snapshots, a limited range of visibility, obstacles that limit the visibility and that moving robots must avoid or push aside, as well as robots that appear and disappear from the scene clearly are all topics that have not yet been studied.

We believe that investigations in these areas will provide useful insights on the ability of weak robots to solve complex tasks.

Acknowledgements The Authors would like to thank Paola Flocchini and Peter Widmayer for their help and suggestions in the preparation of this survey. This research is supported in part by the Natural Sciences and Engineering Research Council of Canada.

References

1. N. Agmon and D. Peleg. Fault-tolerant Gathering Algorithms for Autonomous Mobile Robots. In *Proc. of the 15th ACM-SIAM Symposium on Discrete Algorithms*, pages 1070 – 1078, 2004.
2. H. Ando, Y. Oasa, I. Suzuki, and M. Yamashita. A Distributed Memoryless Point Convergence Algorithm for Mobile Robots with Limited Visibility. *IEEE Trans. on Robotics and Automation*, 15(5):818–828, 1999.

Fig. 3. [illegible] of two vehicles [illegible] and [illegible] formation

[illegible] robots [illegible] power of distributed control from an [illegible] point of view.

[illegible] our robots [illegible] would be interesting [illegible] where the robots have more [illegible] capabilities [illegible] have some limited [illegible] munication [illegible] etc. [illegible] little is known [illegible] like [illegible] et [illegible] about the physical [illegible] [illegible] problems [illegible] [illegible]

[illegible] lin- [illegible] robots [illegible] that [illegible] from the [illegible] yet been [illegible]

We [illegible] insights on the ability [illegible] complex tasks.

Acknowledgements. [illegible] would like [illegible] and Peter Widmayer for [illegible] This research is supported [illegible] Council [illegible] Canada.

References

1. N. Agmon and D. Peleg. [illegible] Gathering Algorithms for Autonomous Mobile Robots. [illegible] ACM-SIAM [illegible] Discrete Algorithms, pages 1070–[illegible]
2. H. Ando, [illegible] Suzuki, and [illegible] Yamashita. A [illegible] Memoryless Point Convergence Algorithm for Mobile Robots with Limited Visibility. IEEE Trans. on Robotics and Automation, [illegible] 15(5):818–828, 1999.

22. P. Flocchini, G. Prencipe, N. Santoro, and P. Widmayer. Gathering of Asynchronous Mobile Robots with Limited Visibility. In *Proceedings 18th International Symposium on Theoretical Aspects of Computer Science*, volume LNCS 2010, pages 247–258, 2001.
23. P. Flocchini, G. Prencipe, N. Santoro, and P. Widmayer. Pattern Formation by Autonomous Robots Without Chirality. In *Proc. 8th Int. Colloquium on Structural Information and Communication Complexity*, pages 147–162, June 2001.
24. P. Flocchini, G. Prencipe, N. Santoro, and P. Widmayer. Gathering of Asynchronous Robots with Limited Visibility. *Theoretical Computer Science*, 337:147–168, 2005.
25. T. Fukuda, Y. Kawauchi, and H. Asama M. Buss. Structure Decision Method for Self Organizing Robots Based on Cell Structures-CEBOT. In *Proc. IEEE Int. Conf. on Robotics and Autom.*, volume 2, pages 695–700, 1989.
26. V. Gervasi and G. Prencipe. Coordination Without Communication: The Case of The Flocking Problem. *Discrete Applied Mathematics*, 143:203–223, 2003.
27. V. Gervasi and G. Prencipe. Robotic cops: The intruder problem. In *Proc. IEEE Conference on Systems, Man and Cybernetics*, pages 2284–2289, 2003.
28. D. Jung, G. Cheng, and A. Zelinsky. Experiments in Realising Cooperation between Autonomous Mobile Robots. In *ISER*, 1997.
29. Y. Kawauchi and M. Inaba and. T. Fukuda. A Principle of Decision Making of Cellular Robotic System (CEBOT). In *Proc. IEEE Conf. on Robotics and Autom.*, pages 833–838, 1993.
30. M. J Matarić. *Interaction and Intelligent Behavior.* PhD thesis, MIT, May 1994.
31. S. Murata, H. Kurokawa, and S. Kokaji. Self-assembling Machine. In *Proc. IEEE Conf. on Robotics and Autom.*, pages 441–448, 1994.
32. F. R. Noreils. Toward a Robot Architecture Integrating Cooperation between Mobile Robots: Application to Indoor Environment. *The Int. J. of Robot. Res.*, pages 79–98, 1993.
33. Y. Oasa, I. Suzuki, and M. Yamashita. A Robust Distributed Convergence Algorithm for Autonomous Mobile Robots. In *IEEE Int. Conf. on Systems, Man and Cybernetics*, pages 287–292, October 1997.
34. L. E. Parker. On the Design of Behavior-Based Multi-Robot Teams. *Journal of Advanced Robotics*, 10(6), 1996.
35. G. Prencipe. On The Feasibility of Gathering by Autonomous Mobile Robots. In *Proc. 12th Int. Colloquium on Structural Information and Communication Complexity*, pages 246–261, 2005.
36. G. Prencipe. The Effect of Synchronicity on the Behavior of Autonomous Mobile Robots. *Theory of Computing Systems*, 38:539–558, 2005.
37. S. Samia, X. Défago, and T. Katayama. Convergence Of a Uniform Circle Formation Algorithm for Distributed Autonomous Mobile Robots. In *In Journés Scientifiques Francophones (JSF), Tokio, Japan*, 2004.
38. K. Sugihara and I. Suzuki. Distributed Algorithms for Formation of Geometric Patterns with Many Mobile Robots. *Journal of Robotics Systems*, 13:127–139, 1996.
39. I. Suzuki and M. Yamashita. Distributed Anonymous Mobile Robots: Formation of Geometric Patterns. *Siam J. Computing*, 28(4):1347–1363, 1999.
40. O. Tanaka. Forming a Circle by Distributed Anonymous Mobile Robots. Technical report, Department of Electrical Engineering, Hiroshima University, Hiroshima, Japan, 1992.

Part III

Contributed Papers

The Unsplittable Stable Marriage Problem

Brian C. Dean, Michel X. Goemans, and Nicole Immorlica

[1] Department of Computer Science, Clemson University. bcdean@cs.clemson.edu
[2] Department of Mathematics, M.I.T. goemans@math.mit.edu
[3] Microsoft Research. nickle@microsoft.com

Abstract. The Gale-Shapley "propose/reject" algorithm is a well-known procedure for solving the classical stable marriage problem. In this paper we study this algorithm in the context of the many-to-many stable marriage problem, also known as the stable allocation or ordinal transportation problem. We present an integral variant of the Gale-Shapley algorithm that provides a direct analog, in the context of "ordinal" assignment problems, of a well-known bicriteria approximation algorithm of Shmoys and Tardos for scheduling on unrelated parallel machines with costs. If we are assigning, say, jobs to machines, our algorithm finds an unsplit (non-preemptive) stable assignment where every job is assigned at least as well as it could be in any fractional stable assignment, and where each machine is congested by at most the processing time of the largest job.

1 Introduction

In the United States, a medical school graduate is required to complete a residency program at a hospital before entering the workforce as a doctor. Since the 1950s, the medical field has turned to a centralized mechanism, called the *National Residency Matching Program* (NRMP), to aid this marketplace [10]. In this program, final-year medical students and hospitals each submit preferences over possible matches, and an algorithm determines which matches will take place. In order for the system to be successful, it is essential that the computed matches be *stable*. That is, there should be no (student, hospital) pair that both prefer each-other to their assigned partners — such a pair would have an incentive to withdraw from the centralized matching system and to make its own plans on the side. Computing a stable matching is a classic problem in economics and computer science, and can be solved in polynomial time by the deferred acceptance algorithm of Gale and Shapley [3].[1]

For many years the NRMP proved to be quite successful. However, in the late 1990s it was observed that many matches were being formed outside the NRMP [12]. The problem stemmed from the fact that many medical students were getting married to one another during medical school, and so had complicated preferences that were ignored by the NRMP. In particular, married

[1] For a discussion of this problem and related questions, see the books by Gusfield and Irving [4] and Roth and Sotomayor [14], or the lecture notes by Knuth [8].

Please use the following format when citing this chapter:

Dean, B.C., Goemans, M.X., Immorlica, N., 2006, in International Federation for Information Processing, Volume 209, Fourth IFIP International Conference on Theoretical Computer Science-TCS 2006, eds. Navarro, G., Bertossi, L., Kohayakwa, Y., (Boston: Springer), pp. 65–75.

A close relative of the stable allocation problem is the well-studied *transportation* problem, where there are linear costs associated with every possible pairing and our objective is to compute a fractional assignment of minimum cost rather than a stable assignment. The stable allocation problem is also known as the ordinal transportation problem since it differs only in that we express the desirability of an assignment in an "ordinal" fashion using ranked preference lists. Unsplittable variants of the transportation problem have been previously considered in the literature, and a celebrated result of Shmoys and Tardos [15] states that from a fractional assignment (where all agents are fully assigned), we can construct an unsplit assignment of no greater cost where each agent is over-capacitated (or *congested*) by at most the maximum demand. Our results can viewed as a direct analog of this result for the ordinal case.

2 The Model

Consider assigning a set $[n] := \{1, 2, \ldots, n\}$ of items to a set $[m]$ of bins. To be somewhat more concrete, let us employ scheduling terminology and assume we are assigning "jobs" to "machines". Job i requires p_i units of processing time, machine j has a capacity of c_j units, and at most u_{ij} units of job i can be assigned to machine j. If $u_{ij} = p_i$ for all (i, j), we follow the terminology of Baiou and Balinski [1] and say our problem is *unconstrained.* All problem data is assumed to be integral.

2.1 Fractional Assignment

We first define a fractional setting where a job may be processed on multiple machines. A fractional assignment x is *feasible* if it satisfies

$$\begin{aligned} &\sum_{j\in[m]} x_{ij} \leq p_i \ \forall i \in [n] \\ &\sum_{i\in[n]} x_{ij} \leq c_j \ \ \forall j \in [m] \\ &0 \leq x_{ij} \leq u_{ij} \ \forall (i,j) \in [n] \times [m]. \end{aligned} \tag{1}$$

In the traditional *transportation* problem (a many-to-many generalization of the bipartite assignment problem), we designate a weight w_{ij} for assigning one unit of job i to machine j, then maximize $\sum w_{ij}x_{ij}$ over (1) using linear programming or network flow techniques (another popular objective is to minimize $\sum w_{ij}x_{ij}$ while insisting that all jobs must be fully assigned). In the *stable allocation problem*, however, we indicate the desirability of an assignment in an "ordinal" fashion by having each job (machine) submit a ranked preference list over all machines (jobs).

Thus, each job $i \in [n]$ has a strict, transitive, and complete preference relation $\pi(i)$ over the set $[m] \cup \emptyset$ where $\{\emptyset\}$ indicates a preference for remaining unmatched. If $\pi(i) = (j_1, \ldots, j_{k-1}, \emptyset = j_k, j_{k+1}, \ldots, j_{m+1})$, then i prefers j_a

job *simultaneously* receives at least as much of an allocation of its first-choice machine as it could in any feasible stable assignment, and it also receives at least as much of an allocation of its second-choice machine as it could in any feasible stable assignment with the same first-choice allocation, and so on. It is always possible to find a job-optimal feasible stable assignment for any problem instance using a strongly-polynomial algorithm of Baiou and Balinski [1].

2.2 Unsplit Assignment

We now consider the "unsplittable" unconstrained stable allocation problem where each job must be entirely assigned to a single machine. Thus the feasible assignments x are precisely the integral solutions to (1) where either $x_{ij} = 0$ or $x_{ij} = p_i$ for all (i, j). As the following simple example shows, an integral stable assignment may not exist.

Example 1. Suppose there are two jobs i_1 and i_2 with demands 1 and 2 respectively, and two machines j_1 and j_2, both with capacity 2. Let $\pi(i_1) = \pi(i_2) = (j_1, j_2)$ and $\pi(j_1) = \pi(j_2) = (i_1, i_2)$. Then the only stable assignment is $x_{i_1 j_1} = 1$, $x_{i_2 j_1} = 1$, and $x_{i_1 j_2} = 1$, but this is not an unsplit assignment.

We therefore consider a relaxation that is directly analogous to a result of Shmoys and Tardos [15] for the bipartite assignment problem with costs. Assuming existence of a feasible fractional assignment of cost C with all jobs fully assigned, Shmoys and Tardos show how to round this solution in polynomial time to obtain an unsplit solution of cost no more than C where each machine is congested (filled beyond its capacity) by at most $p_{max} = \max_i p_i$. Similar results have been achieved in literature on unsplittable flows (see [7, 2, 16] for more background), where our goal is generally to take a fractional solution to a network flow problem and round it to an unsplit flow (where the flow for each commodity follows a single path) without significantly raising the cost of the flow, and without causing excessive congestion on edges.

Definition 5. *An assignment x is* minimally congested *if for every machine j, removal of the least-preferred job (to j) currently assigned to j results in j being utilized at or below its capacity.*

Note that in a minimally congested assignment, each machine is overcapacitated by at most p_{max}. We show how a modified version of the GS algorithm can find, in polynomial time, a stable unsplit assignment that is *job-optimal* among all minimally congested stable unsplit assignments. Suppose x is a job-optimal feasible stable fractional assignment. We prove that in a job-optimal unsplit assignment, each job is assigned to at least the best of its fractional assignments in x (our analog of the condition that cost does not increase).

Our unsplit assignment is stable in that (i) it admits no blocking pairs and (ii) all popular machines are saturated. Note that one must take some care

This theorem follows immediately from the fact that we can interpret the extended GS algorithm for the many-to-many stable allocation problem as nothing more than the standard "one-to-one" GS algorithm applied to an expanded instance where each job i is replaced with p_i unit-sized jobs (each with the same preference list) and each machine j is replaced by c_j unit-sized machines (each with the same preference list). The many-to-many algorithm is sped up by issuing proposals in batches, but it inherets from the one-to-one algorithm the property that the final solution must be job-optimal irrespective of the order of proposals. As an interesting remark, if problem data is irrational, then not only does this reduction to the one-to-one case fail, but it is also not known whether the GS algorithm terminates after a finite number of iterations. We comment on this issue further in the conclusion section.

4 Computing Unsplittable Stable Allocations

In this section we discuss our "ordinal" analog for the stable allocation problem of the result of Shmoys and Tardos for the minimum-cost bipartite assignment problem. Since the constraints $x_{ij} \leq u_{ij}$ do not make sense for an unsplittable stable allocation problem, we henceforth assume we are dealing with an unconstrained stable allocation problem.

Let us modify the GS algorithm as follows. Jobs issue proposals in sequence according to their preference lists, and in each iteration an arbitrary unassigned job i issues a proposal to the next machine j on its preference list. In this case, however, all proposals and rejections are "integral" in that either an entire job is accepted or rejected. Machine j accepts i's proposal, but then proceeds to reject in sequence the least favored jobs assigned to it (possibly including i) until j is at most over-congested by the processing time of a single job — that is, until rejecting the next job would leave the machine being utilized strictly below c_j units of load. Note that such an algorithm results in an assignment where each machine is congested by at most the maximum processing time of a job.

If each machine stores its accepted jobs in a heap based on preference list ranking, this integral variant of the GS algorithm runs in $O(mn \log n)$ time. We now prove some desirable properties of the algorithm. First we show that the assignment output by our algorithm is stable and *job-optimal.* The proof of the following theorem is similar to the traditional proof for the correctness and optimality of the one-to-one GS algorithm.

Theorem 2. *The integral job-proposing GS algorithm computes the* job-optimal *stable unsplit assignment among all minimally congested unsplit stable assignments.*

Proof. Let x^* be the solution output by the GS algorithm. Clearly, x^* is an unsplit assignment that congests each machine by at most p_{max}. Let $x^*(i)$ be the machine to which job i is assigned in x^* and $x^*(j)$ be the set of jobs to

[illegible] ly from the fact that we can interpret the [illegible] GS algorithm [illegible] unsplittable allocation problem as noth- [illegible] standard [illegible] GS algorithm applied to an expanded instance where each job is replaced [illegible] (each with the same [illegible]) and each machine j is replaced [illegible] machines (each [illegible]). The [illegible] property [illegible] optimal [illegible] We comment on this further in the next section.

4 Computing Unsplittable Stable Assignments

[illegible] allocation problem [illegible] without [illegible] allocation problem [illegible].

Let us [illegible] sequence [illegible] unassigned [illegible] list. In this case, [illegible] that of an entire job [illegible] and then proceeds to [illegible] including [illegible] single job [illegible] that [illegible] in an assignment where [illegible] and.

[illegible]

Theorem 2. [illegible] *computes the* [illegible] *stable* [illegible] *stable assign-ments.*

Proof. [illegible]

Proof. The proof follows from Theorem 1 and the fact that jobs propose in decreasing order of their preference list (and so as the algorithm runs the jobs' situations worsen). More formally, consider the sequence of proposals defined by the integral GS algorithm. Call this sequence $(i_1, i_2, \ldots, i_l)$ (note this list includes repetitions and l may be greater than n). Run the fractional GS algorithm with the same order of proposals. We prove by induction that after the proposal of i_k, the current assignment x in the integral variant and x' in the fractional variant satisfy $x(j) = x'(j)$ for all j and a machine is saturated in x if and only if it is in x'. This is clearly true after the proposal of i_1. Assume this is the case after the proposal of i_{k-1} and let j be the machine to which i_k proposes. By inductive assumption, j must be the same machine in both the integral and fractional variants of the algorithm. If j rejects i_k in the integral variant, then it must be that $x(j) >_j i_k$ and $\sum_{i \in x(j)} p_i + \geq c_j$. Thus, in the fractional variant, $\sum_{i \in x'(j)} x'_{ij} = c_j$ and $x'(j) >_j i_k$ so all of i_k's load is rejected. A similar argument holds if j rejects i_k in the fractional variant, and so the inductive hypothesis holds.

Therefore, after the l'th proposal in the integral variant, the final solution x_{int} of the integral variant is at least as preferable as the current solution x' of the fractional variant for each job. Furthermore, as jobs propose in decreasing order of their preference list, the final solution x_{frac} of the fractional variant cannot be preferred to the current solution x' by any job. This completes the proof.

We remark that all the theorems in this paper hold if we instead seek the machine-optimal solution. We merely need to run the Gale-Shapley algorithm with machine-proposals – a machine proposes to the next job on its preference list if it is currently under-utilized (it's load is currently less than its capacity). A job (fractionally) accepts a proposal if it is (fractionally) unassigned or if it prefers the proposing machine to (some of) its current machine(s), in which case it rejects (some of) its current machine(s).

5 Conclusion

In this paper, we studied a natural integral variant of the stable allocation problem in which every job was unsplittably assigned and every machine was not excessively congested. Our results have implications for many economic settings where varying sized agents must be matched to each other. Our work leaves open a number of interesting questions:

Rural hospitals: It is well known that in one-to-one matching, the set of singles remains the same in every stable matching. Roth [11] extended this theorem and showed that in one-to-many matching, an agent not fully utilized in a stable

[illegible] follows [illegible] the fact that jobs propose in [illegible] of their preference list (as long as the algorithm runs the jobs [illegible]). [illegible] consider the sequence of proposals defined by the integral CS [illegible]. Call this sequence ($j_1, j_2, \ldots, j_n$) (note this list [illegible] may be greater than n) [illegible] the fractional CS algorithm with [illegible] induction that after the [illegible] in the integral [illegible] in the first [illegible] if and only if [illegible] proposal of [illegible] proposes. By [illegible] must be the same [illegible] the integral and [illegible] rejects [illegible] the integral variant [illegible]. Thus, in the [illegible] of i's load is rejected [illegible] if j rejects [illegible] the fractional variant, and so the [illegible] holds.

The [illegible] fractional variant, the final solution [illegible] of the [illegible] variant [illegible] as preferable [illegible] the current solution [illegible] of the [illegible] each job. Furthermore, [illegible] proposal in decreasing order of their preference [illegible] of the fractional variant, cannot be preferred to the [illegible]. This completes the proof.

We [illegible] we then [illegible] the [illegible] Gale Shapley algorithm with [illegible] proposals of the [illegible] preference [illegible] (this is [illegible] the [illegible] job [illegible] proposal [illegible] which [illegible]

[illegible]

[illegible] allocation [illegible] every machine [illegible] for many economic [illegible] where [illegible] to each other. Our work [illegible]

[illegible] matching, the set of singles [illegible] extended this theorem and [illegible] fully utilized in a stable

11. A.E. Roth. On the allocation of residents to rural hospitals: a general property of two-sided matching markets. *Econometrica*, 54:425–427, 1986.
12. A.E. Roth. The national residency matching program as a labor market. *Journal of the American Medical Association*, 275(13):1054–1056, 1996.
13. A.E. Roth and E. Peranson. The redesign of the matching market for american physicians: Some engineering aspects of economic design. *American Economic Review*, 89:748–780, 1999.
14. A.E. Roth and M. Sotomayor. *Two-Sided Matching: A Study in Game-Theoretic Modeling and Analysis*. Cambridge University Press, 1990.
15. D.B. Shmoys and É. Tardos. Scheduling unrelated machines with costs. In *Proceedings of the 4th annual ACM-SIAM Symposium on Discrete algorithms (SODA)*, pages 448–454, 1993.
16. M. Skutella. Approximating the single source unsplittable min-cost flow problem. In *Proceedings of the 41st Annual Symposium on Foundations of Computer Science (FOCS)*, pages 136–145, 2000.

11. A. E. Roth. On the allocation of [illegible] to rural hospitals: a general property of two-sided matching markets. *Econometrica*, 54:425–427, 1986.
12. A. E. Roth. The national residency matching program as a labor market. *Journal of the American Medical Association*, [illegible]:1054–1056, 1996.
13. A. E. Roth and E. Peranson. The redesign of the matching market for American physicians: Some engineering aspects of economic design. *American Economic Review*, [illegible].
14. A. E. Roth and M. Sotomayor. *Two-sided Matching: A Study in Game-Theoretic Modeling and Analysis*. Cambridge University Press, 1990.
15. [illegible] Scheduling [illegible]. In [illegible] LNCS, [illegible]
16. A. Subramanian. A new approach to stable matching problems. [illegible] *Computer Science*, [illegible] pages 130–145, [illegible]

Variations on an Ordering Theme with Constraints

Walter Guttmann and Markus Maucher

Fakultät für Informatik, Universität Ulm, 89069 Ulm, Germany
walter.guttmann@uni-ulm.de · markus.maucher@uni-ulm.de

Abstract. We investigate the problem of finding a total order of a finite set that satisfies various local ordering constraints. Depending on the admitted constraints, we provide an efficient algorithm or prove NP-completeness. We discuss several generalisations and systematically classify the problems.

Key words: total ordering, NP-completeness, computational complexity, betweenness, cyclic ordering, topological sorting

1 Introduction

An instance of the betweenness problem is given by a finite set A and a collection C of triples from A, with the task to decide if there is a total order $<$ of A such that for each $(a, b, c) \in C$, either $a < b < c$ or $c < b < a$ [1, problem MS1]. The betweenness problem is NP-complete [2]. Applications arise, for example, in the design of circuits and in computational biology [2, 3].

Similarly, the cyclic ordering problem asks for a total order $<$ of A such that for each $(a, b, c) \in C$, either $a < b < c$ or $b < c < a$ or $c < a < b$ [1, problem MS2]. The cyclic ordering problem, too, is NP-complete [4]. Applications arise, for example, in qualitative spatial reasoning [5].

On the other hand, if $a < b < c$ or $a < c < b$ is allowed, the problem can be solved with linear time complexity by topological sorting [6, Sect. 2.2.3].

Yet another choice, namely $c < a$ or $c < b$, is needed to model an object-relational mapping problem described in Sect. 2. We present a generalisation of topological sorting to solve it.

Starting with Sect. 3, several kinds of generalisations to these problems are explored with respect to their time complexity and interdependence. We prove that each problem is either efficiently solvable or NP-complete by identifying sufficient properties or appropriate reductions. The problems are grouped in three families, treated in Sects. 3, 4, and 5, respectively. Related work is discussed in the conclusion.

Our motivation to investigate the generalised ordering problems is twofold. On the practical side, several instances appear in different branches of computer science, and we are interested in their time complexity. On the theoretical side, the present work is a first step towards addressing the dichotomy of

Please use the following format when citing this chapter:

Guttmann, W., Maucher, M., 2006, in International Federation for Information Processing, Volume 209, Fourth IFIP International Conference on Theoretical Computer Science-TCS 2006, eds. Navarro, G., Bertossi, L., Kohayakwa, Y., (Boston: Springer), pp. 77–90.

requirement $d < e$ modelling that d must be stored before e. We therefore state the decision problem of this, more general version.

Problem 1. INSTANCE: Finite set A, collection B of pairs from A, collection C of triples from A.

QUESTION: Is there a bijection $f : A \to \{1, 2, \ldots, |A|\}$ such that $f(a_1) < f(a_2)$ for each $(a_1, a_2) \in B$, and $f(a_3) < f(a_1)$ or $f(a_3) < f(a_2)$ for each $(a_1, a_2, a_3) \in C$?

Note that the bijection f induces a total order, and vice versa. We prove that problem 1 is efficiently decidable by algorithm T shown in Fig. 2, an extension of topological sorting [6, Sect. 2.2.3]. The algorithm maintains working sets $E \subseteq A$, $F \subseteq B$, and $G \subseteq C$.

```
input:   finite set A, collection of pairs B and triples C from A
output:  total order of A such that the first element of each pair
         in B precedes the second, and the third element of
         each triple in C precedes the first or the second
method:  (E, F, G) ← (A, B, C)
         Order ← empty sequence
         while E ≠ ∅ do
             find e ∈ E such that ∀x, y ∈ E : (e, y) ∉ F ∧ (x, y, e) ∉ G
             if such an e exists then
                 G ← {(x, y, z) ∈ G | x ≠ e ∧ y ≠ e}
                 F ← {(x, y) ∈ F | y ≠ e}
                 E ← E \ {e}
                 prepend e to Order
             else
                 output "there is no order"
                 halt
             end
         end
         output Order
```

Fig. 2. Algorithm T

Theorem 1. *Algorithm T shown in Fig. 2 solves problem 1.*

Proof. Assume algorithm T proposes an order. That order is a permutation of A since during every iteration one element e is removed from E and prepended to the order. To see that the constraints specified by B are satisfied note that each $(a_1, a_2) \in B$ remains in F until the iteration where $a_2 = e$, thus a_2 is prepended to the order. While $(a_1, a_2) \in F$, however, the chosen element e cannot be a_1, hence a_1 precedes a_2 in the order.

[illegible] requirement [illegible] modelling that a must be sorted before [illegible]. We then [illegible] state the decision [illegible] of this more general version:

Problem [illegible] INSTANCE: Finite set A, collection B of pairs from A, collection [illegible].

[illegible] Is there [illegible] bijection f [illegible] $\{1, 2, \ldots\}$ [illegible] $f(a_1) <$ [illegible] $= B$, and [illegible] $f(a_2)$ [illegible] $<$ [illegible]

Note that [illegible] feasibly [illegible]. [illegible] in [illegible] of [illegible], [illegible] 2 [illegible]. The algorithm [illegible] working sets $F \subseteq A$, [illegible] $\subseteq B$ [illegible] $\subseteq C$.

Input: [illegible] collection [illegible] of pairs [illegible] from A [illegible]

Output: [illegible] that the [illegible] of each pair [illegible] in B [illegible] of [illegible] the first [illegible]

[illegible]

while $E \neq \emptyset$ do

[illegible] $\notin F$ [illegible]

[illegible]

output [illegible]

[illegible]

end

[illegible]

return [illegible]

[illegible]

[illegible]

[illegible] permutation of [illegible] and prepended [illegible] is [illegible] the chosen element [illegible] order.

Choose $P = \{(123), (321)\}$ for betweenness, $P = \{(123), (231), (312)\}$ for cyclic ordering, and $P = \mathcal{S}_3 \setminus \{(123), (213)\}$ to get the problem discussed in Sect. 2. The added distinctness condition $a_1 \neq a_2 \neq a_3 \neq a_1$ is easy to check.

The total number of problems in this family is $2^{|\mathcal{S}_3|} = 2^6 = 64$. Already from the small sample just presented it follows that some of these problems are tractable while others are NP-complete. Thus the task arises to classify the remaining problems. All of them are in NP, since a non-deterministic algorithm can guess the order and check in polynomial time that the constraints specified by C are satisfied with respect to the chosen P. This remark applies to all problems discussed in this paper.

To reduce the number of problems that must be investigated, the following symmetry consideration applies. Regard, for example, the problems $P_1 = \{(123), (213)\}$ and $P_2 = \{(231), (321)\}$ that differ just by a consistent renaming of the elements of their permutations. Such a renaming is achieved by composing a permutation from the left, in our case $P_2 = (231) \circ P_1$. Intuitively, this can be compensated by permuting the positions in each triple so that the modified constraints access the original elements. In our example, a triple (a_1, a_2, a_3) from an instance of P_1 would be rearranged to (a_3, a_1, a_2) for P_2. Precisely, symmetry is exploited by permuting each triple and applying the *inverse* permutation to all constraints. It follows that two problems P_1 and P_2 such that $P_2 = \pi \circ P_1$ for some $\pi \in \mathcal{S}_3$ have the same time complexity.

Another kind of symmetry enables a further reduction of the number of problems. Intuitively, reversing each constraint can be compensated by transposing the resulting total order. Precisely, a partial order can be extended to a total order if and only if its transpose can be extended—just take the transpose of the total order. It follows that two problems P_1 and P_2 that differ just by reversing their permutations, that is $P_2 = P_1 \circ (321)$, have the same time complexity. For example, $\mathcal{S}_3 \setminus \{(123), (213)\}$ and $\mathcal{S}_3 \setminus \{(321), (312)\}$ are two such problems.

After applying both kinds of symmetry considerations to the 64 problems, we are left with those shown in Fig. 3. We prove that the classification provided there is correct.

tractable	NP-complete
$\emptyset$	$\{(123), (231)\}$
$\{(123)\}$	$\{(123), (321)\}$
$\{(123), (132)\}$	$\{(123), (132), (231)\}$
$\{(123), (213), (231)\}$	$\{(123), (231), (312)\}$
$\mathcal{S}_3 \setminus \{(123), (213)\}$	$\mathcal{S}_3 \setminus \{(123), (231)\}$
$\mathcal{S}_3$	$\mathcal{S}_3 \setminus \{(123), (321)\}$
	$\mathcal{S}_3 \setminus \{(123)\}$

Fig. 3. Tractability of all problems $\subseteq \mathcal{S}_3$ up to symmetry

QUESTION: Is there a bijection $f : A \rightarrow \{1, 2, \ldots, |A|\}$ such that $f(a_1) < f(a_2)$ for each $(a_1, a_2) \in B$, and for each $(a_1, a_2, a_3) \in C$ there is a $p \in P$ with $f(a_{p(1)}) < f(a_{p(2)}) < f(a_{p(3)})$?

Note that the symmetry considerations presented in Sect. 3 apply as well to this family. The permutation of the positions in the triples is independent of the additional pairs. Symmetry by reversing each constraint can be extended to this, more general case by transposing the relation B to accommodate to the reversed order.

With the results of Sect. 3 in place, the complexity of each problem in the new family can easily be derived. It turns out that the classification remains unchanged.

Theorem 3. *The problems of the family 3 are tractable or NP-complete as shown in Fig. 3.*

Proof. Taking $B = \emptyset$ demonstrates that the new problems are indeed generalisations. All NP-complete problems of Sect. 3 thus remain NP-complete.

On the other hand, the pairs in B feature as additional input for topological sorting. Thus, all tractable problems are solved using the more general algorithm T that already accepts an additional collection of constraining pairs. □

5 Constraints over Disjoint Triples

The third variation we are investigating takes advantage of the expressivity gained by the pairs introduced in Sect. 4. It is rather a specialisation of those problems where we assume that any two triples in the collection C are pairwise disjoint when viewed as sets. This family of problems is also indexed by $P \subseteq \mathcal{S}_3$.

Problem Family 4. INSTANCE: Finite set A, collection B of pairs from A, collection C of pairwise disjoint triples (a_1, a_2, a_3) of distinct elements from A.

QUESTION: Is there a bijection $f : A \rightarrow \{1, 2, \ldots, |A|\}$ such that $f(a_1) < f(a_2)$ for each $(a_1, a_2) \in B$, and for each $(a_1, a_2, a_3) \in C$ there is a $p \in P$ with $f(a_{p(1)}) < f(a_{p(2)}) < f(a_{p(3)})$?

Note that the symmetry considerations presented in Sect. 3 do not affect disjointness, and therefore apply also to this family, the new problems being restrictions of those in Sect. 4. By the latter reason, algorithm T can still be applied to solve the tractable problems. The question remains whether some of the NP-complete problems become more easy. In the remaining part of this section, we answer the question in the negative.

Let us start with the problem $P = \{(123), (231)\}$, which we call the *intermezzo* problem. The requirement for the triples in $(a_1, a_2, a_3) \in C$ therefore reads $f(a_1) < f(a_2) < f(a_3)$ or $f(a_2) < f(a_3) < f(a_1)$. We prove its NP-completeness by reduction from 3SAT using the component design technique described in [1, Sect. 3.2.3].

Question: Is there a bijection $f: A \to \{1, 2, \ldots, |A|\}$ such that $f(a_1) < f(a_2)$ for each $(a_1, a_2) \in B$, and for each $(a_1, a_2, a_3) \in C$ there is a $p \in P$ with $f(a_{p(1)}) < f(a_{p(2)}) < f(a_{p(3)})$?

Note that the symmetry considerations presented in Sect. 3 apply as well to this family. The [illegible] of the position in the triples is independent of the additional [illegible] [illegible] constraints [illegible] can be extended [illegible] [illegible] [illegible] [illegible]

[illegible]

[illegible]

Theorem 8. [illegible] *or NP-complete as shown in Fig.* [illegible]

Proof. [illegible] that the [illegible] problems are indeed generalizations. [illegible] problems of Sect. 3 thus remain NP-complete.

On the other hand, the pairs in B [illegible] for topological sorting. Thus [illegible] [illegible] [illegible] □

5 [illegible]

[illegible]

Problem Family 4. [illegible] [illegible] pairs from A, [illegible] distinct elements from A. [illegible] such that $f(a_1) <$ [illegible] $p \in P$ with [illegible]

[illegible] [illegible] [illegible] whether some [illegible] the remaining [illegible]

Let us [illegible] which we call the *inter-* [illegible] $(a_1, a_2, a_3) \in C$ therefore [illegible] We prove its P-completeness [illegible] using the component design technique described in [illegible]

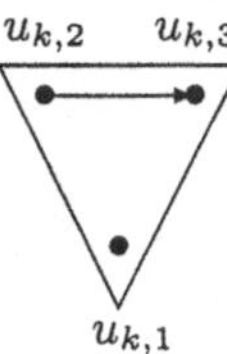

(a) Triple for each literal u_k

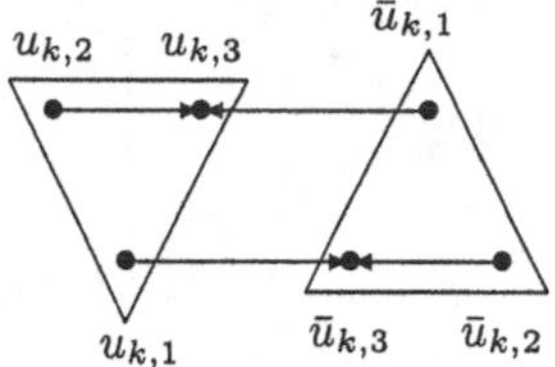

(b) Two triples for each variable u_k

(c) Triple for each occurrence of a literal $c_{i,j}$ in a clause

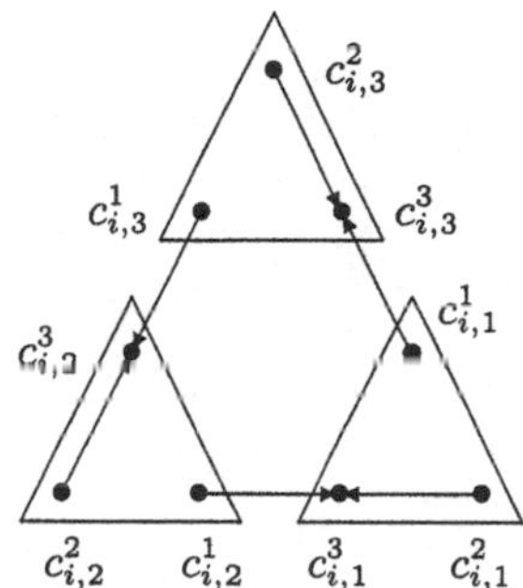

(d) Three triples for each clause c_i

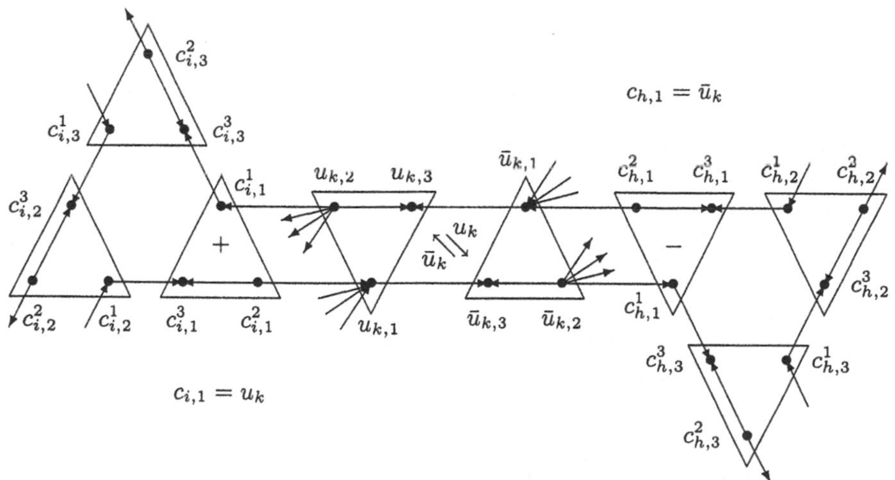

(e) Construction for two clauses and one variable

Fig. 4. Graph showing the construction in the reduction from 3SAT to intermezzo

We obtain the missing fact from the proof of Theorem 2 in Sect. 3 as a consequence of Lemma 1.

Corollary 1. *The problem* $\{(123),(231)\}$ *from the family 2 is NP-complete.*

Proof. Let A', B', and C' characterise an instance of intermezzo. Construct the instance of the problem $\{(123),(231)\}$ from the family 2 where $A = A' \cup \{n\}$ for some $n \notin A'$, and $C = C' \cup \{(n, a_1, a_2) \mid (a_1, a_2) \in B'\}$. This instance has a solution if and only if the corresponding instance of intermezzo has one. □

Continuing the main objective of this section, we reduce intermezzo to the problem $\{(123),(321)\}$ from the current family. Note that the existing NP-completeness proof for betweenness does not apply here because it uses non-disjoint triples [2].

Lemma 2. *The problem* $\{(123),(321)\}$ *from the family 4 is NP-complete.*

Proof. Let A', B', and C' characterise an instance of intermezzo. Construct the instance of betweenness where A extends A' by three new elements a_1', a_2', a_3' for each $(a_1, a_2, a_3) \in C'$. Note that there are $3|C'|$ distinct new elements since the triples in C' are pairwise disjoint. Moreover, C consists of two triples (a_1, a_3', a_3), (a_1', a_2', a_2) for each $(a_1, a_2, a_3) \in C'$. Finally, for each $(a_1, a_2, a_3) \in C'$, B extends B' by inserting three new pairs (a_1', a_1), (a_3', a_2'), (a_2, a_3) and, for each pair (a, a_1), one new pair (a, a_1'). Intuitively, an element a_1 is split into two elements a_1 and a_1' such that a_1' immediately precedes a_1.

Assume there is a total order $\prec'$ of the instance of intermezzo. The order $\prec$ modifies $\prec'$ by replacing, for each $(a_1, a_2, a_3) \in C'$, the occurrence of a_1 in $\prec'$ with

- either $a_1' \prec a_1 \prec a_3' \prec a_2'$ if $a_1 \prec' a_2 \prec' a_3$,
- or $a_3' \prec a_2' \prec a_1' \prec a_1$ if $a_2 \prec' a_3 \prec' a_1$,

such that these four elements succeed without a gap. By definition of intermezzo exactly one of the two cases applies for each triple, thus $\prec$ is a total order of A.

The order $\prec$ satisfies each triple (a_1, a_3', a_3) since $a_1 \prec a_3' \prec a_3$ in the first case and $a_3 \prec a_3' \prec a_1$ in the second case. The order $\prec$ satisfies each triple (a_1', a_2', a_2) since $a_1' \prec a_2' \prec a_2$ in the first case and $a_2 \prec a_2' \prec a_1'$ in the second case. The order $\prec$, being an extension of $\prec'$, satisfies B'. In both cases $a_1' \prec a_1$, $a_3' \prec a_2'$, and $a_2 \prec a_3$ for each triple $(a_1, a_2, a_3) \in C'$, and, since a_1' and a_1 succeed without a gap, $a \prec a_1'$ whenever $a \prec' a_1$. Hence, $\prec$ is a total order of the constructed instance.

Assume there is a total order $\prec$ of the constructed instance. The order $\prec'$ is the restriction of $\prec$ to A. For each triple $(a_1, a_2, a_3) \in C'$, $a_2 \prec' a_3$ since $(a_2, a_3) \in B$. Assume that $a_2 \prec' a_1 \prec' a_3$ for some such triple.

1. By definition of $\prec'$ we also have $a_2 \prec a_1 \prec a_3$.
2. Since $(a_1, a_3', a_3) \in C$ we have $a_1 \prec a_3' \prec a_3$.
3. Since $(a_1', a_1) \in B$ and $(a_3', a_2') \in B$ we have $a_1' \prec a_1 \prec a_3' \prec a_2'$.

[illegible] from the proof of Theorem 2 in Sect. 3 as a [illegible]

Corollary 1. [illegible] *is NP-complete.*

Proof. [illegible] construct the [illegible]

[illegible] NP-complete [illegible] disjoint [illegible]

Lemma 2. [illegible] *is NP-complete.*

Proof. [illegible] Construct the [illegible]

[illegible]

[illegible] total order of A. [illegible]

[illegible] the constructed instance [illegible]

[illegible]

2. Since [illegible]

Since [illegible] $\in B$ we have [illegible]

We have established which of the considered problems are efficiently solvable and which are NP-complete, proving that the classifications coincide for all three problem families that are related as shown in Fig. 5. That picture is completed by the variant that requires disjoint triples but does not permit pairs—this variant can be solved trivially.

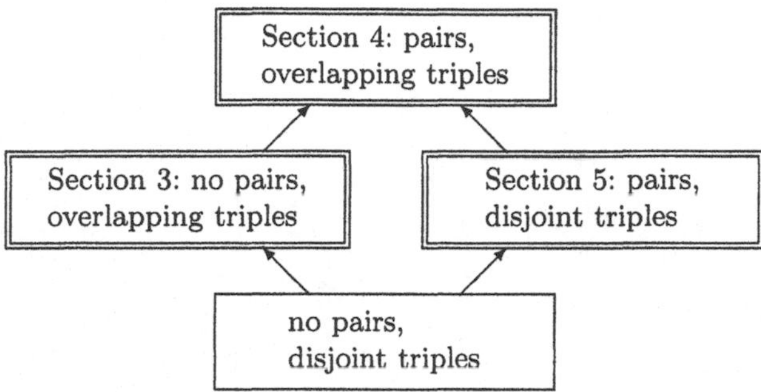

Fig. 5. Variants of problems with triples

The problems discussed in this paper also arise in the context of qualitative spatial reasoning [5]. The algebraic treatment pursued in that area originates in qualitative temporal reasoning, notably with Allen's interval algebra [10]. All subclasses of Allen's interval algebra have been classified as being either NP-complete or tractable [11, 12].

Note that a simple translation from Allen's interval algebra to our formalism fails for two reasons. First, the relative positions of intervals use not only $<$ but also the $\leq$, $=$, and $\neq$ relations. Second, there may be different disjunctions in effect between different pairs of intervals. This could be simulated with the exclusion problem, but that is already NP-complete.

Conversely, a simple translation from our formalism to Allen's interval algebra fails also for two reasons. First, the start and end points of intervals are correlated, whereas no such restrictions apply for our ordering problems with constraints. Second, there is only one clause for each pair of intervals, but our set C models arbitrary conjunctions.

Let us finally mention two further generalisations of the problems presented in this paper. First, the number of elements involved in specifying constraints may be increased beyond three. To this end, a reduction technique can be defined that reveals an interesting structure underlying the ordering problems. It again turns out that large classes of the generalised ordering problems are either tractable or NP-complete, and we intend to address this dichotomy. Second, the strict order may be replaced by a weak order. Both topics are currently under investigation [7].

BuST-Bundled Suffix Trees

Luca Bortolussi[1], Francesco Fabris[2], and Alberto Policriti[1]

[1] Department of Mathematics and Informatics, University of Udine.
`bortolussi|policriti AT dimi.uniud.it`
[2] Department of Mathematics and Informatics, University of Trieste.
`frnzfbrs AT dsm.uniuv.trieste.it`

Abstract. We introduce a data structure, the *Bundled Suffix Tree* (*BuST*), that is a generalization of a Suffix Tree (*ST*). To build a *BuST* we use an alphabet Σ together with a non-transitive relation $\approx$ among its letters. Following the path of a substring β within a *BuST*, constructed over a text α of length n, not only the positions of the exact occurrences of β in α are found (as in a *ST*), but also the positions of all the substrings $\beta_1, \beta_2, \beta_3, \ldots$ that are related with β via the relation $\approx$ among the characters of Σ, for example strings at a certain "distance" from β. A *BuST* contains $O(n^{1+\delta})$ additional nodes ($\delta < 1$) in probability, and is constructed in $O(n^{1+\delta})$ steps. In the worst case it contains $O(n^2)$ nodes.

1 Introduction

A Suffix Tree is a data structure computable in linear time and associated with a finite text $\alpha = \alpha[1], \alpha[2], \ldots, \alpha[n] = \alpha[1...n]$, where $\alpha[i] \in \Sigma$ and $\Sigma = \{a_1, a_2 \ldots, a_K\}$ is the alphabet (that is $|\Sigma| = K$). In the following we suppose the existence of an ordering among alphabet letters and we assume to append a character $\# \notin \Sigma$ at the end of our text, as is customary when working with *ST*'s. A *ST* allows to check in $O(m)$ time if an assigned string β, $|\beta| = m$, is a substring of α; moreover, at the same time it gives the exact positions $j_1, j_2, \ldots, j_r$ of all the r occurrences of β into α in $O(r)$ additional time. Therefore, a *ST* solves the *Exact String Matching Problem* (*ESM*) in linear time with respect to the length n of the searched string. A *ST* solves in linear time also the *Longest Repeated Exact Substring Problem* (*LRES*) of an assigned text α. A complete and detailed treatment of these results can be found in [6].

Even if very efficient in solving the *ESM* and the *LRES* problem, the *ST* data structure suffers of an important drawback when one has to solve an *Approximate String Matching Problem* (*ASM*), or to solve the harder *Longest Repeated Approximate Substring Problem* (*LRAS*). In these cases, one needs to search for strings $\beta_1, \beta_2, \beta_3, \ldots$ substrings of α, such that $\mathbf{d}(\beta, \beta_j) \leq D$, where $\mathbf{d}(\cdot, \cdot)$ is a suitable *distance* (most frequently Hamming or Levenshtein distance) and D is constant or proportional to the length of β. This happens because the structure of a *ST* is not adequate to handle distance in a natural way. This

Please use the following format when citing this chapter:

Bortolussi, L., Fabris, F., Policriti, A., 2006, in International Federation for Information Processing, Volume 209, Fourth IFIP International Conference on Theoretical Computer Science-TCS 2006, eds. Navarro, G., Bertossi, L., Kohayakwa, Y., (Boston: Springer), pp. 91–102.

BuST-Bundled Suffix Trees

[illegible] Francesco [illegible] and Alberto [illegible]

[illegible] of Mathematics and Informatics, University of Udine, [illegible]
[illegible] University of Trieste, [illegible]

Abstract. [illegible] Bundled Suffix Tree [illegible] ($BuST$) [illegible] suffix tree (STT) [illegible] S [illegible] of length m [illegible] the positions of the exact occurrences [illegible] the positions of all [illegible] $S_1, S_2, \ldots$ that are related with [illegible] the relation [illegible] for example [illegible] distance [illegible] $BuST$ contains [illegible] nodes [illegible] in [illegible] it contains [illegible]

1 Introduction

[illegible] when we assume [illegible] A [illegible] positions of S [illegible] additional time [illegible] (LBM) [illegible] A [illegible] solve [illegible] (LRP) [illegible] Problem [illegible] In these cases, the need to [illegible] such that $d(\alpha, S_i) \leq D$, where [illegible] Levenshtein distance, and D [illegible] This happens because the [illegible] natural way. This

[illegible]

[illegible] Bortolussi, L., Fabris, F. and Policriti, A. [illegible] International Federation for Information Processing, Volume 209 [illegible] IFIP International Conference on Theoretical Computer Science—TCS 2006 [illegible] (Boston: Springer), pp. 91–102.

this paper and concerns the calculation of the approximate frequency of appearance of a given subword (with the relative calculation of associated measures of surprise), cf. Section 5. An advantage is that the above mentioned information can be extracted from the *BuST* in the same way this extraction is done with Suffix Trees in the exact case.

The notion of relation between letters of an alphabet is a general concept, susceptible of encoding different properties connected with the specific application domain, e.g. Hamming-like distances or scoring schemes. Moreover, the particular relation used is completely orthogonal with respect to the definition, the construction and the analysis of the data structure. In this presentation we will deal with a restricted type of relation, constructed over an alphabet of macrocharacters, by means of a threshold criterion relative to a selected distance (mainly Hamming distance). The macroletters can have fixed or variable length; this is not a problem as long as they form a prefix-free code. On the other hand, the introduction of macrocharacters brings some rigidity in the type of approximate information that can be encapsulated. For instance, the Hamming-like relation introduced above puts in correspondence two strings if their distance is less than a threshold proportional to their length, and if the errors are distributed among the tuples. Moreover, only strings of length proportional to the macroletters' length can be compared. This rigidity, however, is the price to pay to "localize" the approximate information we are looking for: with the Hamming-like relation, we "localize" a global distance between two strings by splitting it evenly between their tuples.

The paper is organized as follows. In Section 2 we give the definition of the structure and a naive algorithm for its construction. In Section 3 we analyze the dimension of the data structure in the worst and in the average case. In Section 4 we give some hints to an optimal construction algorithm, while Section 5 contains an application for computing approximate surprise indexes. Finally, in Section 6 we draw some conclusions. The interested reader can find complete proofs, details on the optimal construction and further information in [4].

2 Naive construction of a *BuST*

A *ST* is not suitable to handle approximate search in a natural way essentially because of its rigidity in matching characters: they either match and the (unique) path proceeds, or the characters are different and a branching point is necessary. Conversely, in a *BuST* we accept the idea that a path is good not only when characters match, but also when they are in relation.

Let $\Sigma = \{a_1, \ldots, a_k\}$ be an alphabet, and $\approx$ be a symmetric and reflexive binary relation on Σ, encapsulating some form of approximate information.

Definition 1. *Given a string $\beta = \beta[1, \ldots, m]$, we say that $\gamma = \gamma[1, \ldots, m]$ is a* variant *of β if and only if $\beta[i] \approx \gamma[i]$, $\forall i = 1, \ldots, m$, and we write $\beta \approx \gamma$. We denote with $\approx(\beta) = \{\gamma \mid \beta \approx \gamma\}$.*

this [illegible] the calculation of [illegible] frequency of appearance of [illegible] associated measures of [illegible] Section [illegible] advantage [illegible] the above mentioned information can be extracted from the PoST in the same way the extraction is done with suffix [illegible].

[illegible] general concept [illegible] connected with the [illegible] schemes. [illegible] for the [illegible] alphabet [illegible] threshold [illegible] a selected distance [illegible] distance). The [illegible] have fixed or variable length [illegible] a prefix-free code. On the other hand, [illegible] some rigidity in the type of [illegible]. For instance, the [illegible] two strings if [illegible] proportional to [illegible] length, and if the [illegible]. Moreover only strings of length [illegible] reality, however, [illegible] we are looking for [illegible] global distance between two [illegible].

[illegible] the definition of the [illegible]. In [illegible] Section [illegible]. Finally, in Section [illegible] complete proofs [illegible] in [4].

[illegible]

[illegible] is necessary [illegible] that a path is good not only [illegible] but also when they are [illegible].

[illegible] symmetric and reflexive [illegible] information.

Definition 1 [illegible] We [illegible] $(\sigma) = \{\sigma \ldots$ [illegible]

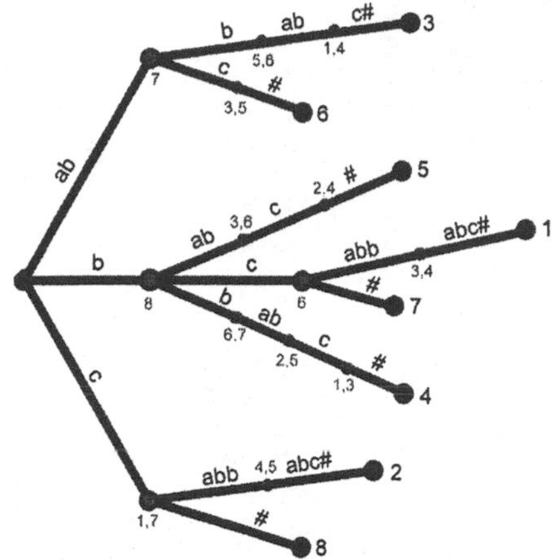

Fig. 1. Bundled Suffix Tree for the sequence $\alpha = bcabbabc\#$, with $a \approx b \approx c$.

The Main property accounts for the most important function of a *BuST*, that is to encode all $\approx$-variants of a substring of α. The Uniqueness property states that once a red node labeled h is inserted, the subtree rooted at this node cannot contain other red nodes with the same label. Maximality and uniqueness together assure that we insert at most one red node at the *deepest* possible position.

Remark 1. If β is the path label of the ST for α, the starting positions of substrings γ of α that are variants of β are found by reading all the labels rooted at the end of β.

Remark 2. The *BuST* is a data structure which is, in some sense, *in the middle* between a Suffix Tree and a Suffix Trie. We recall that a Suffix Trie is similar in shape to a *ST*, but every edge contains as many nodes as the length of its label. While constructing a *BuST*, we insert nodes splitting edges, hence the set of nodes of a *BuST* contains that of a *ST* and resembles to that of the corresponding Suffix Trie. The analogy stops here, as red nodes may have multiple labels and are added using relation $\approx$ as matching primitive.

In order to simplify the following computations, we assume that the relation $\approx$ enjoys the *hypercube-like property* over Σ: for each $a \in \Sigma$, there is a constant number V of $b \in \Sigma$, such that $a \approx b$. When elements of Σ are tuples built over a sub-alphabet Σ_1, we will put $a \approx b$ if and only if $\mathbf{d}(a, b) \leq D$, where $\mathbf{d}(a, b)$ is a suitable distance between tuples and D is a constant. In such cases we will also assume that the constant D is proportional to the length of Σ_1 t-tuples constituting elements of Σ. If we work with the Hamming distance, then the macro-characters b such that $a \approx b$ are all the elements of the Hamming sphere of radius d and centered in a. In such a case the constant V is the *volume* of this Hamming sphere.

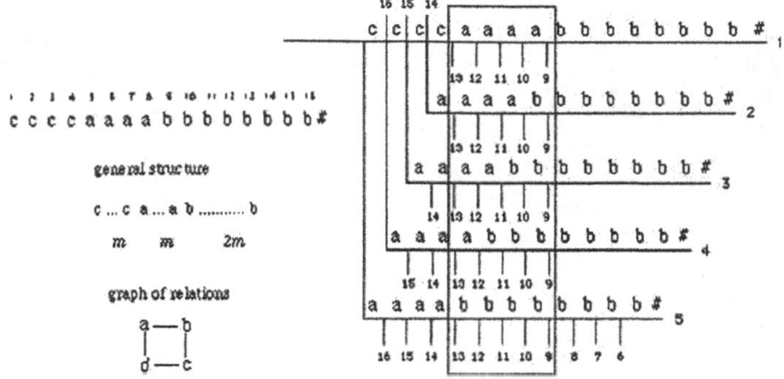

Fig. 2. A worst case BuST for the sequence $\alpha = aaccbbbb\#$

with $\delta = \log V/\log(1/p^+)$. A better estimate of $R(j)$ can be obtained by replacing h_n with z_n, obtaining $R(j) \lesssim n^{\delta'}$, with $\delta' = \log V/\log H(\mathcal{S})$.

Therefore, the total number of red nodes inserted, denoted by R, is bounded on average by:

$$R = \sum_{j=1}^{n} R(j) \lesssim \sum_{j=1}^{n} n^{\delta} = n^{1+\delta}.$$

The value of δ depends on the probability distribution of the source and on the relation between the letters of the alphabet. For instance, for an Hamming-like relation with macrocharacters of length 4 and error rate 25% built over DNA alphabet, and the maximum probability of a DNA letter varying from 0.25 to 0.5, the value of δ remains between 0.46 to 0.92, hence the size of the structure is bound by a subquadratic function.

Observe that the bound we give is coarse, in fact δ can be greater than one, while the size of the data structure cannot be more than quadratic in the length of the processed text. In fact, the number $R(j)$ of red nodes inserted while processing suffix j can be at most one per each path of the Suffix Tree, or equivalently, at most one for each suffix of the text, hence $R(j) \leq n$. Therefore $R \leq n^2$. This theoretical bound can be reached for particular texts, as shown in the following example.

Example 1. Consider a sequence of the form $\alpha = a^n c^n b^{2n}$, over the alphabet $\Sigma = \{a, b, c, d\}$, with $a \approx b \approx c \approx d \approx a$ as relation (it is hypercube like). The lengths of the runs of a,b,c in α are in proportion of $1:1:2$. Note from Figure 2 that, if the length of the text is $4n$, then the rectangular area delimited by the dashed line contains $n(n-1)$ red nodes (the ones with label from $2n+1$ to $4n-1$, repeated n times).

Fig. 2. A worst case BuST for the sequence [illegible]

[illegible] obtained by re[illegible] [illegible]

Therefore the [illegible] number of [illegible] nodes inserted [illegible] is bounded on average [illegible]

[illegible]

The [illegible] of the [illegible] relation [illegible] of the alphabet. [illegible] for an Hamming [illegible] DNA [illegible] DNA [illegible] varying [illegible] the value of [illegible] the size of [illegible] bounded by a sub-quadratic function.

[illegible] that the bound [illegible] greater than [illegible] cannot be [illegible] quadratic in the [illegible] the number [illegible] of [illegible] nodes inserted [illegible] one per [illegible] Therefore [illegible]

[illegible] that [illegible] Figure [illegible] that [illegible] length [illegible] rectangular areas delimited [illegible] the [illegible] with label from [illegible]

Equipped with ISL, and with some extra care to keep correctly into account the maximality property of *BuST*, we can define an algorithm that builds the *BuST* for α starting from its *ST* and processing the text backwards, from the last suffix to the first. Red nodes for suffix i are generated from red nodes for suffix $i+1$, essentially by visiting their parent nodes (in the *ST*) and checking the positions of the tree pointed by ISL departing from there (only for the letters in relation with $\alpha[i]$). Each red node r_{i+1} can be processed in constant time (actually in $O(K^2)$, with $K = |\Sigma|$), thus giving rise to an algorithm (called ISL_BUST) with complexity $O(R)$. The interested reader can find all the details in [4], where the following theorem is proved.

Theorem 1. *ISL_BUST constructs a* BuST *for a text* α *in time* $O(R)$.

5 An Application of *BuST*: detecting approximate unusual words

In this section we present an application of *BuST*s, related to the detection of unusually overrepresented words in a text α. Specifically, we admit as occurrences β' of a word β also strings that are "close" to β, where the concept of closeness means that β' is a variant of β.

Before entering into the details related to the use of *BuST*s, we give a brief overview of a method presented by Apostolico et al. in [2, 1]. The problem tackled is the identification, in a reliable and computationally efficient way, of a subset of strings of a text α that have a particularly high (or low) score of "surprise". Particular care is given in finding a suitable data structure that can represent this set of strings in a space-efficient way, i.e. in a size linear w.r.t. the length of the processed text.

The class of measures of surprise considered is the so called z-score, defined for a substring β of α as $\delta(\beta) = (f(\beta) - E(\beta))/N(\beta)$. Here $f(\beta)$ is the observed frequency of β, $E(\beta)$ is a function that can be interpreted as a kind of expected frequency for β and $N(\beta)$ is a normalization factor. Intuitively, we are computing the (normalized) difference between the expected value for the frequency of β and the observed one. If this score is high, it means that β appears more often than expected, while if it is very low (and negative), than β is underrepresented in α. Conditions on E and N are given to guarantee that, whenever $f(\beta) = f(\beta\gamma)$, then $\delta(\beta) \leq \delta(\beta\gamma)$. In other words, while looking for overrepresented words, we do not have to examine all the $O(n^2)$ substrings of a text α, but we can focus on the longest strings sharing the same occurrences, as they are those having the higher z-score. It is easy to see that those strings correspond exactly to the labels of the (inner) nodes of the suffix tree for α, so we must compute the z-score only for these strings. Their frequency can be computed easily by a traversal of the tree in overall linear time. On the other hand, the computation of E and N can be far from trivial, and its complexity is deeply related to the choice of the probabilistic model adopted for the source. E

that $p'_a = \sum_{b \approx a} p_b$ is the probability of finding a macrocharacter in relation with a, while for a string $a_1 \ldots a_k$ the probability of finding an approximate occurrence under the source model is $\text{Prob}(a_1 \ldots a_k) = \prod_{i=1}^{k} p_{a_i}$. Thus the expected numbers of occurrences in α, $|\alpha| = n$ of a string in relation with β, $|\beta| = m$ is $(n - m + 1)\text{Prob}(\beta)$. Therefore we can adopt the same trick used for computing expectations for the exact case: we precompute a vector $A[i] = \text{Prob}(\alpha[1 \ldots i])$ in linear time using the recursive relation $A[i] = A[i - 1]p_{\alpha[i]}$, then the expectation for $\alpha[i \ldots j]$ can be computed in constant time by $\text{Prob}(\alpha[i \ldots j]) = A[j]/A[i]$.
As normalization factor, we can use the expectation itself, or the first order approximation of the variance. A direct computation of the variance itself seems much more complicated, as here we cannot use anymore the method used in [2] (in essence, we should replace the concept of autocorrelation with the weaker notion of $\approx$-autocorrelation, i.e. we should look for $\approx$-periods of words; we leave this investigation for future work).

With those choices for the source model and for the normalization factor, we are able to compute the z-score δ for each string labeling an inner node (both black and red) of the *BuST* in constant time. Note that if the path in the tree labeled by β ends in the middle of an edge, its frequency is the same as that of the string $\beta\gamma$ labeling the path from the root to the fist node (black or red) below the end of β, and therefore $\delta(\beta\gamma) \geq \delta(\beta)$. So we are guaranteed, in order to find the maximal surprising strings, that we need to compute the index only for the nodes of the *BuST*. In addition the algorithm runs in a time proportional to the size of the *BuST* itself, which is subquadratic on average. Note also that the number of maximal surprising strings (modulo the approximations introduced by the relation) is of the same size of the *BuST*, so we are computing the z-score in optimal size and time.

6 Conclusions

We presented *BuST*, a new index structure for strings, which is an extension of Suffix Trees where the alphabet is enriched with a non-transitive relation, encapsulating some form of approximate information. This is the case, for instance, of a relation induced by the Hamming distance for an alphabet composed of macrocharacters on a base one. We showed that the average size of the tree is subquadratic, despite a quadratic worst case dimension, and we provided a construction algorithm linear in the size of the structure. In the final section, we discussed how *BuST* can be used for computing in a efficient way a class of measures of statistical approximate overrepresentation of substrings of a text α. We have also an implementation of the (naive) construction of the data structure in **C**, which we used to perform some tests on the size of *BuST*, showing that the bound given in Section 3 is rather pessimistic (cf. again [4]).

BuST allow to extract approximate information from a string α in a simple way, essentially in the same way exact information can be extracted from *ST*.

that [illegible] the [illegible] of finding [illegible] in relation with [illegible] of finding an approximate [illegible] source model [illegible] Thus the [illegible] number of occurrences [illegible] of a string in relation with [illegible] Therefore we can adopt the same trick used [illegible] we precompute a vector [illegible] using [illegible] can be computed [illegible]

[illegible] the [illegible] that the [illegible] to [illegible] A direct [illegible] made to [illegible] as here we cannot use [illegible] in [2] [illegible] replace the [illegible] with [illegible] the reader [illegible] should look [illegible] words, we leave [illegible]

With [illegible] for the normalization [illegible] to [illegible] the [illegible] for [illegible] using [illegible] in [illegible] that the path in the [illegible] is the same as that of [illegible] the [illegible] (black [illegible]) below the [illegible] in order to find [illegible] to compute the index only for the [illegible] proportional to the [illegible] that the [illegible] and [illegible]

6 Conclusion

[illegible] final section, we discussed [illegible] can be used for [illegible] way [illegible] class of [illegible] strings of text [illegible] We have [illegible] the [illegible] showing that [illegible]

[illegible] in a simple way [illegible] can be extracted from ST

An O(1) Solution to the Prefix Sum Problem on a Specialized Memory Architecture

Andrej Brodnik[12], Johan Karlsson[1], J. Ian Munro[3], and Andreas Nilsson[1]

[1] Luleå University of Technology
Dept. of Computer Science and Electrical Engineering
S-971 87 Luleå
Sweden
{johan.karlsson,andreas.nilsson}@csee.ltu.se

[2] University of Primorska
Faculty of Education
Cankarjeva 5
6000 Koper
Slovenia
andrej.brodnik@pef.upr.si

[3] Cheriton School of Computer Science
University of Waterloo
Waterloo, Ontario
Canada, N2L 3G1
imunro@uwaterloo.ca

Abstract. In this paper we study the Prefix Sum problem introduced by Fredman. We show that it is possible to perform both update and retrieval in $O(1)$ time simultaneously under a memory model in which individual bits may be shared by several words. We also show that two variants (generalizations) of the problem can be solved optimally in $\Theta(\lg N)$ time under the comparison based model of computation.

1 Introduction

Models of computation play a fundamental role in theoretical Computer Science, and indeed, in the subject as a whole. Even in modeling a standard computer, the random access machine (RAM) model has been subject to refinements which more realistically model cost or, as in this paper, suggest feasible extensions to the model that permit more efficient computation, at least for some problems. Work taking into account a memory hierarchy, either when memory and page sizes are known (cf. [2]) or not (cf. [11]) is an example of the former. Taking into account parallelism, as in the PRAM model (cf. [17,26]), is an obvious example of the latter. More subtle examples include the recent result that the operations of an arbitrary finite Abelian group can be carried out in constant time (We assume a word of memory is adequate to hold the size of the group.) provided one can reverse the bits of a word in constant time [8]. This argues for a more robust set of operations. Here we deal with the way a single level memory is

Please use the following format when citing this chapter:

Brodnik, A., Karlsson, J., Munro, J.I., Nilsson, A., 2006, in International Federation for Information Processing, Volume 209, Fourth IFIP International Conference on Theoretical Computer Science-TCS 2006, eds. Navarro, G., Bertossi, L., Kohayakwa, Y., (Boston: Springer), pp. 103–114.

Fredman showed that, under the comparison based model of computation, an $O(\lg N)$ solution exists for the Prefix Sum problem [9].

The problem can be generalized in several ways and we start by adding another parameter, k to the `Retrieve` operation. This parameter is used to tell the starting point of the array interval to sum over. Hence, `Retrieve(k,j)` returns $\sum_{i=k}^{j} \mathcal{A}(i)$, where $0 \leq k \leq j < N$. This variant is usually referred to as the *Partial Sum* or *Range Sum problem.* The Partial Sum problem can be solved using a solution to the Prefix Sum problem (`Retrieve(k,j) = Retrieve(j) - Retrieve(k-1)`). In fact, the two problems are often used interchangeably.

Furthermore, there is no obvious reason to only allow addition in the `Update` and `Retrieve` operations. We can allow any binary function, $\oplus$, to be used. In fact we can allow the `Update` operation to use one function, $\oplus_u$, and the `Retrieve` operation to use another function, $\oplus_r$. We will refer to this variant of the problem as the *General Prefix Sum problem.*

Moreover, one can allow array position to be inserted at or deleted from arbitrary places. Hence, we can have sparse arrays, e.g. an array where only $\mathcal{A}(5)$ and $\mathcal{A}(500)$ are present. Positions which have not yet been added or have been deleted have the value 0. We refer to this variant as the *Dynamic Prefix Sum problem.* Brodnik and Nilsson [21, pp 65-80] describe a data structure they call a BinSeT tree which can be modified slightly to support all operation of the Dynamic Prefix Sum problem in $O(\lg N)$ time.

The *Searchable Partial Sum* problem extends the set of operations with a `select(j)` operation which finds the smallest i such that $\sum_{k=0}^{i} \mathcal{A}(k) \geq j$ [23]. Hon et al. consider the Dynamic version of the Searchable Partial Sum problem [16]. Another generalization is to use multidimensional arrays and this variant has been studied by the data base community [4,12,13,15,24,25].

Several lower bounds have been presented for the Prefix Sum problem: Fredman showed a $\Omega(\lg N)$ algebraic complexity lower bound and a $\Omega(\lg N/\lg\lg N)$ information-theoretic lower bound [9]. Yao [29] has shown that $\Omega(\lg N/\lg\lg N)$ is an inherent lower bound under the semi-group model of computation and this was improved by Hampapuram and Fredman to $\Omega(\lg N)$ [14]. We side step these lower bounds by considering the RAMBO model of computation [5,10].

As with all RAM based model we need to restrict the size of a word which can be stored and operated on. We denote the word size with b and assume that b is an integer power of 2 which is true for most computers today. A bounded word size also implies a bounded universe of elements that we store in the array. We use M to denote the universe size. Hence all operations $\oplus$ have to be computed modulo M and we require that each of the operands and the result are stored in one word.

We will use n and m to denote $\lceil \lg N \rceil$ and $\lceil \lg M \rceil$ respectively. Hence, $N \leq 2^n$ and $M \leq 2^m$. Both n and m are less than or equal to b, $(n, m \leq b)$. In one of the solutions we actually require that $nm \leq b$.

In Sect. 2 we show a $O(1)$ solution to the Prefix Sum problem under the RAMBO model using a modified Yggdrasil variant. In Sect. 3 we discuss a

Fredman showed that under the [illegible] model of computation, an $O(\lg N)$ solution exists for the [illegible] problem [illegible].

The problem can be generalized in several ways and we start by adding another parameter, k, to the Retrieve operation. This parameter is used to tell the starting point of [illegible] Hence, Retrieve(k, j) returns [illegible] referred to [illegible] Sum problem can [illegible] Retrieve(k, j) = Retrieve$(1, j)$ − Retrieve$(1, k-1)$ [illegible] is an offline [illegible] summary.

Furthermore, [illegible] Retrieve [illegible] function, [illegible] and the [illegible] Update operation [illegible] and the Retrieve operation [illegible] function [illegible]. We will refer to this variant of the problem as the [illegible] Sum problem.

Moreover, [illegible] to be [illegible] arbitrary places [illegible] and [illegible] been [illegible] Sum [illegible] a Binary [illegible] Dynamic [illegible]

The [illegible] with [illegible] Dynamic [illegible] Sum problem [illegible] has been studied [illegible]

[illegible]

[illegible] We use M to denote [illegible] Hence [illegible] have to be computed modulo [illegible] of the [illegible] and the [illegible] in one word.

We will [illegible] respectively. Hence [illegible] $M \leq 2^m$ [illegible] In one [illegible]

In Sect. 2 we [illegible] $O(1)$ solution to the [illegible] problem under the RAMBO model [illegible] a modified Y [illegible] Sect. 3 we discuss [illegible]

```
update(j, Δ)
  if (j == N-1)
    vn1 = vn1 + Δ;
  else
    i = N + j;
    while (i > 1)
      next = i div 2;
      if (i mod 2 == 0)
        ν_next = ν_next + Δ mod M);
      i = next;
```

Alg 1: Updating of a N-m-tree in $O(\lg N)$ time.

```
retrieve(j)
  if (j == N-1)
    sum = vn1;
    i = N + j;
  else
    sum = 0;
    i = N + j + 1;
  while (i > 1)
    next = i div 2;
    if (i mod 2 == 1)
      sum = sum + ν_next mod M;
    i = next;
  return sum;
```

Alg 2: Retrieve in a N-m-tree in $O(\lg N)$ time.

m-Yggdrasil, register `reg[i]` corresponds to the path from node $\nu_{N/2+i}$ to the root of the tree. Each register consists of $nm \leq b$ bits. In total the m-Yggdrasil registers need $(N-1) \cdot m$ bits.

Now, we use the registers from m-Yggdrasil to store the nodes of our tree. The path corresponding to array position j is stored in `reg[j/2]` and hence all nodes along the path can be accessed at once.

We let levels of the tree be counted from the internal nodes above the leaves starting at 0 and ending with $n-1$ at the root. If the ith bit of j is 1 then j is in the right subtree of the node on level i of the path and in the left otherwise. Hence j can be used to determine which nodes along the path should be updated (nodes corresponding to bits of j that are 0) and which nodes should be used when retrieving a sum (nodes corresponding to bits of j that are 1).

When updating the m-Yggdrasil registers (Algorithm 3), for all bits of j, if the ith bit of j is 0 we add Δ to the value of the ith node along the path from j to the root. To do this we shift Δ to the corresponding position ($\Delta << (im)$) and add to `reg[j/2]`. Instead of checking whether the ith bit of j is 0 we can

To support the retrieve method in constant time we use a table `SUM[i]`, ($0 \leq i < 2^{nm}$) with m-bit values that are the sum modulo M of the n m-bit values in i.

To retrieve the sum (Algorithm 5) we read the register **reg** corresponding to j and mask out the parts we need. Then we use the table `SUM` to calculate the sum. Finally, we add `vn1` to the sum if $j = N - 1$.

```
retrieve(j)
  if (j == N-1)
    v = reg[j/2] AND mask(j);
  else
    v = reg[(j+1)/2] AND mask(j+1);
  sum = SUM[v];
  if (j == N-1)
    sum = vn1 + sum;
  return sum;
```

Alg 5: Retrieve in a N-m-tree stored in m-Yggdrasil memory using word size parallelism ($O(1)$ time).

The space needed by the table `SUM` is $2^{nm} \cdot m = N^{\lg M} \cdot m = M^{\lg N} \cdot m$, which is rather large. In order to reduce the space requirement we can reduce, by half, the number of bits used as index into the table. This gives us a space requirement of $\sqrt{M^{\lg N}} \cdot m$. We do this by shifting the top $n/2$ m-bit values from **reg** down and computing the sum modulo M of these values and the bottom $n/2$ values. Then this new $(n/2)m$-bit value is used as index into `SUM` instead.

We can actually repeat this process until we get the m-bit we desire, and hence we do not need the table `SUM` (Algorithm 6). However, this does increase the time complexity to $O(\lg n) = O(\lg \lg N)$. This gives us a trade off between space and time. By allowing $O(\iota)$ steps for the retrieve method we need $M^{\lg N/2^{\iota}} \cdot m$ bits for the table.

Lemma 2 *The retrieve operation of the Prefix Sum problem can be supported in $O(\iota + 1)$ time using $O(M^{\lg N/2^{\iota}} \cdot m + m)$ bits of memory in addition to the N-m-tree. Part of the N-m-tree is stored in m-Yggdrasil memory.*

By adjusting ι we can achieve the following result:

Corollary 1 *The retrieve operation of the Prefix Sum problem can be supported in:*

- *$O(1)$ time using $O(M^{(\lceil \lg N \rceil)/2} \cdot m)$ bits of memory in addition to the N-m-tree, with $\iota = 1$.*
- *$O(\lg \lg N)$ time using $O(m)$ bits of memory in addition to the N-m-tree, with $\iota = \lceil \lg \lg N \rceil$.*

[illegible] support the [illegible] in constant time we use a table SUM[i], $0 \le i <$ [illegible] m-bit [illegible] modulo M of the [illegible] m-bit values in [illegible]

To [illegible] the sum (Procedure 5) we read the [illegible] corresponding [illegible] use the table SUM to calculate [illegible] sum [illegible] M [illegible]

```
[illegible] )
[illegible] ( j = [illegible] -1)
  v = wa[illegible] /2 [illegible] ( j )
[illegible]
  [illegible] (j+1)/2 [illegible] mask( [illegible] ))
  [illegible] SUM[v] [illegible]
  [illegible] = k-1 [illegible]
  [illegible] v [illegible]
  return sum
```

Alg. 5: Retrieving [illegible] store [illegible] word [illegible] parallelism ([illegible])

The space needed [illegible] reduce [illegible] as index [illegible] gives us a space [illegible] from [illegible] the bottom [illegible] row [illegible] However, [illegible] [illegible] [illegible]

[illegible]

By [illegible]

[illegible] problem [illegible]

[illegible]

[illegible] [illegible] with [illegible]

only needs $m+1$ bits to be represented. Hence, if we calculate this value using the strategy above we will not use more than m bits of any word.

Furthermore, a straight forward less than comparison can not be performed using word-size parallelism since all bits of the words are considered. Instead we view the comparison as a check whether the $m+1$st bit is set or not. If it is set the value is larger than or equal to 2^m (cf. [19, 22]). We can actually create a bit mask which consists of m 1s if the $m+1$st bit is set and m 0s otherwise

$$d = (c + 2^m - M \text{ AND } 2^m) - ((c + 2^m - M \text{ AND } 2^m) >> m) \ . \tag{5}$$

This bit mask d can then be used to calculate $res = c \bmod M$. Since res is equal to $c - M$ if the $m+1$st bit of c is set and c otherwise we get

$$res = ((c - M) \text{ AND } d) \text{ OR } (c \text{ AND NOT } d) \ . \tag{6}$$

When computing $c - M$ we must make sure that we do not produce a negative value. This is done by using a similar strategy as for addition above, but we also set any of the bits in $c_{hi,hi}$ to 1 during the computation. If $c - M$ is greater than 0 this will not affect the result and otherwise the result will not be used.

We have a procedure which can be used to compute $(a+b) \bmod M$ without using more than m bits in any word. Hence, word-size parallelism can be used and we get our main result from this section:

Theorem 1 *Using the N-m-tree together with the m-Yggdrasil memory we can support the operations of the Prefix Sum problem in* $O(\iota+1)$ *time using* $(N-1)m$ *bits of m-Yggdrasil memory and* $O(M^{n/2^\iota} \cdot m + m)$ *bits of ordinary memory.*

3 An $O(\lg N)$ Solution to the General and Dynamic Prefix Sum Problem

We can actually partially solve the General Prefix Sum problem using the N-m-tree data structure and the m-Yggdrasil variant of RAMBO. All binary operations such that all elements in the universe have a unique inverse element (i.e. binary operations which form a *Group* with the set of elements in the universe) and only affect the m bits involved in the operation can be supported. This includes for example addition and subtraction but not the maximum function.

To solve the General and Dynamic Prefix Sum problem for semi-group operations we modify the Binary Segment Tree (BinSeT) data structure suggested by Brodnik and Nilsson. It was designed to handle in-advance resource reservation [21, pp 65-80] and if it is slightly modified it can solve both the General and Dynamic Prefix Sum problems efficiently. The original BinSeT stores, in each internal node, μ, the maximum value over the interval, and δ, the change of the value over the interval. Further, it also stores τ, the time of the left most event in the right subtree.

Instead of storing times as interval dividers we store array indices. To solve the Dynamic Prefix Sum problem with addition as operation and we only need

[illegible] calculate the value using [illegible] stored [illegible] word.

[illegible] forward [illegible] can not be performed [illegible] parallelism since all bits of [illegible] considered. Instead [illegible] comparison [illegible] is set [illegible] If [illegible] is [illegible] actually [illegible] which [illegible] of the [illegible]

$$[illegible]$$

[illegible] Since [illegible] is equal [illegible]

$$[illegible] \tag{6}$$

When computing [illegible] we do not produce a negative value. This [illegible] addition [illegible] above but we [illegible] then [illegible] results [illegible]

We have a procedure which can be [illegible] and [illegible] [illegible] more than [illegible]

[illegible] find [illegible] memory [illegible] ordinary memory.

5 An $O(\sqrt{\ldots})$ [illegible] for [illegible] Prefix Sum Problem

We [illegible] partially solved the [illegible] [illegible] structure and [illegible] [illegible] that [illegible] [illegible] and [illegible] [illegible] [illegible] data structure suggested by [illegible] and Nilsson [illegible] resource [illegible] [illegible] solve both the General and Dynamic Prefix Sum [illegible]. The original [illegible] stores, in each [illegible] of the [illegible] the left most event in [illegible]

Instead of storing [illegible] indices. To solve the Dynamic Prefix Sum problem [illegible] operation and we only need

2. Alok Aggarwal and Ashok K. Chandra. Virtual memory algorithms (preliminary version). In *Proceedings of the 20th Annual ACM Symposium on Theory of Computing*, pages 173–185. ACM Press, May 2–4 1988.
3. P. Beame and F. E. Fich. Optimal bounds for the predecessor problem and related problems. *Journal of Computer and System Sciences*, 65(1):38–72, 2002.
4. Fredrik Bengtsson and Jingsen Chen. Space-efficient range-sum queries in OLAP. In Yahiko Kambayashi, Mukesh Mohania, and Wolfram Wöß, editors, *Data Warehousing and Knowledge Discovery: 6th International Conference DaWaK*, volume 3181 of *Lecture Notes in Computer Science*, pages 87–96. Springer, September 2004.
5. Andrej Brodnik. *Searching in Constant Time and Minimum Space (*MINIMÆ RES MAGNI MOMENTI SUNT*)*. PhD thesis, University of Waterloo, Waterloo, Ontario, Canada, 1995. (Also published as technical report CS-95-41.).
6. Andrej Brodnik, Svante Carlsson, Michael L. Fredman, Johan Karlsson, and J. Ian Munro. Worst case constant time priority queue. *Journal of System and Software*, 78(3):249–256, December 2005.
7. Andrej Brodnik and John Iacono. Dynamic predecessor queries. Unpublished manuscript, 2006.
8. Arash Farzan and J. Ian Munro. Succinct representation of finite abelian groups. In *Proceedings of the 2006 International Symposium on Symbolic and Algebraic Computation*, Lecture Notes in Computer Science. Springer, 2006. To appear.
9. Michael L. Fredman. The complexity of maintaining an array and computing its partial sums. *Journal of the ACM*, 29(1):250–260, January 1982.
10. Michael L. Fredman and Michael E. Saks. The cell probe complexity of dynamic data structures. In *Proceedings of the 21st Annual ACM Symposium on Theory of Computing*, pages 345–354. ACM Press, May 14–17 1989.
11. Matteo Frigo, Charles E. Leiserson, Harald Prokop, and Sridhar Ramachandran. Cache-oblivious algorithms. In IEEE, editor, *40th Annual Symposium on Foundations of Computer Science (FOCS)*, pages 285–297. IEEE Computer Society, IEEE Computer Society, October 17–19 1999.
12. Steven P. Geffner, Divyakant Agrawal, Amr El Abbadi, and T. Smith. Relatve prefix sums: An efficient approach for querying dynamic OLAP data cubes. In *Proceedings of the 15th International Conference on Data Engineering*, pages 328–335, 1999.
13. Steven P. Geffner, Mirek Riedewald, Divyakant Agrawal, and Amr El Abbadi. Data cubes in dynamic environments. *Bulletin of the IEEE Computer Society Technical Committee on Data Engineering*, pages 31–40, 1999.
14. Haripriyan Hampapuram and Michael L. Fredman. Optimal biweighted binary trees and the complexity of maintaining partial sums. *SIAM Journal on Computing*, 28(1):1–9, 1998.
15. C. Ho, R. Agrawal, N. Megiddo, and R. Srikant. Range queries in OLAP data cubes. In *Proceedings ACM SIGMOD International Conference on Management of Data*, pages 73–88, 1997.
16. Wing-Kai Hon, Kunihiko Sadakane, and Wing-Kin Sung. Succinct data structure for searchable partial sums. In Toshihide Ibaraki, Naoki Katoh, and Hirotaka Ono, editors, *Algorithms and Computation - ISAAC 2003, 14th International Symposium*, volume 2906 of *Lecture Notes in Computer Science*, pages 505–516. Springer, December 2003.
17. Richard M. Karp and Vijaya Ramachandran. Parallel algorithms for shared-memeory machines. In van Leeuwen [28], chapter 17, pages 869–941.

[illegible] and [illegible] [illegible] memory algorithms [illegible]. [illegible] *Proceedings of the 15th Annual ACM Symposium on Theory of Computing*, pages 173–185. ACM Press, May 2–4 1983.
3. [illegible] and F. E. Fich. Optimal bounds for the predecessor problem and related problems. *Journal of Computer and System Sciences*, 65(1):38–72, 2002.
4. [illegible] and [illegible]. [illegible] range-sum queries in OLAP [illegible] [illegible] and Wolfram [illegible] editors, *Data Ware[illegible]* [illegible] [illegible] [illegible] September [illegible]
5. [illegible]
6. André Frédérik [illegible] [illegible] [illegible] [illegible] [illegible] and [illegible] [illegible] [illegible] [illegible] 18(3):240–255, December 2001.
7. [illegible] Unpublished [illegible]
8. [illegible] [illegible] Theory of Computing [illegible] 2003. [illegible]
9. [illegible]
10. [illegible] Theory [illegible] ACM [illegible]
11. [illegible] [illegible] Computer Society, [illegible]
12. [illegible] OLAP [illegible] *Data Warehousing [illegible]* pages 283–295, 2000.
13. [illegible]
14. [illegible]
15. [illegible] Range queries in OLAP [illegible] SIGMOD [illegible] Management of Data [illegible]
16. [illegible] International Symposium [illegible] pages 507–516 [illegible]
17. [illegible] algorithms for [illegible] In [illegible] pages 500–[illegible]

An Algorithm to Reduce the Communication Traffic for Multi-Word Searches in a Distributed Hash Table

Yuichi Sei[1], Kazutaka Matsuzaki[2], and Shinichi Honiden[3]

[1] The University of Tokyo Information Science and Technology Computer Science Department, Tokyo, Japan sei@nii.ac.jp
[2] The University of Tokyo Information Science and Technology Computer Science Department, Tokyo, Japan matsuzaki@nii.ac.jp
[3] National Institute of Informatics, Tokyo, Japan honiden@nii.ac.jp

Abstract. In distributed hash tables, much communication traffic comes from multi-word searches. The aim of this work is to reduce the amount of traffic by using a bloom filter, which is a space-efficient probabilistic data structure used to test whether or not an element is a member of a set. However, bloom filters have a limited role if several sets have different numbers of elements. In the proposed method, extra data storage is generated when contents' keys are registered in a distributed hash table system. Accordingly, we propose a "divided bloom filter" to solve the problem of a normal bloom filter. Using the divided bloom filter, we aim to reduce both the amount of communication traffic and the amount of data storage.

1 Introduction

Peer-to-peer systems are distributed networks that can share contents or services without the need for a central server. The first peer-to-peer systems, such as Napster [5] and Gnutella [1], lacked scalability. Distributed hash table (DHT) systems such as Chord [19], CAN [15], and Pastry [17] aim to overcome this challenge.

The DHT provides storage and retrieval by using a hash function. When a node participates in the DHT system, it is given a range of hash values for which it is responsible. Then the node finds the hash value of the key[1] of the content it has. It then sends [h(key), the content ID, its address] to any node participating in the DHT. The message is forwarded from node to node until it gets to the node responsible for h(key). Once this has been done, the contents can be found by any user; the user needs only to again hash a key to h(key) and ask any node to find the data corresponding with h(key).

In full-text searching, each node stores the posting list for the word(s) it is responsible for. A query involving multiple words requires that the postings for

[1] We call the hash value of x "h(x)".

Please use the following format when citing this chapter:

Sei, Y., Matsuzaki, K., Honiden, S., 2006, in International Federation for Information Processing, Volume 209, Fourth IFIP International Conference on Theoretical Computer Science-TCS 2006, eds. Navarro, G., Bertossi, L., Kohayakwa, Y., (Boston: Springer), pp. 115–129.

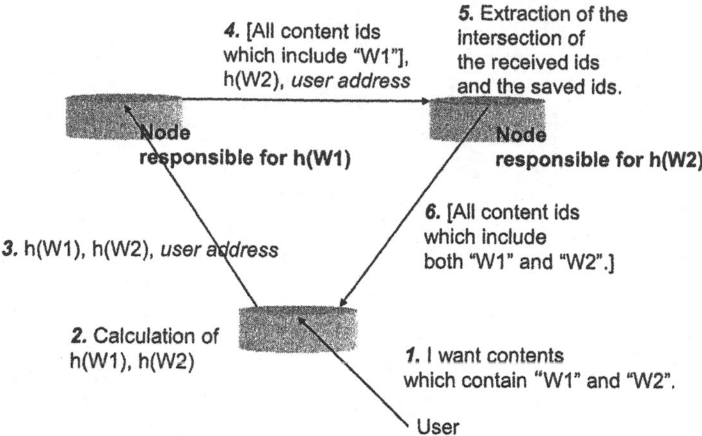

Fig. 1. The process of simple algorithm: normal searching for multi-word text (here, a user want contents which contain the two words "W1" and "W2") on a DHT

Basic description of Bloom Filter Imagine there are set A and set B. To get $A \cap B$ in a simple manner, all the elements of set A are transmitted to the side of set B, and the elements existing in both set A and set B are extracted. At this time, the size of the traffic is the sum of the size of each element in set A. In the method using the bloom filter, set A itself is not transmitted; the bloom filter created by set A is transmitted. The size of the bloom filter is less than the whole size of set A, so the amount of traffic is reduced. The side of set B that received the bloom filter can create s_B satisfying $s_B \supseteq A \cap B$ and $s_B \subseteq B$.

If the test to check whether an element is a member of $A \cap B$ or not to s_B is executed, some false positives (an element that is not a member of $A \cap B$ being returned) occur, but false negatives (an element that is a member of $A \cap B$ being not returned) cannot occur. The false positive rate declines exponentially as the size of bloom filter is increased. Set s_B created by the side of set B is transmitted to the side of set A, and $A \cap B$ is gained.

The execution procedure for the bloom filter is as follows. The idea is to allocate a vector v of m bits, initially all set to 0, and then choose k independent hash functions, $h_1, h_2, ..., h_k$, each with range $1, ..., m$. For each element $a \in A$, the bits at positions $h_1(a), h_2(a), ..., h_k(a)$ in v are set to 1. (A particular bit might be set to 1 multiple times.) Given a query for b, we check the bits at positions $h_1(b), h_2(b), ..., h_k(b)$. If any one of them is 0, certainly b is not in set A. Otherwise, we conjecture that b is in the set, although there is a certain probability that this is incorrect. This is called a "false positive". Parameters k and m should be chosen such that the probability of a false positive (and hence a false hit) is acceptable.

$$\text{FPR} = (1 - (1 - 1/m)^{kn})^k \tag{1}$$
$$\approx (1 - e^{-kn/m})^k. \tag{2}$$

When $k = \ln 2 \times m/n$, Equation (2) has a minimum value. At that time, FPR is $(1/2)^k$. If the target FPR is set to FPR_{target}, $k = \lfloor \log_{1/2} FPR_{target} \rfloor$. Thus,

$$m = \lfloor \lfloor \log_{1/2} FPR_{target} \rfloor \times n / \ln 2 \rfloor. \tag{3}$$

The salient feature of bloom filters is that there is a clear tradeoff between m and the FPR.

Problem with the Bloom Filter If n (the number of elements of a set) and FPR_{target} are given, the filter bit size m can be minimized by setting parameter k to optimum value. This m value should be shared at the system level. This is because if m is different for different filters, the hash functions differ for checking whether or not a given element is a member of the constituent element of the filter. It is thus necessary to re-calculate the hash value of each element per query. We call the bloom filters for which the sizes are the same "fixed-size bloom filters (fBFs)", and we call the bloom filters for which the sizes are different "variable-size bloom filters (vBFs)". We should use fixed-size BFs in order to avoid to calculate many hash values.

However, if the numbers of sets are different, it is a problem that the filter bit size of fBFs is bigger than that of vBFs on average [18]. This is because the FPR increases exponentially as the number of elements of the set increases under the condition that the filter bit size does not change.

In summary, if we use fixed-size BFs, FPR is higher for the same size of variable-size BF on average. If we use variable-size BFs, calculating hash values takes much time. This comparison is further described in 3.2.

2.2 Reducing the amount of traffic in searching for multi-word in DHT

Several studies have been done to reduce the communication traffic in searching for multi-word text in DHT. Two main developments have come from this research. The first development is a device for registering content keys; the second is a device for transmitting content IDs.

In the first approach, in [11], the set of keywords included in the content was also regarded as a DHT key. The authors created combinations with three words or less, and registered the combinations as well as each word in the DHT. However, the number of combinations increases exponentially as the number of words increases.

In [10], the target for search is a Resource Description Framework [7] (RDF). A system that saves "RDF triples" dispersed in DHT was developed. In this system, the RDF triple itself as well as each element of the RDF triple is registered. Because each RDF triple has only three elements, this method prevented much

[illegible] (1)

[illegible] (2)

When [illegible] equation (2) is the minimum value. At that time, [illegible] the false positive rate [illegible]

[illegible] (3)

[illegible]

Problem with the Bloom Filter [illegible] (number of elements of a set) and [illegible] optimized by setting parameters [illegible] optimum [illegible] the system level. This is because [illegible] different [illegible] functions differ for checking whether [illegible] element of the [illegible] each [illegible] hash value of each element per [illegible] the same fixed-size bloom filters [illegible] for which [illegible] order to avoid [illegible]

However, if the number of [illegible] the filter [illegible] because the [illegible] number [illegible] the condition [illegible] change.

[illegible] the same [illegible] hash [illegible]

3.2 Reducing the amount of traffic in searching for multi-word in DHT

[illegible]

In the [illegible] the [illegible] keywords [illegible] contents [illegible] of [illegible] of [illegible] is [illegible]

In [illegible] (EDF) [illegible] DHT was developed. In this system [illegible] of the DHT [illegible] is registered. Because [illegible] this method prevented much

Problem of SfBFA As described in subsection 2.1, the optimum filter bit size depends on the number of elements in the set. In this study, the number of elements in the set is the number of words in the content. Because the numbers of words in the content are different, setting the optimum filter bit size becomes a problem.

The k hash functions used in creating the filter should be shared on the DHT system level, so the size of the filter should also be shared on the system level. The filter bit size can be set to be big enough, but the amount of AndSearchData and traffic will be increased. On the contrary, if the filter bit size is set too small, because of the ascension of FPR, the amount of traffic will also be increased.

We do not use variable-size bloom filters because douing so would mean taking too much time to calculate hash values.

3.2 Divided bloom filter (DBF)

We propose divided bloom filters to overcome the problem of bloom filters.

Each filter bit size can thus be maintained by dividing the set into several sets that have the same number of elements and by creating filters from each set. We call filters created by dividing the original set "divided bloom filters" (DBFs). According to Equation 3, m is proportional to n. For this reason, if the FPR of the bloom filter from original set is α, the FPR of each filter of DBFs is also α.

However, the following problem occurs. When an element b is checked as to whether or not it is a constituent element of the DBF, if it is checked through every divided filter and the number of divided filters is GN,

$$\mathrm{FPR} = 1 - (1 - \alpha)^{GN}. \tag{4}$$

If α is sufficiently small, α to the power of more than two can be ignored, so

$$\mathrm{FPR} \fallingdotseq GN \times \alpha. \tag{5}$$

According to this equation, FPR increases as the number of divisions increases.

The solution needs to identify only one filter that can include element b. By this, FPR is equal to α in total. The only filter that can include element b can be identified by using a DHT hash function without creating extra data storage.

When the node divides the set of words in the content, the node calculates the DHT hash value of each word of the content and divides words into groups according to the DHT hash value. In doing so, the system determines the following parameters in advance.

- MN: average number of words each group can include
- Filter bit size and hash functions used to create filters

The specific process to divide the words of content C is as follows. The value that the DHT hash function can return is $1, 2, ..., DN - 1$.

3.2 Divided bloom filter (DBF)

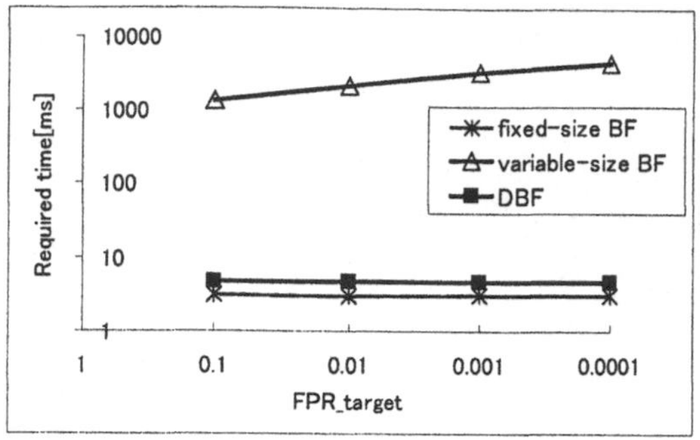

Fig. 3. Required time for checking whether an element is a member of each filter (number of filters is 1,000,000)

1: Figure 2 shows the average FPR of 1,000 sets in each filter method (fixed-size BF, variable-size BF, and DBF). The number of elements of the contents of the sets is from 1 to 1,000. The filter size was determined by FPR_{target}[3]. We changed FPR_{target} from $1/2$ to $1/2^{19}$. MN for the DBFs was set to 100. As FPR_{target} becomes small, we found, the actual FPR of fixed-size BFs becomes much larger than FPR_{target} and that of the DBFs becomes slightly larger than FPR_{target}.

2: Figure 3 shows the simulation result of the required time to check whether an element is a member of a set. We created 1,000,000 filters respectively (fixed-size BF, variable-size BF, and DBF) where the number of elements is 100, and we set $FPR_{target} = 0.1, 0.01, 0.001, \text{and} 0.0001$. We created an element b randomly and measured the required time to determine whether b was a member of each filter. In regards to fixed-size BFs and DBFs, according to Figure 3, the required times do not vary with change in FPR_{target}. In regards to variable-size BF, we recalculated k hash values for each filter. Hence, the required time was very long. In regards to DBFs, the required time was much less than that of variable-size BFs and close to that of fixed-size BFs.

3.3 Saving divided bloom filter algorithm (SDBFA)

We call the method where the node registers a DBF as well as its content ID, its address, and the hash value of the key a "saving divided bloom filter algorithm" (SDBFA).

If this SDBFA is used, the approximate minimum length of the filter satisfying the target FPR can be obtained even if different contents have different numbers of words.

[3] That is, we set the filter size to the size of variable-size BFs whose FPR is FPR_{target}.

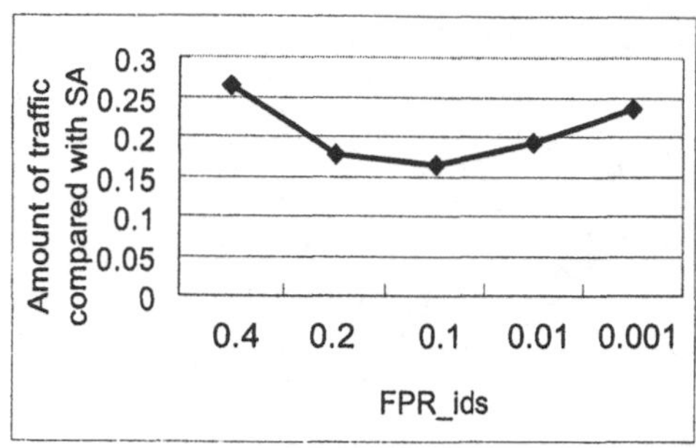

Fig. 4. Average amount of traffic using TfBFA compared with that using SA

4.2 Experimental results

The searches were repeated 1000 times. From here on, we call the FPR_{target} of filters created from content IDs "FPR_{ids}" and call the FPR_{target} of filters created from words included in the contents "FPR_{words}".

In the experiment on TfBFA, we set FPR_{ids} to 0.4, 0.2, 0.1, 0.01, and 0.001. Figure 4 shows the result. The amount of traffic for each of the FPR_{ids}, respectively, was 0.26, 0.17, 0.16, 0.19, and 0.24 compared with that of SA. If the FPR_{ids} is small, the filter bit size that node N(W1) transmits to node N(W2) in Table 1-TfBFA becomes bigger. To the contrary, if the filter bit size is large, the number of content IDs that node N(W2) transmits to node N(W1) becomes larger.

In regards to SfBFA, we set FPR_{words} to 0.4, 0.2, 0.1, 0.01, and 0.001 (Figure 5-Left on the extreme right point and Figure 5-Right on the extreme right point). Figure 5-Left shows the amount of traffic involved in searching for multi-word text, and Figure 5-Right shows the amount of AndSearchData in registering one content to the nodes.

In regards to SDBFA, FPR_{words} was set to the same value as in the experiments with SfBFA, and MN was set to 10, 20, 50, and 100 (Figure 5 except for each extreme right point.) In Figure 5-Left, SDBFA (which uses DBF) can be seen to have reduced the amount of traffic more than SfBFA (which uses a normal bloom filter). As shown in Figure 5-Right, the amount of AndSearchData with the method using a normal bloom filter is not so different from that with the method using DBF. When $FPR_{words} = 0.1$, the goal of 12.1% traffic compared with SA was realized by using DBF. Figure 5-Right shows that the average amount of AndSearchData per content was the same as that with SfBFA. The amount of AndSearchData is the same as that of SDBFA.

In regards to STDBFA, FPR_{words} was set to 0.1 and MN to 10 for registering contents' keys, and FPR_{ids} was set to 0.1 and MN to 2, 5, 10, 20, and 50 for transmission of content IDs (Figure 6.) In Figure 6, the condition $MN = 20$ can be seen to have reduced the amount of traffic the most.

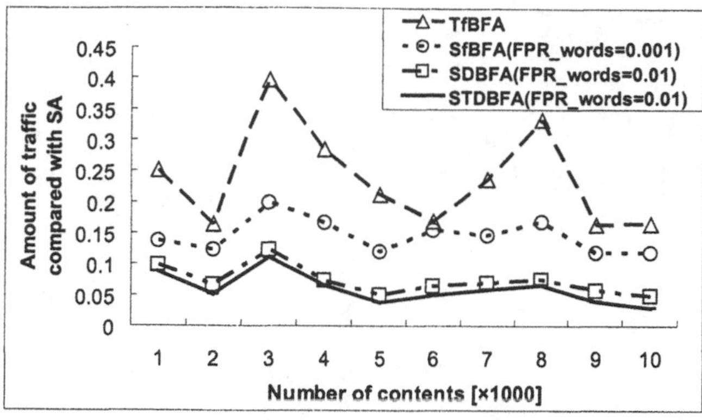

Fig. 7. Amount of traffic with change in the number of contents

	Amount of traffic compared with SA	Amount of data storage per content [KB]
TfBFA	0.237	
SfBFA	0.144	1095
Desired Value	0.121	
SDBFA	0.072	730
STDBFA	0.059	730

Table 2. Comparison of the results for all algorithms

like movies or music. At this time, the keys for DHT are the texts inserted in multimedia contents by languages that describe metadata (like MPEG7 [3]). If mounting metadata into multimedia contents could be done automatically, contents would have much metadata. If a DHT system for these multimedia contents were constructed, the amount of traffic generated in searching for multiword text would grow larger. However, we believe that our proposed method would also be able to reduce the amount of traffic in such a system.

Some DHT algorithms taking mobility and wireless environments into account have been developed (e.g., M-CAN [14] and Warp [22]). Compared to traditional P2P, characteristics of MP2P include unreliable connection, limited bandwidth, and the constraints of mobile devices. Hence, we believe that our proposed method can better apply to these DHTs.

Note that in the experiments in this work, the virtual user queried random words. However, we should perform experiments by creating a user model from real DHT systems or histories of real search engines.

Fig. 7. Amount of traffic in exchanging [illegible] contents

Table [illegible]. Comparison of [illegible]

11. Austin T. Clements, Dan R. K. Ports, and David R. Karger. Arpeggio: Metadata searching and content sharing with chord.
12. D. Eastlake 3rd and P. Jones. US Secure Hash Algorithm 1 (SHA1). RFC 3174, September 2001.
13. J. LI, B. LOO, J. HELLERSTEIN, F. KAASHOEK, D. KARGER, and R. MORRIS. the feasibility of peer-to-peer web indexing and search, 2003.
14. Gang Peng, Shanping Li, Hairong Jin, and Tianchi Ma. M-can: a lookup protocol for mobile peer-to-peer environment. In *ISPAN*, pages 544–550, 2004.
15. Sylvia Ratnasamy, Paul Francis, Mark Handley, Richard Karp, and Scott Schenker. A scalable content-addressable network. In *Proceedings of the ACM Conference on Applications, Technologies, Architectures, and Protocols for Computer Communications*, pages 161–172, August 2001.
16. Patrick Reynolds and Amin Vahdat. Efficient peer-to-peer keyword searching. In *Middleware*, pages 21–40, 2003.
17. Antony I. T. Rowstron and Peter Druschel. Storage management and caching in PAST, a large-scale, persistent peer-to-peer storage utility. In *Symposium on Operating Systems Principles*, pages 188–201, 2001.
18. Michael A. Shepherd, William J. Phillips, and C.-K. Chu. A fixed-size bloom filter for searching textual documents. *Comput. J.*, 32(3):212–219, 1989.
19. Ion Stoica, Robert, David Karger, Frans Kaashoek, and Hari Balakrishnan. Chord: A scalable Peer-To-Peer lookup service for internet applications. In *Proceedings of the 2001 ACM SIGCOMM Conference*, pages 149–160, 2001.
20. Chunqiang Tang, Zhichen Xu, and Sandhya Dwarkadas. Peer-to-peer information retrieval using self-organizing semantic overlay networks. In *SIGCOMM*, pages 175–186, 2003.
21. Jiangong Zhang and Torsten Suel. Efficient query evaluation on large textual collections in a peer-to-peer environment. In *Peer-to-Peer Computing*, pages 225–233, 2005.
22. Ben Y. Zhao, Ling Huang, Anthony D. Joseph, and John Kubiatowicz. Rapid mobility via type indirection. In *IPTPS*, pages 64–74, 2004.

Exploring an Unknown Graph to Locate a Black Hole Using Tokens

Stefan Dobrev[1], Paola Flocchini[1], Rastislav Královič[1,2]*, and Nicola Santoro[3]

[1] SITE, University of Ottawa, {sdobrev,flocchin}@site.uottawa.ca
[2] Dept. of Computer Science, Comenius University, kralovic@dcs.fmph.uniba.sk
[3] School of Computer Science, Carleton University, santoro@scs.carleton.ca

Abstract. Consider a team of (one or more) mobile agents operating in a graph G. Unaware of the graph topology and starting from the same node, the team must explore the graph. This problem, known as *graph exploration*, was initially formulated by Shannon in 1951, and has been extensively studied since under a variety of conditions. The existing investigations have all assumed that the network is *safe* for the agents, and the solutions presented in the literature succeed in their task only under this assumption.
Recently, the exploration problem has been examined also when the network is *unsafe*. The danger examined is the presence in the network of a *black hole*, a node that disposes of any incoming agent without leaving any observable trace of this destruction. The goal is for at least one agent to survive and to have all the surviving agents to construct a map of the network, indicating the edges leading to the black hole. This variant of the problem is also known as *black hole search*. This problem has been investigated assuming powerful inter-agent communication mechanisms: *whiteboards* at all nodes. Indeed, in this model, the black hole search problem can be solved with a minimal team size and performing a polynomial number of moves.
In this paper, we consider a less powerful *token* model. We constructively prove that the black hole search problem can be solved also in this model; furthermore, this can be done using a minimal team size and performing a polynomial number of moves. Our algorithm works even if the agents are *asynchronous* and if both the agents and the nodes are *anonymous*.

1 Introduction

1.1 The Problem

The problem of exploring an unknown graph using a team of one or more mobile agents (or robots) is a classical fundamental problem that has been extensively studied since its initial formulation in 1951 by Shannon [19]. It requires the agents, starting from the same node, to visit within finite time all

* Partially supported by grant VEGA 1/3106/06.

Please use the following format when citing this chapter:

Dobrev, S., Flocchini, P., Královič, Santoro, N., 2006, in International Federation for Information Processing, Volume 209, Fourth IFIP International Conference on Theoretical Computer Science-TCS 2006, eds. Navarro, G., Bertossi, L., Kohayakwa, Y., (Boston: Springer), pp. 131–150.

ployed e.g. in [6, 8, 9, 10, 11, 13, 14]. In the whiteboard models, the black hole search problem can be solved with a minimal team size and performing a polynomial number of moves (e.g., [8, 9, 10, 11]).

The problem of exploring a dangerous graph has never been investigated in the less powerful *token* model, which is instead commonly employed in the exploration of safe graphs. In the classical token model, each agent has available a token that can be carried, can be placed in the center on a node, or removed from it. All tokens are identical (i.e., indistinguishable) and no other form of marking or communication is available. In our variation (*enhanced token model*) we allow tokens to be placed also on a node in correspondence to a port. Notice that the classical token model can be implemented with 1-bit whiteboards, while our variation is not as weak; in fact, it could be implemented by having a $\log d$-whiteboard on a node with degree d.

The principal question targeted by our research was the impact of the communication model to the solvability and complexity of the BHS problem: to what extent can be the whiteboard model weakened, and still allow the polynomial solvability of BHS? With this goal in mind, we examine the problem of performing black hole search in the enhanced token model. Several immediate computational and complexity questions naturally arise. In particular, are the weaker communication and marking capabilities provided by enhanced tokens sufficient to solve the problem ? If so, how can the problem be solved? at what costs? In this paper we provide definite answer to these questions.

1.2 Our Results

In this paper we present an algorithm that works in the token model and solves the BHS problem with the minimal number of agents and with a polynomial number of moves. Our algorithm works even if the agents are *asynchronous*, and if both the agents and the nodes are *anonymous*. More precisely, we consider an unknown, arbitrary, anonymous network and a team of exploring agents starting their identical algorithm from the same node (*home-base*). The agents are anonymous, they move from node to neighboring node asynchronously (i.e., it takes a finite but unpredictable time to traverse a link).

Each agent has available an indistinguishable token (or pebble) that can be placed on, or removed from, a node; on a node, the token can be placed either in the center or on an incident link. In our algorithm there are never two tokens placed on the same location (node center or port), nor an agent ever carries more than one token.

Using only this tool for marking nodes and communicating information, we show that with $\Delta + 1$ agents the exploration can be successfully completed. In fact, we present an algorithm that will allow at least one agent to survive and, within finite time, the surviving agents will know the location of the black hole with the allowed level of accuracy. The number of moves performed by the agents when executing the proposed protocol is shown to be polynomial. The proposed algorithm is rather complex.

not the location of the BH) [11]. In the case of specific graphs, including many important interconnection networks, the number of moves can be reduced to linear [8].

In all these investigations, the nodes of the network have available a *whiteboard*, i.e., a local storage area that the agents can use to communicate information. Access to the whiteboard is gained in mutual exclusion and the capacity of the whiteboard is always assumed to be at least of $\Omega(\log N)$ bits.

In the synchronous environments, the investigations have produced optimal solutions for trees [5]; approximation results have been obtained for arbitrary graphs in [5, 16].

2 The Model

The network $G = (V, E)$ is a simple undirected graph with node-connectivity two or higher; let $N = |V|$ and $M = |E|$ be the number of nodes and of edges of G, respectively, $d(x)$ denote the degree of x, and Δ denote the maximum degree in G. If $(x, y) \in E$ then x and y are said to be neighbors. The nodes of G are *anonymous* (i.e., without unique names). At each node x there is a distinct label (called port number) associated to each of its incident links (or ports). Without loss of generality, we assume that the labels at $x \in V$ are the consecutive integers #1, #2, ..., #$d(x)$.

Operating in G is a team of $\Delta + 1$ anonymous agents. The agents know the number of nodes of the network, can move from node to a neighboring node in G, have computing capabilities and limited amount of memory ($O(M \log N)$ bits suffice for our algorithm). We also assume that agents know the degree Δ of the BH.

Each agent has a token that can be placed on on a node and removed from it; tokens are identical and their placement can be used to mark nodes and ports/links. More precisely, a node can be marked by a token in different modalities: in the center, or in correspondence of one of the incident ports.

The agents obey the same set of behavioral rules (the "algorithm") and initially, they are all located at the same node h, called *home-base* (home-base).

The agents can be seen as automata, where one computational step of an agent A in a node v is defined as follows. Based on the state (local memory) of A and on the presence of tokens at v and incident links (examined atomically):
- change the state (local memory of A)
- remove (or place) at most one token from v or an incident link and
- start waiting (for a token to disappear) or leave v via one of the incident links.

The computational steps are atomic and mutually exclusive, i.e. no more than one agent computes in the same node at the same time. The links satisfy FIFO property, i.e. the agents entering a link $e = (u, v)$ at u will arrive at v and execute the computational steps in the same order they entered e. The agents are *asynchronous* in the sense that waiting (for a token to disappear) and traversing a link can take an unpredictable (but finite) amount of time.

[illegible] of the [illegible] the Ring [illegible]. In the case of [illegible] graphs, including many [illegible] the number of moves can be reduced to [illegible] [8].

In all these investigations, the nodes of the network have available a white-board [illegible] the agents can use to communicate informa[illegible] [illegible] to the [illegible] is achieved in mutual exclusion, and the capacity of the whiteboard [illegible] level of [illegible].

[illegible]

[illegible] The Model

[illegible] $G = (V, E)$ [illegible] with node-connectivity two [illegible] $n = |V|$ and [illegible] of nodes and of edges of G, respectively; [illegible] and [illegible] maximum degree in G. [illegible] The nodes of G are anonymous [illegible] none of them has a distinct label [illegible] numbers each of its incident links (or ports). Without loss of generality, we assume that the labels [illegible] consecutive integers [illegible]

[illegible] the number of nodes [illegible] have [illegible] or [illegible] memory ($O(\log [illegible])$ [illegible] suffice for our algorithm. We [illegible] assume [illegible] the degree of [illegible]

[illegible] that [illegible] [illegible] tokens [illegible] not [illegible] and remove [illegible] ports links. More precisely, [illegible] in different models [illegible]

The [illegible]

[illegible]

[illegible]

[illegible] link and [illegible] waiting [illegible] the needed link.

The [illegible] no more than one [illegible] the same [illegible] links satisfy [illegible] will arrive at [illegible] and [illegible] entered it. The [illegible] waiting [illegible] to disappear [illegible] amount of time.

algorithm requires that no agent enters a *dangerous* port, ensuring in this way that at most Δ agents enter the black hole. We will thus say that a dangerous port *blocks* the (other) agents.

Initially, all ports incident to the home-base are *unexplored*. The local map of an agent is constructed by adding edges in a sequential manner according to Algorithm 1: The searching for an unexplored port is straightforward: any

Algorithm 1 General algorithm of an agent

```
loop
    traverse the local map and look for an unexplored port p
    if unexplored port p found then
        EXPLORE(p)
        continue the main loop
    else
        if local map contains N-1 vertices and there are at most Δ outgoing edges
            then
            TERMINATE
        else
            SUSPEND
        end if
    end if
end loop
```

traversal of the explored part using only the edges identified as *safe* in the local map will do.

In the execution of EXPLORE(p), the agent explores the edge incident to port p, determines whether it leads to a new node or to an already discovered one[2], and updates the local map. Duc to complex interaction of anonymity with asynchrony, in some cases the agent might be unsure of whether an edge leads to a new node or to an already visited one. However, the agent is able to recognize this uncertainty, and will add this edge to the local map as *quasi-safe* instead of *safe*.

Eventually, no unexplored port is found. If $N-1$ nodes has been visited, the remaining node is the BH and the algorithm can terminate. Otherwise, the access to the unexplored part of the graph is blocked by *dangerous* ports. Since G is two-connected, at least one of those ports does not lead to the BH and the token will eventually be removed from it, making it *unexplored*. In order to avoid live-lock, the agent that failed to find an *unexplored* port suspends itself using procedure SUSPEND until such a progress has been made. The basic idea of SUSPEND is to go to the home-base, set a flag there (by using a token) indicating that an agent is waiting for wake-up, verify that no progress has been made before the flag has been set up, and then wait to be woken-

[2] p might lead to the BH as well, in which case the agent disappears there and does not continue the algorithm

[illegible] requires that an agent enters a dangerous port containing in this way [illegible] the black hole will they say that a dangerous port [illegible].

[illegible] all ports incident to the node [illegible] are explored. The local map [illegible] by adding edges [illegible] according [illegible].

Algorithm [illegible]

[illegible]

4 [illegible]

5 [illegible]

6 [illegible]

7 [illegible]

8 [illegible]

[illegible] in the local [illegible]

In the [illegible] to [illegible] whether it leads [illegible] not [illegible] discovered [illegible] the local map. [illegible] with [illegible] whether no edge [illegible] to a new node [illegible] agent [illegible] able to [illegible] of [illegible].

[illegible] the [illegible] ports [illegible] the [illegible] to find an unexplored port [illegible] progress has been made. The [illegible] verify that no progress [illegible] to be reason[illegible]

[illegible] the algorithm.

Notice that recognizing if v is already in the local map would be an easy task if either the agents were able to recognize their own tokens, or they were able to recognize the home-base. In fact, if agents were able to recognize their tokens, then A could simply put its token at v and scan the explored subgraph: if it finds its token, v is already explored, otherwise it is a new node. If the agents were able to recognize the home-base, then A could determine whether v is a new node as follows. For each node w in the local map, A guesses that $v = w$ and verifies whether that is really true: Let α be a sequence of port labels specifying a safe path (determined by looking in the local map) from w to the home-base. Starting from v, A follows[3] the port labels specified by α. If A finishes in the home-base, then $v = w$, otherwise A makes another guess. If all guesses fail, v is a new node. However, in our model the agents can not recognize their tokens nor the home-base. Still, the basic structure is to guess for all already explored nodes w whether $v = w$ and to verify the guess, although the verification is much more involved.

Let β_w (we will use β when w is clear from the context) be a sequence of port labels starting with the label of the port from u to v and then following a path (using only edges marked as *safe* in the agent's map) from w through the primary SR and ending in u. Clearly, if $v = w$ then β specifies a simple cycle in the graph (and therefore $|\beta| \leq n$, even if actually $v \neq w$).

Agent A verifies whether $v = w$ by following the labels specified by a cyclic repeating of β (we will call it β^*) for up to N^2 edges or until A finds a difference between what it sees in the current node and what it should see (according to its map) if $v = w$. The number of steps is chosen large enough so that following β^* creates a cycle even if $v \neq w$ (as we will see later, using only β is not enough). This means (as will be proven later) that if no discrepancy has been found for N^2 steps, u and v indeed lie on a cycle C passing through the correct SR, with the labels specified by β^*. Unfortunately, it is still possible that, although no discrepancy is found, $v \neq w$: this could happen if $|C|$ is a multiple of $|\beta|$. In this case the agent verifies whether $v = w$ or not in the procedure VERIFY, which will be described later.

The N^2 steps along β^* must be done in cautious manner, not entering *dangerous* ports, since it may be the case that $v \neq w$ and β^* leads to the BH.

The cautious walk is complicated by the fact that a port to be taken (let its label be λ) from a node w' might be *dangerous.* If this happens, the agent cannot afford to wait in w' until the token is removed, because this edge might indeed lead to the BH. Instead, it wants to ensure that, if $v = w$ then the token will be removed allowing A to continue its cautious walk through λ. To do so, A goes backwards for $|\beta|$ steps reaching a safe node through safe links; this node might indeed be w' (this happens if the guess $v = w$ is correct), or it could be a different node w''. Agent A waits here until there is no token on the port labelled λ. Although not sure about the identity of the node, the agent knows

[3] cautious walk needs to be used, as v might be different from w, and α from v might lead to the BH

Verification

The test of a candidate vertex w in the procedure EXPLORE may end, after traversing the sequence β^* for N^2 steps, in a situation where the agent knows that either β or its multiple forms a safe cycle connecting u and v. The procedure VERIFY is used to verify whether the cycle consists of just one repetition of β (in which case $v = w$).

Algorithm 3 VERIFY – let p be the SR, if the hypothesis about w is true

```
PosCount = NegCount = 0
loop
    go to home-base, wait until it becomes empty, and go to the primary SR
    if the SR is empty then
        put token and exit loop
    else
        wait until the SR becomes empty
    end if
end loop
while PosCount < 2ΔMN^3 + ΔMN and NegCount < 2ΔMN^3 + ΔMN do
    if known, go to the other SR and wait until it becomes empty
    go to the home-base, wait until it becomes empty
    go to p
    if there is a token then
        PosCount = PosCount + 1
    else
        NegCount = NegCount + 1
    end if
    go to the primary SR and if empty update the knowledge of storerooms using
        rule R4 and restart algorithm
end while
take token
if PosCount ≥ 2ΔMN^3 + ΔMN then
    return TRUE
else
    return FALSE
end if
```

The idea of VERIFY is to use a token in the primary SR for breaking symmetry on the β^*-cycle. An agent A performing a VERIFY first makes sure that it is not interfering with any other agent by waiting until both the home-base and the SR's it knows to be safe are empty. It then puts its token in the primary SR and walks[4] along the β^*-cycle for $|\beta|$ steps to a vertex w' and checks whether there is a token in w'. The idea is that if $v = w$ then w' is the SR and contains the token, if $v \neq w$ then w' should be empty as it is not the correct SR.

[4] Note that it is not needed to use cautious steps, as the cycle identified by β^* has already been traversed and is known to be safe

SR) and A will take it (or the token of yet another agent).

Algorithm 4 GRAB-TOKEN – starts in home-base

1: if there is a token in home-base, get it and exit GRAB-TOKEN
2: go to primary SR, if there is a token there, get it and exit GRAB-TOKEN
3: go to the home-base and if there is a token there, get it and exit GRAB-TOKEN
4: go to the other SR and get token

Suspend & Wake-Up

Recall that an agent A performs SUSPEND when further exploration progress is blocked by *dangerous* links, but A knows that eventually at least one of those link will become unblocked. The basic idea is to put the token in the home-base to signal "I want to be waken-up", check whether a progress has been made before the token was put down (to prevent deadlock, as an agent performing WAKE-UP after removing its token from a dangerous edge might have arrived to the home-base before the token was put there) and, if not, then wait until the token disappears. An agent performing WAKE-UP simply moves a token from the home-base (if there is any) to its primary SR.

The problems arise because several agents might be executing SUSPEND, WAKE-UP and VERIFY simultaneously, and because the agents do not necessarily agree on the correct SR. Dealing with that constitutes the most technical part of the algorithm. The basic idea is to wait until any activity going on (detected by non-empty home-base or SR) looks to have finished and then restart SUSPEND. Still, there are many possible cases how the agents can steal each other's tokens and/or misinterpret what is going on. The reasons behind the design of SUSPEND and WAKE-UP will become fully apparent only when reading the formal proofs in the next section.

The idea of WAKE-UP is to wake-up an agent suspended at home-base by moving its token to a SR. In order to make GRAB-TOKEN work, the waking-up agent first places its token in the SR and then removes the token from the home-base. If the home-base is empty or the SR is full, WAKE-UP does nothing, because either there is nobody suspended, or it has been already waken-up and just has to pick up its token. When an agent suspended at home-base sees that its token has disappeared, it will search around and find its token (using GRAB-TOKEN)

4 Correctness and Complexity

Let us call an agent *informed* if its knowledge about which storerooms are safe is correct. If the BH is located in one of the storerooms, all agents (that have finished initialization) are informed; otherwise an informed agent knows that

[illegible]

Algorithm [illegible] home-base [illegible]

[illegible]

[illegible] Wait [illegible]

[illegible] blocked by [illegible] but it knows that eventually at least one of [illegible] [illegible] the home-base [illegible] simply moves a token [illegible] home-base [illegible]

The [illegible] executing Super[illegible] [illegible] the agents do not neces- [illegible] the most technical [illegible] when reading the formal proofs [illegible] section.

[illegible]

[illegible]

4 Correctness and Complexity

[illegible] is correct. If the [illegible] of the [illegible] agents (that have finished [illegible]) [illegible] informed, [illegible] agent knows the

Theorem 1. (Main Theorem) *At least one agent successfully terminates with a correct map.*

Due to the lack of space, we present only the key lemmas, we omit some proofs and we only informally sketch some reasonings.

Let us start with some basic observations. Since a token is put in a vertex only in SUSPEND, WAKE-UP or VERIFY, we get:

Claim. 1.A token is in the vertex v only if v is a home-base or a SR.

The most technical part of the algorithm is the implementation of the communication between agents by means of tokens. We are specifically interested in agents who have put their token in the home-base or in the SR and are now without a token; we will call them *empty-handed* to distinguish them from agents who do not have a token because they are performing a cautious step. From the definition of *cautious step*, from Claim 1, and by construction we get:

Claim. 2. There are as many empty-handed agents as tokens in the home-base and storerooms.

An agent performing procedure GRAB-TOKEN visits the home-base and possibly some SR's a constant number of times in a search for a token. For the correctness of the algorithm it is important to prove that a token is always found.

Lemma 1. *An agent always gets a token in procedure* GRAB-TOKEN.

Proof. Consider, for the sake of contradiction, an agent A executing GRAB-TOKEN that has not found a token. Let t_0 be the time when A sees that its primary SR x is empty and starts to travel back to home-base. Let $t_1 > t_0$ be the time when A arrives to the home-base, finds it empty again, and starts to travel to SR y. By Claim 2, at time t_0 there must be at least one token T in home-base or SR y. However, since A does not find T, T must have disappeared after t_0 before A gets there. The only way for T to disappear is if it is taken by some empty-handed agent B. However, since B is empty-handed, there must be another token T' in some vertex (home-base or SR) at the time when B grabs T. The idea is to argue about T and T' and show that A would find one of them. In particular, we first prove that at some point in time after t_0 both home-base and SR y are full, and then prove that from this fact it follows that A finds a token.

Let us focus on the time t' when B put T' and thus became empty-handed. We distinguish three cases. First, consider $t' > t_1$. B could not have removed T from the home-base before time t_1, therefore at time t_1 (and t' as well, as it is B that removes it) T must be in SR y. Since A started traveling from the home-base to SR y at time $t_1 < t'$ and due to the FIFO property, B cannot get to SR y before A and so A finds T in SR y – contradiction.

Proof. A vertex v is added as new only if the test $w = v$ in EXPLORE failed for every candidate w. We show that if the test fails then indeed $w \neq v$. The test for a given w can fail:
- By having the port γ still dangerous after executing the loop on lines 5..9 for $2\Delta MN^3$ times. However, if $w = v$, then between each iteration of that loop the port γ is cleared which is a contradiction with Lemma 2. Hence, $w \neq v$.
- By noticing (in line 14) difference between what the map tells what should be seen if $v = w$ and what really is visible. Clearly, in such case $v \neq w$.
- By having VERIFY return false. VERIFY returns false if the agent A has not found the token in the vertex p (which is equal to its correct SR x if $v = w$) for at least $2\Delta MN^3$ times. Note that A always leaves SR x with its token there. We distinguish two cases:
(i) If x=SR1 the lemma follows from the second part of Lemma 4: no other agent steals A's token from SR1, so if $v = w$ then A always sees a token in p and, subsequently, VERIFY never returns FALSE.
(ii) Let x=SR2. Which agent could remove A's token from SR2? From Lemmas 4 and 5 we know that A's token was not removed from SR2 by an agent D executing VERIFY from SR1, because in that case B's token remains in SR1. It cannot be the case that A's token was removed by an agent B executing VERIFY from SR2, because that agent would have first placed its token in SR2. Therefore, A's token was removed by an agent B executing a GRAB-TOKEN as a part of SUSPEND or WAKE-UP. However, for each removal of a token from a SR by an agent B executing SUSPEND there must have been a wake-up of some other agent that kicked out a token from the home-base to a SR (otherwise B would have picked up its token in the home-base). The only exception are the cases when an agent becomes informed and first takes a token from its old primary SR, which can happen at most Δ times. The lemma follows from the fact that there are less then $2\Delta MN^3$ wake-ups.

Using the previous lemma, we can argue that an agent disappears in a BH only during a cautious step:

Lemma 7. *If A enters* BH, *the link e upon which it arrived is marked by its token.*

Since no agent enters a link marked by a token and the degree of the BH is at most Δ, we get:

Theorem 2. *At most Δ agents die.*

The next lemmas are needed to show that no deadlock can occur, i.e. every agent is always able to continue its algorithm after some finite time. First, we prove that no deadlock occurs when an agent is waiting for a disappearance of a token:

Lemma 8. *A token from the home-base eventually disappears.*

[illegible] A [illegible] added as new [illegible] EXPLORE failed for [illegible]. We show that if the test fails then indeed [illegible]. The test [illegible].

[illegible] having [illegible] still [illegible] after executing the loop on lines 5–9 for [illegible] times. However, if [illegible] each iteration of that loop, the [illegible] with Lemma 2. Hence [illegible].

[illegible] what [illegible] which [illegible].

[illegible] We will [illegible] two cases.

[illegible] follows from the [illegible] of [illegible] other [illegible] always sees a token in [illegible].

[illegible]

[illegible] GRAB-TOKEN [illegible] a token from a [illegible] wake-up of some [illegible] (otherwise [illegible]). The only exception are the cases [illegible].

Using [illegible] we can [illegible] only during [illegible].

[illegible]

[illegible]

Theorem 4. [illegible]

The [illegible] occur, i.e. [illegible] after some finite time. First, we [illegible] waiting for a disappeared [illegible].

[illegible] A token [illegible] disappears.

Lemma 12. *Each informed agent has a correct map.*

Proof. It follows from Lemma 6 that if an agent A adds a new vertex v to its map, then indeed v has not been in A's local map before. So it remains to be proven that if an informed agent A adds an edge (u, w) between two visited vertices to its map, then there is an edge (u, w) in the graph. Adding an edge (u, w) requires that the hypothesis $v = w$ tested in EXPLORE and VERIFY returns TRUE.

We first prove that after successfully finishing N^2 iterations of the loop on line 4 in EXPLORE the sequence β^* defines a (not necessarily simple) cycle connecting v and u, whose length is a multiple of $|\beta|$. Let $\beta = (\beta_1, \beta_2, \ldots, \beta_k)$ where each β_i specifies two port numbers: a consistent traversal must arrive via port p_1 and leave via port p_2. Since $k \leq N$, by traversing β^* for N^2 steps it must happen that the agent visits a particular vertex q twice with the same position in the sequence β; say β_i. Clearly, from now on the agent walks in cycle. Let q be the first such vertex. However, since β_i specifies also the arriving port number, it means that the agent has both times arrived to q using the same port, i.e. it already started in the cycle.

To conclude, we prove that if VERIFY returns TRUE for some informed agent it must be that the cycle formed by β^* has length $|\beta|$ and hence $v = w$. If VERIFY returns TRUE it means that A saw a token in p at least $2\Delta MN^3$ times and between every two successive visits of p there was a time when home-base was free and, if there are two storerooms, also a time when SR2 was free. If p was not SR1, it must be that either p is home-base or p is SR1 and each of the $2\Delta MN^3$ times some agent put its token at p (which was removed before the next visit of A in p).

We conclude the proof by showing that a token is put in p less then $2\Delta MN^3 + \Delta MN$ times. There are two possible situations when an agent B could put its token to p: either B performs a VERIFY in SR2 (there are at most ΔMN such cases: B must be a non-informed agent and it puts its token once per each call of VERIFY before getting informed), or B performs a SUSPEND-WAKE-UP pair. However, in the latter case there must be a cautious step that triggers this WAKE-UP which, according to Lemma 2, accounts for another $2\Delta MN^3$ possibilities.

By Lemmas 1-12, the main theorem (Theorem 1) follows.

Let us now consider the number of moves. By Lemmas 10,11 plus the fact that each of the Δ agents performs at most M iterations of the loop in Algorithm 1, we have

Theorem 4. *The* BH *can be located using* $O(\Delta^2 M^2 N^7)$ *moves.*

References

1. I. Averbakh and O. Berman. A heuristic with worst-case analysis for minimax routing of two traveling salesmen on a tree. *Discr. Appl. Math.*, 68:17–32, 1996.

[illegible] 12 [illegible] 4 [illegible] next step.

[illegible] a new vertex [illegible] before. So it remains to be [illegible] that [illegible] two [illegible] Adding an edge [illegible]

[illegible] with the same [illegible] the agent [illegible] both [illegible]

[illegible] when [illegible] was [illegible] was [illegible] before the [illegible]

[illegible] and [illegible] per each [illegible]

[illegible] the loop in Algo[illegible]

Theorem 4. [illegible]

References

[1] Averb[illegible] for minimax [illegible] of [illegible] 17–22, 1996.

Fast Cellular Automata with Restricted Inter-Cell Communication: Computational Capacity

Martin Kutrib[1] and Andreas Malcher[2]

[1] Institut für Informatik, Universität Giessen
Arndtstr. 2, D-35392 Giessen, Germany
kutrib@informatik.uni-giessen.de
[2] Institut für Informatik, Johann Wolfgang Goethe Universität
D-60054 Frankfurt am Main, Germany
a.malcher@em.uni-frankfurt.de

Abstract. A d-dimensional cellular automaton with sequential input mode is a d-dimensional grid of interconnected interacting finite automata. The distinguished automaton at the origin, the communication cell, is connected to the outside world and fetches the input sequentially. Often in the literature this model is referred to as iterative array. We investigate d-dimensional iterative arrays and one-dimensional cellular automata operating in real and linear time, whose inter-cell communication is restricted to some constant number of bits independent of the number of states. It is known that even one-dimensional one-bit iterative arrays accept rather complicated languages such as $\{a^p \mid p \text{ prim}\}$ or $\{a^{2^n} \mid n \in \mathbb{N}\}$ [16]. We show that there is an infinite strict double dimension-bit hierarchy. The computational capacity of the one-dimensional devices in question is compared with the power of communication-restricted two-way cellular automata. It turns out that the relations are quite different from the relations in the unrestricted case. On passing, we obtain an infinite strict bit hierarchy for real-time two-way cellular automata and, moreover, a very dense time hierarchy for every k-bit cellular automata, i.e., just one more time step leads to a proper superfamily of accepted languages.

Key words: Cellular automata; Iterative arrays; Restricted communication; Formal languages; Computational capacity; Parallel computing

1 Introduction

Devices of homogeneous, interconnected, parallel acting automata have extensively been investigated from a computational capacity point of view. The specification of such a system includes the type and specification of the single automata (sometimes called cells), their interconnection scheme (which can imply a dimension to the system), a local and/or global transition function and the input and output modes. Multidimensional devices with nearest neighbor con-

Please use the following format when citing this chapter:

Kutrib, M., Malcher, A., 2006, in International Federation for Information Processing, Volume 209, Fourth IFIP International Conference on Theoretical Computer Science-TCS 2006, eds. Navarro, G., Bertossi, L., Kohayakwa, Y., (Boston: Springer), pp. 151–164.

strict bit hierarchy for real-time two-way cellular automata and, moreover, a very dense time hierarchy for every k-bit cellular automata, i.e., just one more time step yields to a proper superfamily of accepted languages.

2 Definitions and Preliminaries

We denote the rational numbers by $\mathbb{Q}$, the integers by $\mathbb{Z}$, the non-negative integers by $\mathbb{N}$, and the positive integers $\{1, 2, ...\}$ by $\mathbb{N}_+$. The empty word is denoted by λ, the reversal of a word w by w^R, and for the length of w we write $|w|$. The set of words over some alphabet A whose lengths are at most $l \in \mathbb{N}$ is denoted by $A^{\leq l}$. Set inclusion and strict set inclusion are denoted by $\subseteq$ and $\subset$, respectively.

A d-dimensional iterative array is a d-dimensional array (i.e. $\mathbb{N}^d$) of finite automata, sometimes called cells, where each of them is connected to its nearest neighbors in every dimension. For convenience we identify the cells by their coordinates. Initially they are in the so-called quiescent state. The input is supplied sequentially to the distinguished communication cell at the origin. For this reason, we have different local transition functions. The state transition of all cells but the communication cell depends on the current state of the cell itself and the current states of its neighbors. The state transition of the communication cell additionally depends on the current input symbol (or if the whole input has been consumed on a special end-of-input symbol). In an iterative array with k-bit restricted inter-cell communication, during every time step each cell may communicate only k bit of information to its neighbors. These bits depend on the current state and are determined by so-called bit-functions. The finite automata work synchronously at discrete time steps.

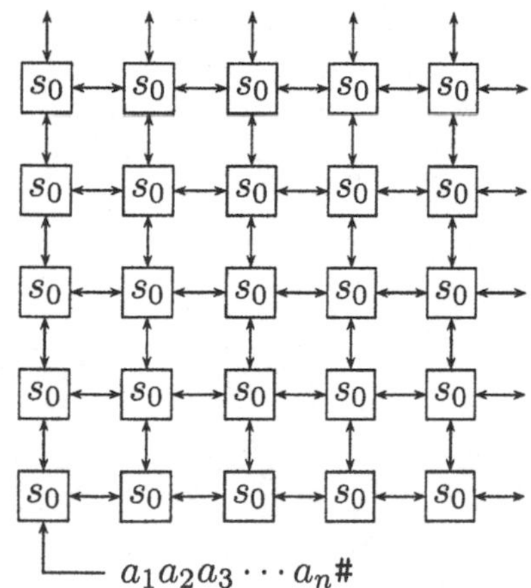

Fig. 1. A two-dimensional iterative array.

(2) $L(\mathcal{M}) = \{w \in A^* \mid w$ *is accepted by* $\mathcal{M}\}$ *is the* language accepted *by* $\mathcal{M}$.
(3) Let $t : \mathbb{N} \to \mathbb{N}$, $t(n) \geq n+1$, *be a mapping. If all* $w \in L(\mathcal{M})$ *are accepted with at most* $t(|w|)$ *time steps, then* L *is said to be of* time complexity t.

The family of all languages which can be accepted by an IA_k^d with time complexity t is denoted by $\mathscr{L}_t(\mathrm{IA}_k^d)$. If t equals the function $n+1$, acceptance is said to be in *real time* and we write $\mathscr{L}_{rt}(\mathrm{IA}_k^d)$. The *linear-time* languages $\mathscr{L}_{lt}(\mathrm{IA}_k^d)$ are defined according to $\mathscr{L}_{lt}(\mathrm{IA}_k^d) = \bigcup_{i \in \mathbb{Q}, i \geq 1} \mathscr{L}_{i \cdot n}(\mathrm{IA}_k^d)$.

Definition 3. *Let* $L \subseteq A^*$ *be a language over an alphabet* A *and* $l \in \mathbb{N}_+$ *be a constant.*

(1) Two words $w \in A^*$ *and* $w' \in A^*$ *are* l*-right-equivalent with respect to* L *if for all* $y \in A^{\leq l}$: $wy \in L \iff w'y \in L$.
(2) $N_r(l, L)$ *denotes the number of* l*-right-equivalence classes with respect to* L.
(3) Two words $w \in A^{\leq l}$ *and* $w' \in A^{\leq l}$ *are* l*-left-equivalent with respect to* L *if for all* $y \in A^*$: $wy \in L \iff w'y \in L$.
(4) $N_\ell(l, L)$ *denotes the number of* l*-left-equivalence classes with respect to* L.

Lemma 4. *Let* $k, d \in \mathbb{N}_+$ *be constants.*

(1) If $L \in \mathscr{L}_{rt}(IA_k^d)$, *then there exists a constant* $p \in \mathbb{N}$ *such that*

$$N_r(l, L) \leq p^{(l+1)^d}$$

and
(2) if $L \in \mathscr{L}_t(IA_k^d)$, *then there exists a constant* $p \in \mathbb{N}$ *such that*

$$N_\ell(l, L) \leq p \cdot 2^{k \cdot d \cdot l}$$

for all $l \in \mathbb{N}_+$ *and all time complexities* $t : \mathbb{N} \to \mathbb{N}$.

Proof. Let $\mathcal{M} = \langle S, A, F, s_0, d, k, b_1, \ldots, b_{2d}, \delta, \delta_0 \rangle$ be a real-time IA_k^d that accepts L. In order to determine an upper bound for the number of l-right-equivalence classes we consider the possible configurations of $\mathcal{M}$ after reading all but $|y| \leq l$ input symbols. The remaining computation depends on the last $|y|$ input symbols, the current state of the communication cell, and the states of the cells which can send information that is received by the communication cell during the last $|y|+1$ time steps. These are at most $(|y|+1)^d$ cells. So, in total there are at most $|S|^{1+(|y|+1)^d} \leq |S|^{2(l+1)^d}$ different possibilities. Setting $p = |S|^2$, we obtain $N_r(l, L) \leq p^{(l+1)^d}$.

Now let $\mathcal{M}$ be a IA_k^d that accepts L with time complexity t. In order to determine an upper bound to the number of l-left-equivalence classes we consider the possible configurations of $\mathcal{M}$ after reading prefixes w whose lengths are at most l. A computed configuration depends on the information which is sent to the array by the communication cell, and the current state of the communication cell. So, there are at most $(2^{k \cdot d})^{|w|-1} \cdot |S| \leq |S| \cdot 2^{k \cdot d \cdot l}$ different configurations. Setting $p = |S|$, we obtain $N_\ell(l, L) \leq p \cdot 2^{k \cdot d \cdot l}$. In particular, the number of equivalence classes is independent of the time complexity t. □

[illegible] is accepted [illegible] the language accepted by $\mathcal{M}$ [illegible] are accepted [illegible] time steps, then L [illegible] of time complexity t.

The family of all languages which [illegible] be accepted by an IA^d_k with time complexity t [illegible] IA_k [illegible] function [illegible] acceptance [illegible] $\mathcal{L}_t(IA^d_k)$. The [illegible] time [illegible] $\mathcal{L}_{rt}(IA^d_k)$ [illegible] (IA) [illegible]

Definition [illegible]

(1) [illegible] with respect to [illegible] for all [illegible]

(2) [illegible] denotes the number of [illegible] equivalence classes with respect to E_ℓ.

(3) [illegible] with respect to [illegible] for all [illegible]

(4) [illegible] denotes the number of [illegible] equivalence classes with respect to E_ℓ.

[illegible] be constant.

[illegible]

[illegible]

[illegible] that accepts L [illegible] the number of ℓ-right [illegible] equivalence classes we consider [illegible] possible configurations of $\mathcal{M}$ after reading all but [illegible] one symbol. The [illegible] the last [illegible] symbols, the [illegible] state of the [illegible] the cells [illegible] during [illegible] the [illegible]

[illegible] we obtain [illegible] whose lengths are at most [illegible] information which is sent [illegible] state of the communication [illegible] different configurations [illegible] we obtain [illegible] In particular, the number of equivalence classes is independent of the time complexity [illegible]

$$p^{(3m(d+1)+2(d+3)+2+1)^d} \leq p^{(6md+2d+9)^d} \leq p^{(17md)^d} \leq 2^{\lceil \log(p) \rceil (17d)^d m^d}$$

classes. We choose m such that $m > \lceil \log(p) \rceil (17d)^d$, and obtain strictly less than

$$2^{mm^d} = 2^{m^{d+1}}$$

classes. From the contradiction we obtain $L_{dim}(d+1) \notin \mathscr{L}_{rt}(\text{IA}_k^d)$.

Now we turn to the construction of a real-time IA_1^{d+1} which accepts $L_{dim}(d+1)$. First we observe that the structure of accepted words is regular. Therefore, the communication cell can check it and, moreover, can decode the checked input over $\{a, b\}$ uniquely to a word from $M(d+1)$. For convenience, we explain the acceptance also in terms of these words. Basically, the idea is to store the prefix u in such a way that the symbol $u[x_{d+1}] \cdots [x_1]$ is stored in cell $(x_{d+1} - 1, x_d - 1, \ldots, x_1 - 1)$. While subsequently reading the suffix $¢e^{x_{d+1}}\$ \cdots \$e^{x_1}\$e^{2x}\$v$ symbol $u[x_{d+1}] \cdots [x_1]$ is addressed and sent to the communication cell where it is compared with v. Accordingly, we call the first phase the storage and the second phase the retrieval phase.

We name cells dependent on their coordinates. A cell is said to be of level j, if its last j coordinates are 0, i.e., $(i_1, \ldots, i_{d+1-j}, 0, \ldots, 0)$. Note that a level j cell is also of level $j' < j$, and the communication cell is the sole level $d+1$ cell. A cell with maximal level j activates its neighbors $(i_1, \ldots, i_{d+1-j}, 0, \ldots, 0, 1)$, $(i_1, \ldots, i_{d+1-j}, 0, \ldots, 1, 0), \ldots, (i_1, \ldots, i_{d+1-j}, 1, \ldots, 0, 0)$, and $(i_1, \ldots, i_{d+1-j} + 1, 0, \ldots, 0)$, i.e., sends a non-zero signal for the first time. Therefore, each cell is uniquely activated by one of its neighbors and, moreover, can determine its maximal level by this neighbor. A cell with maximal level $j \leq d$ may activate at most $j+1$ neighbors.

Activation takes place during the storage phase, in which cells mark a path to the current storage position by state components. When the communication cell reads $h(a)$ (resp. $h(b)$), it sends the two bits 10 (resp. 11) along the path until the position is reached. Now the corresponding cell $(i_1, \ldots, i_{d+1})$ stores symbol a (resp. b), activates its neighbor $(i_1, \ldots, i_{d+1} + 1)$ to be the next storage position by sending the bits 01, and extends the current path to the newly activated neighbor.

Whenever the communication cell reads $h(\$)$, it sends the bits 01 along the path. In this situation the cells on the path count the number of at most d consecutive 01 signals, and possibly reroute the path as follows. A cell lets pass $p-1$ signals, where p is the number of already activated neighbors. If there is another signal, it activates the next neighbor according to the above given ordering, and reroutes the path to it. Clearly, there cannot be more signals than the number of activated neighbors minus one, since the next predecessor cell of higher level does not let pass so many of them.

When the communication cell reads $h(¢)$, it sends the bits 00 to the array. This signal is distributed to all activated cells recursively. It is the beginning of the retrieval phase. During this phase a path to the addressed symbol is set up. To this end, the communication cell sends along the path a bit 1 for each read $h(e)$, and the bits 00 for each of the next $d+1$ separators $h(\$)$.

On the other hand, consider two different prefixes $w = u_1 \cdots u_l\$$ and $w' = u'_1 \cdots u'_l\$$. Since they are different, there is an x such that $u_x \neq u'_x$. Therefore, $we^{2l+4}\$e^x\$e^{2x}\$u_x \in L_{bit}(d, k+1) \iff w'e^{2l+4}\$e^x\$e^{2x}\$u_x \notin L_{bit}(d, k+1)$. For all $d, k \in \mathbb{N}_+$, there are

$$(2^{d\cdot(k+1)} - 1)^l = (2^d 2^{d\cdot k} - 1)^l \geq (2 \cdot 2^{d\cdot k} - 1)^l \geq$$
$$(2^{d\cdot k} + 1)^l > (2^{d\cdot k} + \frac{1}{2})^l = ((1 + \frac{1}{2^{d\cdot k+1}})2^{d\cdot k})^l$$

different words of this form. Since $\frac{1}{2^{d\cdot k+1}} > 0$, we may choose l in such a way that $(1 + \frac{1}{2^{d\cdot k+1}})^l > p$. This implies the following lower bound on the number of induced equivalence classes:

$$N_\ell(l, L_{bit}(d, k+1)) > p \cdot 2^{d\cdot k\cdot l}$$

From the contradiction we obtain $L_{bit}(d, k+1) \notin \mathscr{L}_{rt}(\mathrm{IA}^d_k)$.

It remains to be shown that $L_{bit}(d, k+1) \in \mathscr{L}_{rt}(\mathrm{IA}^d_{k+1})$. As in the proof of Theorem 5, a corresponding iterative array stores the symbols u_i in a storage phase, and in a retrieval phase symbol u_x is addressed and sent back to the communication cell that compares it with v. The input symbols are binary encoded by $(k+1) \cdot d$ bits, respectively, such that the code of a_i is $i+1$.

First, we present the construction for $d = 1$, which is generalized subsequently. During the storage phase, a symbol u_i is read and its code is sent to the array. It is stored in cell i at time step $2i$. At time $2i+1$ cell $i+1$ is activated by cell i. So, cell $i+1$ can store symbol u_{i+1} at time $2(i+1)$. The following behavior stops the storage phase. It is constructed with an eye towards generalizations to higher dimensions. When the communication cell reads the symbol \$ it sends a 0 to the array. When this 0 is to be stored in cell $m+1$ at time $2(m+1)$, the cell recognizes the end of the storage phase, waits for three time steps, and sends a signal from right to left that informs all cells passed through about the end of the phase. The signal arrives at the communication cell at time step $2(m+1) + 3 + (m+1) = 3m+6$, i.e., when the input prefix $u_1 \cdots u_m\$e^{2m+4}\$$ has been read.

Now the retrieval phase starts. To this end, the communication cell sends signals 1 to the array as long as it reads the next input part e^x. When it reads the following \$ it sends a 2. Each cell which receives a 1 for the first time deletes the 1 from the stream. The unique cell that receives the 2 immediately after receiving a 1 for the first time, identifies itself to be the addressed cell x. It sends its stored symbol u_x to the left. The symbol arrives at the communication cell at time $3x$ after the beginning of the retrieval phase, i.e., before the v appears in the input.

We turn to higher dimensions. Roughly, the idea is to split the encodings of the input symbols u_i into d blocks of length k bits, respectively. These blocks are distributed to the d neighbors of the communication cell. This would lead to a straightforward generalization. But the problem arises that we cannot stop the storage phase since signal 0 (and any other signal) may appear as a block

On the other hand, consider two different prefixes [illegible] and [illegible]. Since they are different, there [illegible] such that [illegible]. Therefore, [illegible] for all [illegible] $\in \mathbb{N}_+$ there are [illegible]

[illegible]

[illegible] choose [illegible] a way [illegible] bound on the number [illegible] cases:

[illegible]

[illegible] of the [illegible] [illegible] Au the [illegible] of [illegible] symbol [illegible] the input symbol [illegible] binary [illegible] of [illegible]

First, we present [illegible] whose [illegible] Since the [illegible] code is sent to [illegible] cell [illegible] is [illegible] The fol- [illegible] towards [illegible] cell made [illegible] time [illegible] for three time steps, and [illegible] that information [illegible] passed through [illegible] the [illegible] arrives at the [illegible] the input [illegible]

[illegible] signal [illegible] codes [illegible] [illegible] that [illegible] [illegible] the communication [illegible] at time [illegible] before the [illegible] appears in the input.

We [illegible] the encodings of the input symbols [illegible]. These blocks are distinguished [illegible] this would lead to a situation [illegible] we cannot stop the storage phase since signal 0 and any other signal may appear as a block

cell 1 is the communication cell that indicates acceptance or rejection, and the array is bounded to the n cells which are initially active. Real time is defined to be n time steps. A *one-way cellular automaton* (OCA_k) is a cellular automaton in which each cell receives information from its immediate neighbor to the right only. So, the flow of information is restricted from right to left. The relations between these devices and iterative arrays in general are depicted in the left part of Figure 3. Now we turn to explore the relations for restricted devices.

Theorem 10. *For all $k \in \mathbb{N}_+$, there is a regular language which is not accepted by any real-time k-bit CA.*

Proof. Let $L_k = \{xvx \mid v \in \{a\}^* \text{ and } x \in \{a_0, \dots, a_{2^{2k}}\}\}$ be the regular witness language. Assume contrarily, L_k is accepted by some real-time CA_k with state set S, bit functions $b_1, b_2 : S \to \{0,1\}^k$ giving the bits communicated to the left and to the right, and local transition function $\delta : \{0,1\}^k \times S \times \{0,1\}^k \to S$.

First we partition the input states $\{a_0, \dots, a_{2^{2k}}\}$ according to b_1, i.e., two states s_1 and s_2 are in the same class if and only if $b_1(s_1) = b_1(s_2)$. Since there are $2^{2k}+1$ input states and the range of b_1 has 2^k elements, there is at least one class S_1 with at least 2^k+1 states. Next, S_1 is partitioned according to $b_1(\delta(b_2(a), s, b_1(\#)))$. Therefore, there is at least one subclass of S_1 that has at least two states, say a_i and a_j.

For an accepting computation on input $a_i a^n a_i$, for some $n \in \mathbb{N}_+$, we consider the relevant states of the cells $n-1$, n, $n+1$ at time steps 0, 1, 2. In particular, $c_0(n-1) = a$, $c_0(n) = a_i$, $c_0(n+1) = \#$, $c_1(n-1) = a'$, $c_1(n) = a_i'$, $c_2(n-1) = a''$. Due to the real-time restriction, states $c_1(n+1)$, $c_2(n)$, and $c_2(n+1)$ cannot affect the overall computation result. Since a_i and a_j are in the same class S_1, for input $a_i a^n a_j$ we obtain $c_0(n-1) = a$, $c_0(n) = a_j$, $c_0(n+1) = \#$, $c_1(n-1) = a'$, $c_1(n) = a_j'$. Since a_i and a_j are in the same subclass we obtain $c_2(n-1) = a''$. Therefore, input $a_i a^n a_j$ not belonging to L_k would be accepted. □

It is not hard to see that language L_k is accepted by a real-time CA_{k+1} as well as by a CA_k in time $n+1$. So, we obtain a strict bit hierarchy for two-way real-time cellular automata.

Theorem 11. *Let $k \in \mathbb{N}_+$ be a constant, then $\mathscr{L}_{rt}(CA_k) \subset \mathscr{L}_{rt}(CA_{k+1})$.*

Moreover, by modification of the witness language, i.e., by increasing the underlying alphabet, we obtain a very dense strict time hierarchy. That is, if we allow just one more time step, we obtain a strictly more powerful device.

Theorem 12. *Let $k \in \mathbb{N}_+$, $r \in \mathbb{N}$ be constants, then*

$$\mathscr{L}_{rt+r}(CA_k) \subset \mathscr{L}_{rt+r+1}(CA_k).$$

Since, trivially, any regular language is accepted by some real-time IA_1, the next theorem completes the incomparability results.

Theorem 13. *Let $k \in \mathbb{N}_+$ be a constant. There is a language belonging to the difference $\mathscr{L}_{rt}(OCA_1) \setminus \mathscr{L}_{lt}(IA_k)$.*

takes $x + 1$ time steps until the carryovers reach the new cell that extends the counter.

In addition, at time step 1 the rightmost cell sends a signal 1 to the left. The input is to be accepted if and only if this signal appears in a cell exactly at a time step at which this cell becomes the new most significant bit of the counter, i.e., at time steps $2^x + x$. In this case the signal 1 is passed through the counter in order to cause the leftmost cell to accept. Since the previous counter length was x, the total input length is $2^x + x + x$. □

For the sake of completeness, the following theorem is presented without proof.

Theorem 15. *Let $k \in \mathbb{N}_+$ be a constant, then $\mathscr{L}_{lt}(IA_k) \subset \mathscr{L}_{lt}(CA_k)$.*

References

1. Buchholz T, Klein A, Kutrib M (1999) Iterative arrays with a wee bit alternation. In: Fundamentals of Computation Theory 1999, LNCS 1684, pp 173–184
2. Buchholz T, Klein A, Kutrib M (2000) Iterative arrays with small time bounds. In: Mathematical Foundations of Computer Science 1998, LNCS 1893, pp 243–252
3. Buchholz T, Klein A, Kutrib M (1999) Iterative arrays with limited nondeterministic communication cell. In: Words, Languages and Combinatorics III, pp 73–87
4. Chang JH, Ibarra OH, Palis MA (1987) Parallel parsing on a one-way array of finite-state machines. IEEE Trans Comput C-36:64–75
5. Cole SN (1969) Real-time computation by n-dimensional iterative arrays of finite-state machines. IEEE Trans Comput C-18:349–365
6. Fischer PC (1965) Generation of primes by a one-dimensional real-time iterative array. J ACM 12:388–394
7. Ibarra OH, Palis MA (1985) Some results concerning linear iterative (systolic) arrays. J Parallel Distributed Comput 2:182–218
8. Ibarra OH, Palis MA (1988) Two-dimensional iterative arrays: Characterizations and applications. Theoret Comput Sci 57:47–86
9. Iwamoto C, Hatsuyama T, Morita K, Imai K (1999) On time-constructible functions in one-dimensional cellular automata. In: Fundamentals of Computation Theory 1999, LNCS 1684, pp 317–326
10. Malcher A (2004) On the descriptional complexity of iterative arrays. IEICE Transactions on Information and Systems E87-D:721–725
11. Seidel SR (1979) Language recognition and the synchronization of cellular automata. Technical Report 79-02, Department of Computer Science, University of Iowa, Iowa City
12. Smith III AR (1972) Real-time language recognition by one-dimensional cellular automata. J Comput System Sci 6:233–253
13. Terrier V (1995) On real time one-way cellular array. Theoret Comput Sci 141:331–335
14. Umeo H (2001) Linear-time recognition of connectivity of binary images on 1-bit inter-cell communication cellular automaton. Parallel Comput 27:587–599

[illegible] time steps until the [illegible] were [illegible] the new cell [illegible] the [illegible].

In addition, [illegible] time step the rightmost cell sends a signal [illegible] to the left. [illegible] is [illegible] only if this signal [illegible] cell exactly [illegible] of the [illegible] to [illegible] the [illegible] pattern [illegible], the [illegible] length [illegible].

[illegible] the following [illegible] result [illegible].

Theorem 13. [illegible] (CA) [illegible] (CA) [illegible]

References

1. [illegible]
2. [illegible]
3. [illegible] (pp 78–87)
4. [illegible]
5. [illegible]
6. [illegible]
7. [illegible]
8. [illegible]
9. [illegible]
10. [illegible] 721–725
11. [illegible] Technical Report [illegible] University of [illegible]
12. [illegible] cellular automata [illegible]
13. [illegible] cellular arrays. Theor. Comput. Sci. [illegible]
14. [illegible] images on 1-bit inter-cell communication cellular automata [illegible] 27:567–595

Asynchonous Distributed Components: Concurrency and Determinacy

Denis Caromel and Ludovic Henrio

CNRS – I3S – Univ. Nice Sophia Antipolis – INRIA Sophia Antipolis
Inria Sophia-Antipolis,2004 route des Lucioles – B.P. 93
F-06902 Sophia-Antipolis Cedex
{caromel, henrio}@sophia.inria.fr

Abstract. Based on the **imp**ς-calculus, ASP (Asynchronous Sequential Processes) defines distributed applications behaving deterministically. This article extends ASP by building hierarchical and asynchronous distributed components. Components are hierarchical - a composite can be built from other components, and distributed - a composite can span over several machines. This article also shows how the asynchronous component model can be used to statically assert component determinism.

1 Introduction

The advent of components in programming technology raises the question of their formal ground, intrinsic semantics, and above all their compositional semantics. It represents a real challenge as practical component models are usually quite complex, featuring distribution over local or wide area networks. But, few formal models for component were proposed so far [4, 20, 3, 14]. Since the first ideas about software components, usually dated in 1968 [1], the design of a reusable piece of software has technically evolved. From the first off-the-shelf modules, a component has become a complex piece of parameterized code with attributes to be set. Its behavior can be adapted with various non functional aspects (life-cycle, persistence, etc.). Finally, such piece of code is to be deployed in a hosting infrastructure, sometimes it can also be retrieved for replacement with a new version. In recent years, one crucial new aspect of component has been introduced: not only the interfaces being offered are specified, but also the needed interfaces.

A first key aspect of our work is to take into account this feature: the model being proposed allows to specify that a software components *provides* well defined interfaces, and *requires* well defined services or interfaces. A second and important contribution is to take into account components that are distributed over several machines. A given component can span as a unique entity over several hosts in the network. This work go further than a distributed-component infrastructure just allowing two components to talk over the network. Finally, the components being proposed are hierarchical (allowing a compositional spec-

Please use the following format when citing this chapter:

Caromel, D., Henrio, L., 2006, in International Federation for Information Processing, Volume 209, Fourth IFIP International Conference on Theoretical Computer Science-TCS 2006, eds. Navarro, G., Bertossi, L., Kohayakwa, Y., (Boston: Springer), pp. 165–183.

Stefani et al. [6, 20] introduced the kell calculus that is able to model components and especially sub-components control. We rather demonstrate how to build distributed components that behave deterministically and for which the deterministic behavior is statically decidable. Moreover, the properties shown here rely on properties of communications and semantics of the calculus that are not ensured directly by the kell calculus, and its adaptation would be more complicated than the new calculus presented here. However, those two approaches being rather orthogonal, one could expect to benefit of both by adapting a kell calculus-like control of components with an (adaptation of) ASP as the underlying calculus. Bruneton, Coupaye and Stefani also proposed a hierarchical component model: Fractal [12], together with its reference implementation Julia [7]. Our work can also be considered as a foundation for distributed Fractal components, focusing on the hierarchical aspect rather than on the component control.

2.2 ASP Calculus: Syntax and Informal Semantics

The ASP calculus [10], is an extension of the **imp**ς-calculus [2, 15] with two primitives (*Serve* and *Active*) to deal with distributed objects. The ASP calculus is implemented as a Java library (ProActive [11]). ASP strongly links the concepts of thread and of object, it is minimally characterized by:

- *Sequential activities*: each object is manipulated by a single thread,
- Communications are *asynchronous method calls*, and
- *Futures* as first class objects representing awaited results.

$a, b \in L ::= x$	variable,
$\quad \mid [l_i = b_i; m_j = \varsigma(x_j, y_j)a_j]^{i \in 1..n}_{j \in 1..m}$	object definition,
$\quad \mid a.l_i$	field access,
$\quad \mid a.l_i := b$	field update,
$\quad \mid a.m_j(b)$	method call,
$\quad \mid clone(a)$	superficial copy,
$\quad \mid Active(a, m_j)$	activates a. m_j defines the service policy
$\quad \mid Serve(M)$	serves a request among the set M of method labels, $M = \{m_1, \ldots, m_k\}$

Fig. 1. ASP Syntax (l_i are fields names, m_j are methods names)

ASP is formalized as follows. An *activity* (denoted by α, β, γ, ...) is composed of a thread manipulating a set of objects put in a store. The primitive *Active*(a, m) creates a new activity containing the object a which is said *active*, m is a method called upon the activity creation. Every request (method call) sent to an activity is actually sent to this master object. An activity also

Second, section 2 introduces [illegible] that is able to model components and especially component control. We [illegible] demonstrate how to [illegible] components that behave deterministically, and for which the [illegible] behaviour is statically decidable. Moreover, the properties shown [illegible] of the calculus that are [illegible] by the [illegible] [illegible] component control [illegible] implementation [illegible] controls [illegible] the component control.

2.1 ASP Calculus: [illegible]

[illegible]

[illegible]

Fig. 1. [illegible]

A [illegible] is com- [illegible] The primitive [illegible] request invoked [illegible] object. An activity also

In the following, α_P denotes the activity α of configuration P. Without any restriction, and to allow comparison based on activities identifiers, we suppose that the freshly allocated activity names are chosen deterministically: the first activity created by α will have the same identifier for all executions.

Potential Services Let $\mathcal{M}_{\alpha_P}$ be an approximation of the set of M that can appear in the $Serve(M)$ instructions that the activity α may perform in the future. In other words, if an activity *may* perform a service on a set of method labels, then this set must belong to $\mathcal{M}_{\alpha_P}$:

$$\exists Q,\ P \xrightarrow{*} Q \wedge a_{\alpha_Q} = \mathcal{R}[Serve(M)] \Rightarrow M \in \mathcal{M}_{\alpha_P}$$

This set can be specified by the programmer or statically inferred.

Interfering Requests Two requests on methods m_1 and m_2 are said to be *interfering* in α in a program P if they both belong to the same potential service, that is to say if they can appear in the same $Serve(M)$ primitive:

$$\text{Requests on } m_1 \text{ and } m_2 \text{ are interfering if } \{m_1, m_2\} \subseteq M \in \mathcal{M}_{\alpha_p}$$

Equivalence Modulo Replies $\equiv_F$, defined in [9], is an equivalence relation considering references to futures already calculated as equivalent to local reference to the part of store which is the (deep copy of the) future value.

More precisely, $\equiv_F$ is an equivalence relation on parallel configurations modulo the renaming of locations and futures and permutations of requests that cannot interfere. Moreover, a reference to a future already calculated (but not locally updated) is equivalent to a local reference to the (part of the store which is the) deep copy of the future value.

Deterministic Object Networks If two interfering requests cannot be sent to the same destination (β below) at the same moment then the program behaves deterministically. Of course, two such request would originate from two different activities (α_Q). "there is at most one" is denoted by $\exists^1$.

Definition 1 (DON) *A configuration P, is a* Deterministic Object Network *(DON(P)) if it cannot be reduced to a configuration where two interfering requests can be sent concurrently to the same destination activity:*

$$\begin{aligned}P \xrightarrow{*} Q \Rightarrow \forall \beta \in Q,\ \forall M \in \mathcal{M}_{\beta_Q},\\ \exists^1 \alpha_Q \in Q, \exists m \in M, \exists \iota, \iota',\ \ a_{\alpha_Q} = \mathcal{R}[\iota.m(\iota')] \wedge \sigma_{\alpha_Q}(\iota) = AO(\beta)\end{aligned}$$

Theorem 1 (DON determinism).

$$\begin{cases} DON(P) \wedge \\ P \xrightarrow{*} Q_1 \wedge \\ P \xrightarrow{*} Q_2 \end{cases} \Rightarrow \quad \exists R_1, R_2, \begin{cases} Q_1 \xrightarrow{*} R_1 \wedge \\ Q_2 \xrightarrow{*} R_2 \wedge \\ R_1 \equiv_F R_2 \end{cases}$$

[illegible] In the following, [illegible] configuration [illegible]. Without any restrictions [illegible] to allow [illegible] survives identifiers, we suppose that the [illegible] identifiers [illegible] chosen deterministically, the first activity created by [illegible] will hold the same identifier for all executions.

Potential Services. [illegible] set of M that can appear in the [illegible] future [illegible] method [illegible] this set [illegible]

$$[illegible]$$

The set can be specified by the programmer or statically inferred.

Interfering Requests. Two requests on the same activity are said to be interfering [illegible] if they both belong to [illegible] potential [illegible] to say if they [illegible] in the [illegible] predicate:

[illegible] requests [illegible] are interfering [illegible] M_α

Equivalence Modulo Replies. [illegible] equivalence relation [illegible] considering [illegible] futures already [illegible] equivalent to local references [illegible] value. More precisely [illegible] parallel configurations [illegible] requests, but [illegible] calculated (but not [illegible]) [illegible]

Confluence [illegible] Networks [illegible] to the same [illegible] have [illegible] different [illegible]

Definition [illegible]

$$[illegible]$$

Theorem 1 (DON [illegible]

$$[illegible]$$

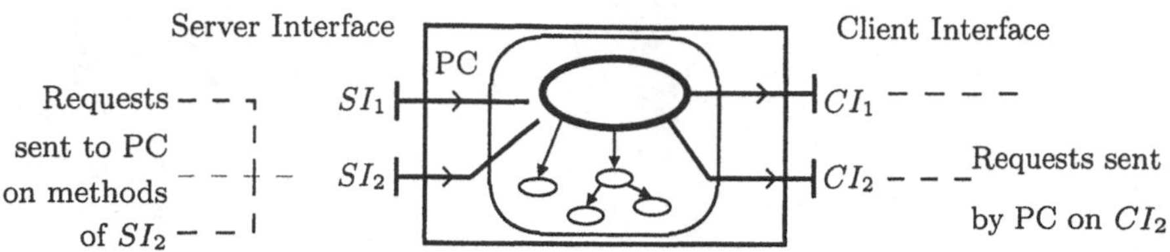

Fig. 2. A primitive component PC

$$CC ::= {}_{Name} \ll C_1, \ldots, C_m; \varepsilon_S; \psi; \varepsilon_C \gg$$

Where a component C_i is either a primitive or a composite one: $C ::= PC \mid CC$, and each client interface CI inside CC can only be connected once, leading to the following definition:

$\varepsilon_S : Exported(CC) \rightarrow \bigcup_{sc \in C_1 \ldots C_m} Exported(sc)$ *is a total function*

$\psi : \bigcup_{sc \in C_1 \ldots C_m} Imported(sc) \rightarrow \bigcup_{sc \in C_1, \ldots C_m} Exported(sc)$ *is a partial function*

$\varepsilon_C : \bigcup_{sc \in C_1 \ldots C_m} Imported(sc) \rightarrow Imported(CC)$ *is a partial surjective function*

Such that $dom(\psi) \cap dom(\varepsilon_C) = \emptyset$

We define: $Exported(CC) = dom(\varepsilon_S)$ and $Imported(CC) = codom(\varepsilon_C)$.

Defining ε_S as a function allows to export a given internal server interface as several external ones, but imposes each incoming request to be communicated to a single destination (each imported interface is bound to a single server interface of an internal component). Similarly, a client interface is exported only once for communications to have a single determinate destination: ε_C is a function (each client interface of an internal component is plugged at most once to an exported interface). ψ is a function so that internal communications are determinate too (each client interface of an internal component is plugged at most once to another internal server interface). And finally, also to ensure unicity of communication destination, ε_C and ψ have disjunct domain so that an internal client interface cannot be both bound internally and exported.

Correct Connections Figure 3 sums up the possible bindings that are allowed according to Definition 3. The component shown in the figure is a valid CC but not a DCC (DCC will be defined in Section 6.2, Definition 8).

Incorrect Connections Figure 4 shows the impossible bindings that correspond to the restrictions of Definition 3. The condition of Definition 3 that prevents the composition from being correct is written above each sub-figure.

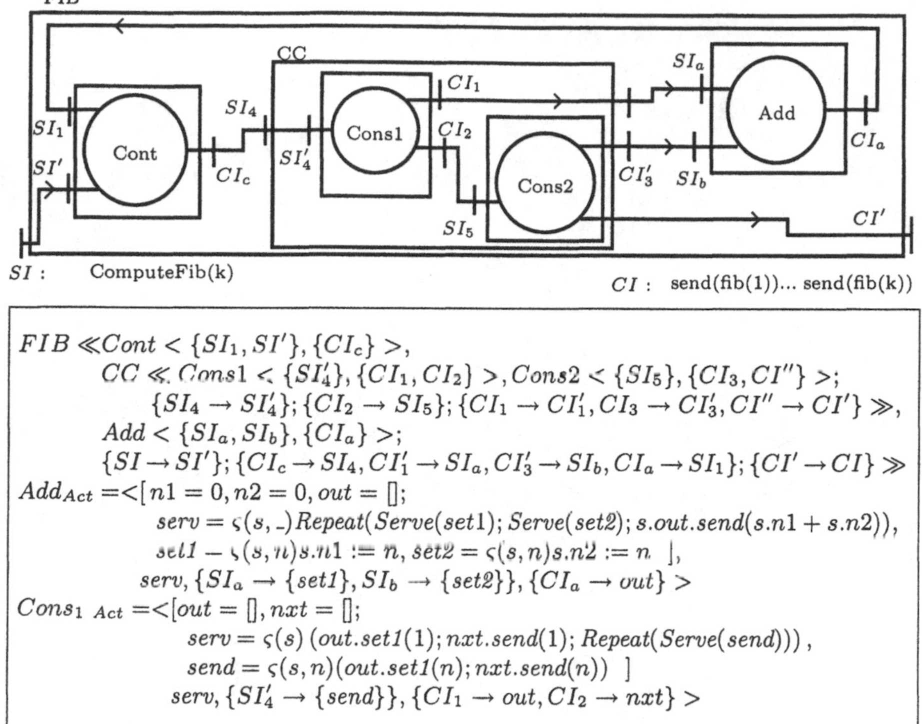

$$
\begin{array}{l}
FIB \ll Cont < \{SI_1, SI'\}, \{CI_c\} >, \\
\quad CC \ll Cons1 < \{SI'_4\}, \{CI_1, CI_2\} >, Cons2 < \{SI_5\}, \{CI_3, CI''\} >; \\
\quad\quad \{SI_4 \rightarrow SI'_4\}; \{CI_2 \rightarrow SI_5\}; \{CI_1 \rightarrow CI'_1, CI_3 \rightarrow CI'_3, CI'' \rightarrow CI'\} \gg, \\
\quad Add < \{SI_a, SI_b\}, \{CI_a\} >; \\
\quad \{SI \rightarrow SI'\}; \{CI_c \rightarrow SI_4, CI'_1 \rightarrow SI_a, CI'_3 \rightarrow SI_b, CI_a \rightarrow SI_1\}; \{CI' \rightarrow CI\} \gg \\
Add_{Act} =<[n1 = 0, n2 = 0, out = [];\\
\quad\quad serv = \varsigma(s, \_) Repeat(Serve(set1); Serve(set2); s.out.send(s.n1 + s.n2)), \\
\quad\quad set1 = \varsigma(s, n) s.n1 := n, set2 = \varsigma(s, n) s.n2 := n \ ], \\
\quad serv, \{SI_a \rightarrow \{set1\}, SI_b \rightarrow \{set2\}\}, \{CI_a \rightarrow out\} > \\
Cons_{1\ Act} =<[out = [], nxt = []; \\
\quad\quad serv = \varsigma(s)\ (out.set1(1); nxt.send(1); Repeat(Serve(send)))\ , \\
\quad\quad send = \varsigma(s, n)(out.set1(n); nxt.send(n)) \ ] \\
\quad serv, \{SI'_4 \rightarrow \{send\}\}, \{CI_1 \rightarrow out, CI_2 \rightarrow nxt\} >
\end{array}
$$

Fig. 5. A composite component for computing Fibonacci numbers

and *Cons2* forward their input to their two client interfaces (upon initialization they respectively send 1 and 0 to their client interfaces); they are merged in a composite component. *Add* simply sends on its output interface the addition of what the component receives on its two server interfaces. A controller *Cont* exports a server interface ($ComputeFib(k)$) taking an integer k and forwarding $k-1$ times its input on the other interface SI_1 to CI_c.

Primitive components for *Add* and $Cons_1$ are specified by Add_{Act} and $Cons_{1\ Act}$, the others can be specified similarly (*Repeat* performs an infinite loop, ";" expresses sequential composition, both can be expressed directly in ASP). $Cons_2$ can be specified by renaming inputs and outputs of $Cons_1$.

Finally, the FIB composite component is built by interconnecting those components as shown and expressed in the figure. For example, requests sent by $Cons_1$ on CI_1 are first exported on interface CC'_1 of CC and then sent, according to the bindings of FIB, to the interface SI_a of *Add*. *Cons2* sends *send* requests to the exported client interface, thus FIB produces $Fib(1) \dots Fib(k)$.

Fig. 5. A [illegible]

[illegible]

$$\Psi_{PC} : \emptyset \rightarrow \emptyset$$

$$\Psi_{CC} : \bigcup_{C \sqsubseteq CC} \mathit{Imported}(C) \rightarrow \bigcup_{C \sqsubseteq CC} \mathit{Exported}(C)$$
$$\Psi_{\mathrm{Name}\ll C_1,\ldots,C_m;\varepsilon_S;\psi;\varepsilon_C\gg} = \psi \oplus \Psi_{C_1} \oplus \ldots \oplus \Psi_{C_m}$$

In the general case, μ_C and Ψ_C are partial functions. In the case of a complete component C, for any client interface CI of C or a component inside C, either $\mu_C(CI)$ or $\Psi_C(CI)$ is defined.

Φ follows bindings, exportations and importations, to define the bindings between *primitive components*:

$$\Phi_C : \bigcup_{PC \sqsubseteq C} \mathit{Imported}(PC) \rightarrow \bigcup_{PC \sqsubseteq C} \mathit{Exported}(PC)$$
$$\Phi_C = \xi_C \circ \Psi_C \circ \mu_C$$

For a *complete closed* component C, Φ_C is a *total surjective* function.

We define below the deployment of the composite component CC: this static deployment creates as many activities as there are primitive components and binds their interfaces accordingly. Let PC_n range over primitive components defined inside CC: $PC_n = \mathrm{Name}_n < \{SI_{ni}\}^{i \in 1..k_n}, \{CI_{nj}\}^{j \in 1..l_n} >$ s.t. $PC_n \sqsubset CC$; and $PC_{n\,Act} = \mathrm{Name}_{n\,Act} < a_n, srv_n, \varphi_{S_n}, \varphi_{C_n} >$ range over their activities. We denote $N_s(SI_p)$, the index of the primitive component defining the interface SI_p: $N_S(SI_{ni}) = n$. The term defined in Figure 6 deploys the composite component CC defined above (the mutually recursive definition of activities *let rec*...*and*... can be built from core ASP terms). This deployment phase does not rely on any request and thus is entirely deterministic.

$$\begin{array}{l}
\mathit{let\ rec}\ c_1{=}\mathit{Active}((a_1.\varphi_{C_1}(CI_{11}) := c_{N_S(\Phi_{CC}(CI_{11}))}). \cdots .\varphi_{C_1}(CI_{1k_1}) := c_{N_S(\Phi_{CC}(CI_{1k_1}))}, srv_1) \\
\mathit{and}\ c_2{=}\mathit{Active}(a_2.\varphi_{C_2}(CI_{21}) := c_{N_S(\Phi_{CC}(CI_{21}))}. \cdots .\varphi_{C_1}(CI_{2k_2}) := c_{N_S(\Phi_{CC}(CI_{2k_2}))}, srv_2) \\
\mathit{and}\ \ldots \\
\mathit{and}\ c_n{=}\mathit{Active}(a_n.\varphi_{C_n}(CI_{n1}) := c_{N_S(\Phi_{CC}(CI_n))}. \cdots .\varphi_{C_n}(CI_{nk_n}) := c_{N_S(\Phi_{CC}(CI_{nk_n}))}, srv_n)
\end{array}$$

Fig. 6. Deployment of a composite component

This is sufficient to give a semantics to the components with all useful connections bound; but, here, components are not runtime entities and this translation neither is modular, nor gives any way of manipulating dynamically the components (e.g. component reconfiguration is far from trivial). An active object representation of each composite component will make them accessible and reconfigurable at runtime.

Composite Components Each CC contains the same CI fields as PCs, together with SI fields storing destinations to which received method calls must be forwarded.

For each composite component $\text{Name} \ll C_1, .., C_m; \varepsilon_S; \psi; \varepsilon_C \gg$, we define $N'_S(SI_i)$ the unique number such that $C_{N'_S(SI_i)}$ defines the server interface SI_i; and similarly $N'_C(CI_j)$ such that $C_{N'_C(CI_j)}$ is the sub-component containing the client interface CI_j. Figure 8 describes the instantiation of a composite component: it creates an activity for this component, binds the client interfaces according to ε_C and ψ, and the server interfaces according to ε_S.

$$
\begin{array}{l}
[\![\text{Name} \ll C_1, .., C_m; ; \varepsilon_S; \psi; \varepsilon_C \gg]\!] \triangleq \\
\quad \mathit{let}\ c_1 = [\![C_1]\!]\ \mathit{in} \qquad \ldots \qquad \mathit{let}\ c_m = [\![C_m]\!]\ \mathit{in} \\
\quad \mathit{let}\ \text{Name} = \mathit{Active}([\\
\qquad \forall SI_i \in dom(\varepsilon_S),\ SI_i = [CDest = c_{N'_S(\varepsilon_S(SI_i))}, IDest = \varepsilon_S(SI_i)], \\
\qquad \forall CI_j \in codom(\varepsilon_C),\ CI_j = [CDest = [], IDest = []], \\
\qquad started = false; \\
\qquad \forall CI_j \in codom(\varepsilon_C),\ setCI_j = \varsigma(s, Cdst', Idst')((s.CI_j).CDest := Cdst').IDest := Idst', \\
\qquad \forall SI_i \in dom(\varepsilon_S),\ setSI_i = \varsigma(s, Cdst', Idst')((s.SI_i).CDest := Cdst').IDest := Idst', \\
\qquad Call = \varsigma(s, CI\_SI, m_j, x)s.CI\_SI.CDest.Call(s.CI\_SI.IDest, m_j, x), \\
\qquad start = \varsigma(s)s.started = true, \\
\qquad srv = \varsigma(s)Repeat(if\ started\ then\ Serve(Call) \\
\qquad \qquad \qquad \qquad else\ Serve(\forall CI_j \in dom(\varepsilon_C)\ setCI_j, \forall SI_i \in dom(\varepsilon_S)\ setSI_i, start)) \\
\quad] \qquad , srv) \quad \mathit{in} \\
\qquad \forall CI_j \in dom(\psi),\ c_{N'_C(CI_j)}.setCI_j(c_{N'_S(\psi(CI_j))}, \psi(CI_j)) \\
\qquad \forall CI_j \in dom(\varepsilon_C),\ c_{N'_C(CI_j)}.setCI_j(\text{Name}, \varepsilon_C(CI_j)); \\
\qquad c_1.start(); \ldots; c_m.start(); \text{Name}
\end{array}
$$

Fig. 8. Composite Component Deployment

Once deployed, the main component has to be started:
$[\![\text{Name} \ll \ldots \gg]\!].start()$

The deployment phase relies on *setact*, and *setCI* requests but the order of these requests is always the same as first the *setact* requests are sent during the primitive component creation; and then the *setCI* are sent by the unique embedding composite component, and thus the deployment phase is deterministic.

This translation reveals the importance of the first class nature of futures. Indeed, every request transits through several primitive and composite components; if futures could not be transmitted between activities, then every component activity would be blocked as soon as a request transits through it, leading almost systematically to a deadlock. Of course, the first class nature of futures is also a major advantage from a functional point of view for both translations.

5.3 Perspective: Reconfiguration and Component Controllers

In the last translation extra activities are added (a kind of component membranes), and requests must transit through them. But this additional cost is

Composite [illegible] each [illegible] contains the same CI fields as PCs, [illegible] together with S[illegible] fields storing destination [illegible] for received method calls must be forwarded.

For each composite component [illegible], we define [illegible] the [illegible] defines the service interface [illegible] similarly [illegible] such [illegible] component containing the [illegible] interface [illegible] of a composite [illegible] interfaces [illegible]

[illegible]

[illegible]

[illegible] shows the [illegible] [illegible]

The [illegible] but the order of these requests is always the same [illegible] are sent during the [illegible] component [illegible] the unique [illegible] phase is [illegible]

[illegible]

[illegible]

[illegible] Correspondence [illegible] and Component Controllers

In the last [illegible] component [illegible] but this additional cost is

$$SDON(P) \Leftrightarrow \left(\left. \begin{array}{l} (\dot{\alpha}, \dot{\beta}, m_1) \in \mathcal{G}(P) \\ (\dot{\alpha}', \dot{\beta}, m_2) \in \mathcal{G}(P) \\ \dot{\alpha} \neq \dot{\alpha}' \end{array} \right\} \Rightarrow \forall M \in \mathcal{M}_{\dot{\beta}_P}, \{m_1, m_2\} \not\subseteq M \right)$$

Theorem 2 (SDON determinism). *SDON terms behave deterministically.*

Proof : It is sufficient to prove that $SDON(P) \Rightarrow DON(P)$, or that $\neg DON(P) \Rightarrow \neg SDON(P)$. Suppose P is not a DON, then it may send in the future two concurrent requests, and thus there is an activity β of a configuration Q such that $P \xrightarrow{*} Q$ and:

$$\exists M \in \mathcal{M}_{\beta_P}, \exists \alpha \neq \alpha', \exists m_1, m_2 \in M, \begin{cases} a_\alpha = \mathcal{R}[\iota.m_1(\iota')] \wedge \sigma_\alpha(\iota) = AO(\beta) \\ a_{\alpha'} = \mathcal{R}[\iota_2.m_2(\iota_2')] \wedge \sigma_{\alpha'}(\iota_2) = AO(\beta) \end{cases}$$

Then, as $\mathcal{G}(P)$ is an approximated call graph:

$$\exists M \in \mathcal{M}_{\beta_P}, \exists \alpha \neq \alpha', \exists m_1, m_2 \in M_{\beta_P}(\dot{\alpha}, \dot{\beta}, m_1) \in \mathcal{G}(P) \ \wedge \ (\dot{\alpha}', \dot{\beta}, m_2) \in \mathcal{G}(P)$$

and, as $\forall \alpha, \neg Part(\dot{\alpha})$, and by definition of $\mathcal{M}_{\dot{\beta}_P}$:

$$\exists \dot{\alpha} \neq \dot{\alpha}' \wedge (\dot{\alpha}, \dot{\beta}, m_1) \in \mathcal{G}(P) \ \wedge \ (\dot{\alpha}', \dot{\beta}, m_2) \in \mathcal{G}(P) \ \wedge \ m_1, m_2 \in M \wedge M \in M_{\dot{\beta}_P}$$

Finally, P is not a SDON. □

Of course, not every DON is a SDON, but SDON can be considered as the best approximation of DON that does not require control flow analysis.

6.2 Deterministic Components

We define a deterministic assemblage of components based on the fact that PCs provide an abstraction for activities and thus the SDON definition can be entirely expressed in terms of specifications of PCs and connections of interfaces. Indeed, suppose that for any two methods of the same SI cannot interfere, then a component system is deterministic if each SI can be accessed by a single activity (that is by a single component). Then, ensuring that only one CI is finally plugged to each SI is sufficient to ensure confluence.

As each PC can be considered as an abstraction of an activity, for each PC, we denote $\mathcal{M}_{PC}$ is the potential service of the activity defined by PC_{Act}.

Definition 7 (Deterministic Primitive Component (DPC))
A primitive component $PC = {}_{Name} < \{SI_i\}^{i \in 1..k}, \{CI_j\}^{j \in 1..l} >$ *is a DPC if its activity* ${}_{Name_{Act}} < a, srv, \varphi_S, \varphi_C >$ *associates its server interfaces to disjoint subsets of the served methods of the embedded active object; and such that two interfering requests necessarily belong to the same SI:*

$$\forall M \in \mathcal{M}_{PC}, \forall m_1, m_2 \in M \ (m_1 \in \varphi_S(SI_i) \wedge m_2 \in \varphi_S(SI_j)) \Rightarrow i = j$$

[illegible]

Theorem 2 (SDON [illegible] determinacy [illegible]

Proof: [illegible]

[illegible]

3 [illegible] Components

[illegible] the fact that [illegible]

[illegible]

Definition [illegible] **Determinable Primitive Components (DPC))**

[illegible]

PCs (statically defined), thus we can consider PCs as the abstract domain for activities. This abstraction does not merge activities: $\forall PC$, $\neg Part(PC)$. We denote $comp(SI)$ the PC such that $SI \in Exported(PC)$ and similarly $comp(CI)$ the PC such that $CI \in Imported(PC)$. An approximation of $\mathcal{G}(P)$ becomes:

$$\{(PC, PC', m) | CI \in dom(\Phi) \wedge PC = comp(CI) \wedge PC' = comp(\Phi(CI)) \\ \wedge PC'_{Act} =< a, s, \varphi_S, \varphi_C > \wedge m \in \varphi_S(\Phi(CI))\}$$

And thus the SDON property is verified (with $PC'_{Act} =< a, s, \varphi_S, \varphi_C >$):

$$\left.\begin{array}{l}(PC, PC', m_1) \in \mathcal{G}(P) \\ (PC_2, PC', m_2) \in \mathcal{G}(P) \\ PC \neq PC_2\end{array}\right\} \Rightarrow \forall k \in 1,2,\ m_k \in \varphi_S(SI_k) \wedge PC' = comp(SI_k) \wedge SI_1 \neq SI_2 \\ \Rightarrow \forall M \in \mathcal{M}_{PC'},\ \{m_1, m_2\} \not\subseteq M$$

Indeed, $m_1, m_2 \in M$ and $M \in \mathcal{M}_{PC'}$ would imply $SI_1 = SI_2$ because PC' is a DPC. Finally a DCC behaves deterministically when deployed with the first translational semantics. □

DCC assemblage allows to statically ensure deterministic behavior of components, only based on the following requirements.

- Potential services can be statically determined, or are statically specified (every served set has been declared as a potential service).
- SI interfaces are respected: they only receive requests on the methods they define; this could be checked by typing techniques [2] on ASP source terms.
- Requests follow bindings and are not modified while following these bindings.
- There is a bijection between primitive components and functional activities.

The two first requirements correspond to static analysis or specification; whereas the two last ones must be guaranteed by the components semantics which is the case for both translational semantics of Section 5.

We have shown in [9] that every Process Network can be translated into a (deterministic) ASP term, which can then be fit into a deterministic assemblage of components. Such a bijection between process networks and DCCs will finally provide a large number of DCCs.

7 Conclusion

This article defines a *hierarchical* component calculus that provides a very convenient abstraction of activities and method calls. This abstraction allows static verification of *determinism* properties. Our component model is aimed at *distribution*, featuring *asynchronous remote method invocations*, and *futures* as generalized references passing through components. Primitive components are defined as a set of *Server Interfaces* (SI) and *client interfaces* (CI), together with an ASP term for the primitive component content. Intuitively, each SI corresponds to a set of methods, each CI to a field. Composite components are recursively made of primitives and other composites, with a partial binding between SIs and CIs, and some SIs and CIs exported.

Crnkovic, Judith A. Stafford, Heinz W. Schmidt, and Kurt C. Wallnau, editors, *CBSE*, volume 3054 of *Lecture Notes in Computer Science*. Springer, 2004.
8. Luca Cardelli and Andrew D. Gordon. Mobile ambients. *Theoretical Computer Science*, 240(1):177–213, 2000. An extended abstract appeared in *Proceedings of FoSSaCS '98*, pages 140–155.
9. Denis Caromel and Ludovic Henrio. *A Theory of Distributed Objects*. Springer-Verlag New York, Inc., 2005. To appear.
10. Denis Caromel, Ludovic Henrio, and Bernard Paul Serpette. Asynchronous and deterministic objects. In *Proceedings of the 31st ACM SIGACT-SIGPLAN symposium on Principles of programming languages*, pages 123–134. ACM Press, 2004.
11. Denis Caromel, Wilfried Klauser, and Julien Vayssière. Towards seamless computing and metacomputing in Java. *Concurrency: Practice and Experience*, 10(11–13):1043–1061, 1998. ProActive available at `http://www.inria.fr/oasis/proactive`.
12. Bruneton E., Coupaye T., and Stefani J.B. Recursive and dynamic software composition with sharing. In *Proceedings of the 7th ECOOP International Workshop on Component-Oriented Programming (WCOP'02)*, 2002.
13. Cormac Flanagan and Matthias Felleisen. The semantics of future and an application. *Journal of Functional Programming*, 9(1):1–31, 1999.
14. Dimitra Giannakopoulou, Jeff Kramer, and Shing Chi Cheung. Behaviour analysis of distributed systems using the tracta approach. *Automated Software Engg.*, 6(1), 1999.
15. Andrew D. Gordon, Paul D. Hankin, and Sren B. Lassen. Compilation and equivalence of imperative objects. *FSTTCS: Foundations of Software Technology and Theoretical Computer Science*, 17:74–87, 1997.
16. Robert H. Halstead, Jr. Multilisp: A language for concurrent symbolic computation. *ACM Transactions on Programming Languages and Systems (TOPLAS)*, 7(4):501–538, 1985.
17. Gilles Kahn. The semantics of a simple language for parallel programming. In J. L. Rosenfeld, editor, *Information Processing '74: Proceedings of the IFIP Congress*, pages 471–475. North-Holland, New York, 1974.
18. Uwe Nestmann and Martin Steffen. Typing confluence. In Stefania Gnesi and Diego Latella, editors, *Proceedings of FMICS'97*, pages 77–101. Consiglio Nazionale Ricerche di Pisa, 1997. Also available as report ERCIM-10/97-R052, European Research Consortium for Informatics and Mathematics, 1997.
19. Thomas Parks and David Roberts. Distributed Process Networks in Java. In *Proceedings of the International Parallel and Distributed Processing Symposium (IPDPS2003)*, Nice, France, April 2003.
20. Alan Schmitt and Jean-Bernard Stefani. The kell calculus: A family of higher-order distributed process calculi. *Lecture Notes in Computer Science*, 3267, Feb 2005.

[illegible] Bradford, [illegible] and Albert C. Wallner, editors. [illegible] volume [illegible] of Lecture Notes in Computer Science. Springer 2000.

6. [illegible] Mobile ambients. Theoretical Computer Science, 240(1):177–213, [illegible] abstract appeared in Proceedings of [illegible]

[illegible] A Theory of Distributed Objects. Springer, New York, Inc., 2005. [illegible]

[illegible]

12. [illegible] dynamic software components with [illegible]

[illegible]

14. [illegible]

15. Andrew D. [illegible] Compilation [illegible] Transactions of Software Technology and [illegible]

[illegible]

[illegible] Computing [illegible] ACM [illegible]

18. [illegible]

[illegible] 2005.

Decidable Properties for Regular Cellular Automata

Pietro Di Lena

Department of Computer Science, University of Bologna, Mura Anteo Zamboni 7, 40127 Bologna, Italy. dilena@cs.unibo.it

Abstract. We investigate decidable properties for regular cellular automata. In particular, we show that regularity itself is an undecidable property and that nilpotency, equicontinuity and positively expansiveness become decidable if we restrict to regular cellular automata.

1 Introduction

Cellular Automata (CA) are often used as a simple model for complex systems. They were introduced by Von Neumann in the forties as a model of self-reproductive biological systems [16]. Mathematical theory of CA was developed later by Hedlund in the context of symbolic dynamics [7].

To a cellular automaton one associates the shift spaces generated by the evolution of the automaton on suitable partitions of the configuration space. Adopting Kůrka's terminolgy we call *column subshifts* this kind of shift spaces (see [12] chapter 5). A general approach to the study of a cellular automaton is to study the complexity of its column subshifts (see [5, 13, 10]).

Regularity has been introduced by Kůrka for general dynamical systems [14]. A CA is regular if every column subshift is sofic, i.e. if the language of every column subshift is regular. Kůrka classified CA according to the complexity of column subshift languages [13]. In Kůrka's classification the main distiction is whether the cellular automaton is regular or not. He compared language classification with two other famous CA classifications such as equicontinuity and attractor classification.

In this paper we study the decidability of topological properties for CA. In particular, we show that regularity is not a decidable property (Theorem 7) which implies that the membership in Kůrka's language classes is undecidable. In contrast, we show that some topological properties which are in general undecidable become decidable if we restrict to the class of regular CA. For instance, we show that for regular CA nilpotency, equicontinuity and positively expansiveness are decidable properties (Theorem 6). Moreover, we provide an answer to a question raised in [3] showing that the topological entropy is computable for one-sided regular CA (Theorem 5).

The paper is organized as follows. Section 2 is devoted to the introduction of the notation and general definitions while Section 3 contains our results.

Please use the following format when citing this chapter:

Di Lena, P., 2006, in International Federation for Information Processing, Volume 209, Fourth IFIP International Conference on Theoretical Computer Science-TCS 2006, eds. Navarro, G., Bertossi, L., Kohayakwa, Y., (Boston: Springer), pp. 185–196.

The topological entropy $h(X) = \lim_{n\to\infty} \log|\mathcal{B}_n(X)|/n$ of a shift space X is a measure of the complexity of X. While the topological entropy is not computable for general subshifts, it is for sofic shifts (see [15]).

The language of a sofic shift is denoted as *regular* in the context of *formal language theory* (see [9] for an introduction). The class of regular languages is the class of languages which can be recognized by a *deterministic finite state automaton* (DFA). Formally, a DFA is a 5-tuple (Q, A, δ, q_0, F) where Q is a finite set of states, $F \subseteq Q$ is the set of *accepting* states, $q_0 \in Q$ is the *initial state*, A is a finite alphabet and $\delta : Q \times A \to Q$ is a partial transition function (i.e. it can be defined only on a subset of $Q \times A$). The language represented by a DFA is the set of words generated by following a path starting from the initial state and ending to an accepting state.

For every regular language there exists an unique smallest DFA, where smallest refers to the number of states. In general, most of the questions concerning regular languages are algorithmically decidable. In particular, it is decidable if two distinct DFA represent the same language.

From a DFA representing the language of a sofic shift S it is possible to derive a labeled graph presentation of S in the following way:

1. the set of vertices V consists of the pairs $(q, a) \in Q \times A$ s.t. $\delta(q, a) \in Q$.
2. there exists an edge $(q, a) \to (q', a')$, $(q, a), (q', a') \in V$, if $\delta(q, a) = q'$
3. $\forall v = (q, a) \in V$, $\zeta(v) = a$.

2.2 Cellular Automata

A *cellular automaton* is a dynamical system $(A^{\mathbb{Z}}, F)$ where A is a finite alphabet and F is a σ-commuting, continuous function. $(A^{\mathbb{Z}}, F)$ is generally identified by a block mapping $f : A^{2r+1} \to A$ such that $F(x)_i = f(x_{[i-r,i+r]}), i \in \mathbb{Z}$. According to Curtis-Hedlund-Lyndon Theorem [7], the whole class of continuous and σ-commuting functions between shift spaces arises in this way.

We refer to f and r respectively as *local rule* and *radius* of the CA.

A CA is *one-sided*, if the local rule is of the form $f : A^{r+1} \to A$ where $\forall x \in A^{\mathbb{Z}}, i \in \mathbb{Z}, F(x)_i = f(x_{[i,i+r]})$. A one-sided CA is usually denoted with $(A^{\mathbb{N}}, F)$.

We recall the definition of some topological properties of CA. Let d denote the metric on $A^{\mathbb{Z}}$ defined in Section 2.1.

Definition 1. *Let $(A^{\mathbb{Z}}, F)$ be a CA.*

1. $(A^{\mathbb{Z}}, F)$ *is* nilpotent *if*

$$\exists N > 0, \exists x \in A^{\mathbb{Z}}, \sigma(x) = x, \ s.t.\ \forall n \geq N, F^n(A^{\mathbb{Z}}) = x.$$

2. $(A^{\mathbb{Z}}, F)$ *is* equicontinuous at $x \in A^{\mathbb{Z}}$ *if*

$$\forall \epsilon > 0, \exists \delta > 0 \ s.t.\ \forall y \in A^{\mathbb{Z}}, d(x, y) < \delta, \exists n > 0 \ s.t.\ d(F^n(x), F^n(y)) < \epsilon.$$

3. $(A^{\mathbb{Z}}, F)$ *is* equicontinuous *if* $\forall x \in A^{\mathbb{Z}}$, $(A^{\mathbb{Z}}, F)$ *is equicontinuous at* x.

3 Results

In this section we investigate decidable properties of regular CA. Most of our effort will be devoted to show that if $S \subseteq (A^{2r+1})^{\mathbb{N}}$ is a sofic shift and $(A^{\mathbb{Z}}, F)$ is a CA with radius r, it is possible to decide whether $S = \Sigma_{2r+1}$ (Theorem 3). This strong result has a lot of consequences. The most relevant one is that for regular CA it is possible to compute column subshifts of every given width (Theorem 4). The (dynamical) complexity of a CA is strictly related to the complexity of column subshifts languages. Actually we show that, thanks to the computability property, it is possible to decide if a regular CA is nilpotent, equicontinuous or positively expansive (Theorem 6). Moreover, it turns also out, that it is possible to compute the topological entropy for one-sided regular CA (Theorem 5). The negative consequence of computability/decidability results is that regularity itself is an undecidable property (Theorem 7).

In order to show our fundamental decidability result (Theorem 3) we need to define the concept of *cellular automaton extension* of a sofic shift and to show some basic properties.

Definition 6. *Let $(A^{\mathbb{Z}}, F)$ be a CA with radius r. Let $\mathcal{G} = (V, E, \zeta)$ be a labeled graph with $\zeta : V \to A^{2r+1}$. For $t > 0$, let the* (F,t)-extension *of $\mathcal{G}$ be the labeled graph $\mathcal{G}_{(F,t)} = (V_t, E_t, \zeta_t)$, with $\zeta_t : V_t \to A^{2r+t}$, defined in the following way (see figure 1):*

- vertex set:

$$V_t = \{(v_1, .., v_t) \in V^t \mid \exists a \in A^{2r+t}, \zeta(v_i) = a_{[i,2r+i]}, 1 \leq i \leq t\}$$

- edge set:

$$E_t = \{(e_1, .., e_t) \in E^t \mid \exists v, v' \in V_t, i(e_j) = v_j, t(e_j) = v'_j, f(\zeta(v_j)) = \zeta(v'_j)_{r+1}\}$$

- labeling function:

$$\forall v = (v_1, ..., v_t) \in V_t, \zeta_t(v) = a \text{ where } a_{[i,2r+i]} = \zeta(v_i), 1 \leq i \leq t.$$

Definition 7. *Let $(A^{\mathbb{Z}}, F)$ be a CA. Let $t > 0, k > 1$ and let $a, b \in \mathcal{B}_t(\Sigma_k)$ such that $a = a_1...a_k$, $b = b_1...b_k$ where $a_i, b_i \in A^t$ and $a_{i+1} = b_i, 1 \leq i < k$. Then, we say that x, y are* compatible blocks *and we denote with $a \odot b = a_1...a_k b_k$ their* overlapping concatenation.

Moreover, let $x, y \in \Sigma_k$ such that $x = x_1..x_k, y = y_1...y_k$ where $x_i, y_i \in A^{\mathbb{N}}$ and $x_{i+1} = y_i, 1 \leq i < k$. We say that x, y are compatible sequences *and, abusing the notation, we denote with $x \odot y = x_1...x_k y_k$ their* overlapping concatenation.

The following two lemmas will be used extensively.

2 Results

In this section we investigate [illegible] properties of regular CA. Most of our effort will be devoted to show that if $S \subseteq (A^{\mathbb{Z}}, \sigma)$ is a sofic shift and $(A^{\mathbb{Z}}, F)$ is a CA with radius r, [illegible] decide whether $S = \Sigma_{F,r}$ (Theorem [illegible]). This [illegible] result has a lot of consequences, the most relevant one is that [illegible] regular CA [illegible] compute column subshifts of every given width (Theorem [illegible]). [illegible] of a CA is strictly related to the complexity of column subshifts [illegible] the complexity properties [illegible] regular CA [illegible] it is possible to compute the topological entropy of [illegible] regular CA (Theorem [illegible]). [illegible] consequence of [illegible] results is that [illegible] property (Theorem [illegible]).

In order to show our fundamental [illegible] result [illegible] we need [illegible] the concept of [illegible] shifts and [illegible] some [illegible] properties.

Definition [illegible] be a CA with radius [illegible] (V, E) [illegible] be a labeled [illegible] $G = (V, E)$ [illegible] with [illegible] the following way [illegible]

$$[illegible]$$

[illegible]

$$E = \{(e, [illegible]) [illegible]\}$$

[illegible]

$$[illegible] \leq 1$$

Definition [illegible] with [illegible] where [illegible] < 1. [illegible] will be [illegible] overlapping [illegible]

Moreover [illegible] overlapping [illegible] compatible sequences [illegible] overlapping [illegible]

The following [illegible] lemmas will be used extensively [illegible]

Proposition 1. *Let $(A^{\mathbb{Z}}, F)$ be a CA with radius r and let $\mathcal{G}, \mathcal{G}'$ be two distinct labeled graph presentations of the same sofic shift $S = S_{\mathcal{G}} = S_{\mathcal{G}'} \subsetneq (A^{2r+1})^{\mathbb{N}}$. Then, for any $t > 0$, $S_{\mathcal{G}_{(F,t)}} = S_{\mathcal{G}'_{(F,t)}}$.*

Proof. We show that $S_{\mathcal{G}_{(F,t)}} \subseteq S_{\mathcal{G}'_{(F,t)}}$. The proof for the converse inclusion can be obtained by exchanging $\mathcal{G}$ with $\mathcal{G}'$.

First of all, note that, by definition of $(F,1)$-extension, $S_{\mathcal{G}_{(F,1)}} = S_{\mathcal{G}'_{(F,1)}}$. Let $x \in S_{\mathcal{G}_{(F,t)}}$ and let $x_1, ..., x_t \in S$ such that $x = x_1 \odot ... \odot x_t$. Then, $x_1, ..., x_t \in S_{\mathcal{G}'_{(F,1)}}$ and, by Lemma 2, it follows that $x \in S_{\mathcal{G}'_{(F,t)}}$. □

Thanks to Proposition 1 we can refer directly to the extension of a sofic shift S rather than to the extension of a labeled graph presentation of S.

Definition 8. *Let $(A^{\mathbb{Z}}, F)$ be a CA with radius r. Let $S \subsetneq (A^{2r+1})^{\mathbb{N}}$ be a sofic shift and let $\mathcal{G}$ be a labeled graph presentation of S. For $t > 0$, let denote with $S_{(F,t)} = S_{\mathcal{G}_{(F,t)}}$ the* (F,t)-extension *of the sofic shift S.*

We now show some useful properties of the (F,t)-extensions of sofic shifts.

Lemma 3. *Let $(A^{\mathbb{Z}}, F)$ be a CA with radius r. Let $S \subsetneq (A^{2r+1})^{\mathbb{N}}$ be a sofic shift. Then $\forall t > 0$,*

a. *if $\Sigma_{2r+1} \subset S$ then $\Sigma_{2r+t} \subsetneq S_{(F,t)}$,*
b. *if $\Sigma_{2r+1} = S$ then $\Sigma_{2r+t} = S_{(F,t)}$,*
c. *if $\Sigma_{2r+1} \supset S$ then $\Sigma_{2r+t} \supset S_{(F,t)}$.*

Proof. **a.** Let $x \in \Sigma_{2r+t}$ such that $x = x_1 \odot .. \odot x_t$ where $x_i \in \Sigma_{2r+1}$, $1 \leq i \leq t$. Then, $x_i \in S_{(F,1)}$, $1 \leq i \leq t$ and, by Lemma 2, $x_1 \odot .. \odot x_t \in S_{(F,t)}$.

b. By point a, $\Sigma_{2r+t} \subsetneq S_{(F,t)}$, thus we just have to show that $S_{(F,t)} \subsetneq \Sigma_{2r+t}$ or, equivalently, that $\mathcal{L}(S_{(F,t)}) \subsetneq \mathcal{L}(\Sigma_{2r+t})$. Let $k > 0$ and let $a \in \mathcal{B}_k(S_{(F,t)})$. Let $a_1, ..., a_t \in \mathcal{B}_k(S)$ be such that $a_1 \odot ... \odot a_t = a$. By hypothesis, $a_1, ..., a_t \in \mathcal{B}_k(\Sigma_{2r+1})$ then, by Lemma 1, it follows that $a_1 \odot ... \odot a_t \in \mathcal{B}_k(\Sigma_{2r+t})$.

c. Since $\Sigma_{2r+1} \supset S$, appling the same reasoning of point b, it is possible to conclude that $\Sigma_{2r+t} \supseteq S_{(F,t)}$. We have just to show that the inclusion is strict. Since $\Sigma_{2r+1} \supset S$, there exists a block $b_1 \in \mathcal{L}(\Sigma_{2r+1})$ such that $b_1 \notin \mathcal{L}(S)$. Then, let $b \in \mathcal{L}(\Sigma_{2r+t})$ such that $b = b_1 \odot b_2 \odot ... \odot b_t$ for some $b_2, ..., b_t \in \mathcal{L}(\Sigma_{2r+1})$. Trivially, $b \notin \mathcal{L}(S_{(F,t)})$. □

The following theorem easily follows from Lemma 3 and provides a strong characterization for regular CA. It is a two-sided extension of a theorem proved by Blanchard and Maass for one-sided CA [1].

Theorem 2. *Let $(A^{\mathbb{Z}}, F)$ be a CA with radius r. Then $(A^{\mathbb{Z}}, F)$ is regular if and only if Σ_{2r+1} is a sofic shift.*

Proof. The necessary implication is trivial. Then, suppose Σ_{2r+1} is a sofic shift. For every $d < 2r + 1$, Σ_d is a factor of Σ_{2r+1} then it is a sofic shift. For every $d > 2r + 1$, by Lemma 3 point b, Σ_d can be represented by a labeled graph then it is a sofic shift. □

In general, if Σ_d is a sofic shift for $d < 2r + 1$ it is not possible to conclude that the CA is regular (see [10]).

Proposition 4. *Let $(A^{\mathbb{Z}}, F)$ be a CA with radius r and let $S \subseteq (A^{2r+1})^{\mathbb{N}}$ be a sofic shift. Then it is decidable if S is F-extendible.*

Proof. Given a labeled graph representation of S, it is possible to compute $S_{(F,2)}$ and it is possible to compute labeled graph representations for $\Phi_{[1,2r+1]}(S_{(F,2)})$ and $\Phi_{[2,2r+2]}(S_{(F,2)})$. Given labeled graph representation of S, $S' = \Phi_{[1,2r+1]}(S_{(F,2)})$ and $S'' = \Phi_{[2,2r+2]}(S_{(F,2)})$ it is easy to build three finite state automata whose recognized languages are respectively $\mathcal{L}(S), \mathcal{L}(S')$ and $\mathcal{L}(S'')$. Then, the proof follows from Proposition 2 and from the decidability of the equivalence between finite state automata. □

Proposition 5. *Let $(A^{\mathbb{Z}}, F)$ be a CA with radius r and let $S \subseteq \Sigma_{2r+1}$ be a sofic shift. Then it is decidable if $\Sigma_{2r+1} = S$.*

Proof. We provide a proof for the following claim which trivially is algorithmically checkable.

> *Let $M = (Q, A^{2r+1}, q_0, F, \delta)$ be the smallest DFA recognizing the language $\mathcal{L}(S)$. Let $N = (|Q| \cdot |A|^{2r+1})^{2r+1}$. Then $\Sigma_{2r+1} = S$ if and only if $\mathcal{B}_N(\Sigma_{4r+1}) = \mathcal{B}_N(S_{(F,2r+1)})$.*

By Lemma 3, the necessary condition is trivially true. Obviously, if $\Sigma_{4r+1} = S_{(F,2r+1)}$ then $\Sigma_{2r+1} = S$. Thus, we show by induction on $k > 0$ that $\mathcal{B}_k(\Sigma_{4r+1}) = \mathcal{B}_k(S_{(F,2r+1)})$.

a. (Base Case) By hypothesis, $\mathcal{B}_N(\Sigma_{4r+1}) = \mathcal{B}_N(S_{(F,2r+1)})$. Moreover, since the language of a subshift is factorial, $\mathcal{B}_k(\Sigma_{4r+1}) = \mathcal{B}_k(S_{(F,2r+1)})$, $\forall k \leq N$.

b. (Inductive Case) Suppose $\mathcal{B}_K(\Sigma_{4r+1}) = \mathcal{B}_K(S_{(F,2r+1)})$, $K \geq N$. We have to show that $\mathcal{B}_{K+1}(\Sigma_{4r+1}) = \mathcal{B}_{K+1}(S_{(F,2r+1)})$.
Let $\mathcal{G} = (V, E, \zeta)$ be the labeled graph presentation of S derived from the smallest DFA M according to the procedure described at the end of section 2.1. Note that the number of vertices of $\mathcal{G}$ is less then or equal to $|Q| \cdot |A|^{2r+1}$. Moreover, let $\mathcal{G}_{(F,2r+1)}$ be the $(F, 2r+1)$-extension of $\mathcal{G}$. Note that the number of vertices of $\mathcal{G}_{(F,2r+1)}$ is less then or equal to N.
Let $a \in \mathcal{B}_{K+1}(\Sigma_{4r+1})$ and let $a^1, ..., a^{2r+1} \in \mathcal{B}_{K+1}(\Sigma_{2r+1})$ such that $a = a^1 \odot ... \odot a^{2r+1}$. Since, by inductive hypothesis, $\mathcal{B}_K(\Sigma_{4r+1}) = \mathcal{B}_K(S_{(F,2r+1)})$, it follows that $\mathcal{B}_{K+1}(\Sigma_{2r+1}) = \mathcal{B}_{K+1}(S)$ and, trivially, that $a^1, ..., a^{2r+1} \in \mathcal{B}_{K+1}(S)$. Then there exist uniques legal paths

$$u_1^1 \to ... \to u_{K+1}^1, ..., u_1^{2r+1} \to ... \to u_{K+1}^{2r+1}$$

in $\mathcal{G}$, where $u_1^i = (q_0, a_1^i)$ and $\zeta(u_k^i) = a_k^i, \forall i \in [1, 2r+1], 1 \leq k \leq K+1$.
We show that there exists $x \in S_{(F,2r+1)}$ such that $x_{[0,K]} = a$. Let $y \in S_{(F,2r+1)}$ such that $y_{[0,K-1]} = a_{[0,K-1]}$. One such y exists since, by inductive hypothesis, $\mathcal{B}_K(\Sigma_{4r+1}) = \mathcal{B}_K(S_{(F,2r+1)})$. Then there exists an unique path $v_0 \to v_1 \to ..$ in $\mathcal{G}_{(F,2r+1)}$ such that $\zeta_{2r+1}(v_i) = y_i$, $i \in \mathbb{N}$ and such that $v_0 = ((q_0, c_{[1,2r+1]}), ..., (q_0, c_{[2r+1,4r+1]}))$ where $c = y_0 \in A^{4r+1}$. Since $K > N$ there exist $0 \leq i < j < K$ such that $v_i = v_j$. Then,

Proposition [illegible] *be a* [illegible] *is decidable.*

Proof. Given a labeled [illegible] of Σ, it is possible to compute [illegible] is possible to compute [illegible] [illegible]

Proposition [illegible] Σ [illegible] *Then it is decidable* [illegible]

Proof. We provide a proof for the following [illegible] which [illegible] is algorithmically checkable: [illegible]

[illegible]

[illegible] Obviously [illegible]

a. Case [illegible] the [illegible] of a [illegible] [illegible] We have to show that [illegible]

Let $\mathcal{G}$ [illegible] the smallest DFA [illegible] at the end of section 2.1. Note that the number of vertices of $\mathcal{G}$ is [illegible] Moreover, let [illegible] the number of [illegible]

[illegible]

[illegible] Then there is [illegible]

[illegible]

[illegible] $K+1$. We show that [illegible] Let [illegible] exists since, by induction [illegible] Then there exists an integer [illegible] and [illegible] Since [illegible] Then,

Theorem 6. *Let $(A^{\mathbb{Z}}, F)$ be a regular CA. Then the following topological properties are decidable.*

1. *Nilpotency*
2. *Equicontinuity*
3. *Positively Expansiveness*

Proof. By Theorem 4, given $(A^{\mathbb{Z}}, F)$, it is possible to compute Σ_{2r+1}.

1. It is easy to see that $(A^{\mathbb{Z}}, F)$ is nilpotent if and only if there exists $a \in A^{2r+1}$ and $N > 0$ such that $\forall n \geq N, \forall x \in \Sigma_{2r+1}$, $\sigma^n(x) = a$. Given a labeled graph representation of Σ_{2r+1}, this last condition is trivially algorithmically checkable.
2. It is easy to see that $(A^{\mathbb{Z}}, F)$ is equicontinuous if and only if $\mathcal{L}(\Sigma_{2r+1})$ is a bounded periodic language and that, given a labeled graph representation of Σ_{2r+1}, it is algorithmically checkable if $\mathcal{L}(\Sigma_{2r+1})$ is bounded periodic.
3. Every positively expansive CA is conjugated to (Σ_{2r+1}, σ) where Σ_{2r+1} is a shift of finite type and, in particular, it is an n-full shift (see [12]). Since, for positively expansive CA, $n = |F^{-1}(x)|$ for every $x \in A^{\mathbb{Z}}$, n is a computable number. The proof follows from the decidability of the conjugacy problem for one-sided shifts of finite type (see [15]). □

To conclude, we show that, as a negative consequence of the decidability of properties in Theorem 6, regularity is an undecidable property which implies that the membership in Kůrka's language classes is undecidable.

Theorem 7. *It is undecidable whether a CA is regular.*

Proof. Assume it is decidable if a CA is regular. Then, since nilpotent CA are regular, by Theorem 6, it is possible to decide if a CA is nilpotent. □

4 Conclusions and open problems

We investigated decidable properties for regular cellular automata. We showed that regularity itself is not a decidable property (Theorem 7) and that, conversely, for regular cellular automata nilpotency, equicontinuity and positively expansiveness are decidable properties (Theorem 6). Moreover we aswered a question raised in [3] showing that the topological entropy is computable for one-sided regular CA (Theorem 5). It is unknown if almost equicontinuity and sensitivity are or not decidable properties for regular CA (since to be almost equicontinuous or sensitive is a dicotomy for CA, this two properties are either both decidable or both not decidable).

References

1. F. Blanchard, A. Maass. Dynamical Behaviour of Coven's Aperiodic Cellular Automata. Theor. Comput. Sci., 163, 291–302 (1996).

Symbolic Determinisation of Extended Automata

Thierry Jéron, Hervé Marchand, and Vlad Rusu

Irisa/Inria Rennes, Campus de Beaulieu, 35042 Rennes France.
{Thierry.Jeron | Herve.Marchand | Vlad.Rusu} @irisa.fr

Abstract. We define a symbolic determinisation procedure for a class of infinite-state systems, which consists of automata extended with symbolic variables that may be infinite-state. The subclass of extended automata for which the procedure terminates is characterised as *bounded lookahead extended automata*. It corresponds to automata for which, in any location, the observation of a bounded-length trace is enough to infer the first transition actually taken. We discuss applications of the algorithm to the verification, testing, and diagnosis of infinite-state systems.

Key words: symbolic automata, determinisation

1 Introduction

Most existing models of computation are nondeterministic, but they include restricted, deterministic versions as subclasses. A natural question is comparing the expressiveness of the general, nondeterministic class with that of the corresponding restricted, deterministic subclass. For example, it is well known that nondeterministic and deterministic *finite automata* on *finite words* are equivalent, but for finite automata on *infinite* words, the equivalence depends on the acceptance condition (e.g., *Müller* versus *Büchi* acceptance); and for *pushdown* and *timed automata*, the nondeterministic version is strictly more expressive than the deterministic one [1, 2].

Besides this theoretical interest, the distinction between nondeterministic and deterministic models has practical consequences. For example, *verification* consists in checking whether an *implementation* of a system satisfies a *specification*; both views of the system are modeled by automata of some kind. This problem can be seen as a language inclusion problem, which in turn can be encoded into a language emptyness problem (i.e., checking the emptyness of the language recognised by a product between the implementation and the *complement* of the specification). The complement of the specification is an automaton that accepts exactly the words that are rejected by the specification, and is easily computed if the specification is deterministic (by complementing the specification's acceptance condition). Otherwise, if the specification is nondeterministic, it has to be *determinised*, i.e., turned into an equivalent deterministic machine.

Please use the following format when citing this chapter:

Jéron, T., Marchand, H., Rusu, V., 2006, in International Federation for Information Processing, Volume 209, Fourth IFIP International Conference on Theoretical Computer Science-TCS 2006, eds. Navarro, G., Bertossi, L., Kohayakwa, Y., (Boston: Springer), pp. 197–212.

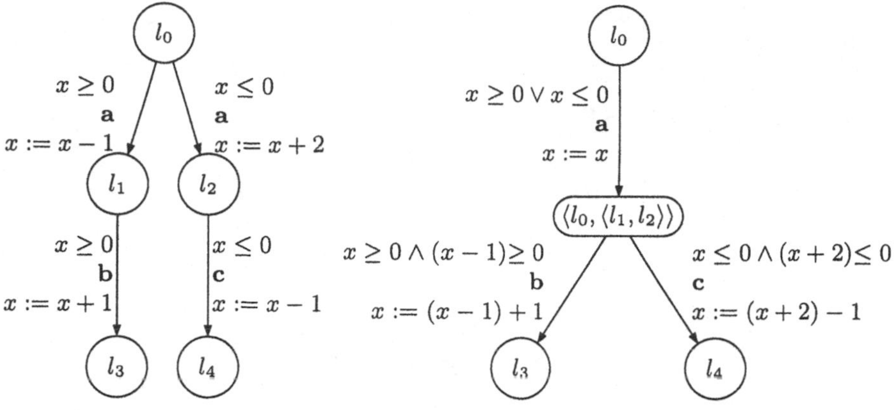

Fig. 1. Left: extended automaton $\mathcal{S}$ Right: extended automaton $det(\mathcal{S})$

from l_0 to $\langle l_0, \langle l_1, l_2 \rangle \rangle$ of $det(\mathcal{S})$ does not "know" which assignment to perform. To solve this problem, the idea is to *postpone* assignments until it becomes clear which one of the transitions of the nondeterministic choice was actually taken, and then to "catch up" with the assignments in order to preserve the semantics.

Hence, if b occurs after a, then the transition from l_0 to l_1 was taken (hence, $x := x - 1$ sould have been performed), but if c occurs after a, the transition from l_0 to l_2 was taken (hence $x := x + 2$ should have been performed). Note how the assignments are simulated in $det(\mathcal{S})$: the transition labeled by b (resp. by c) has $x - 1$ (resp. $x + 2$) substituted for x in its guard and assignments. To match the behaviour of $\mathcal{S}$, in which the transition labeled by b (resp. c) are fireable only after a transition labeled a has been fired with $x \geq 0$ (resp. $x \leq 0$) holding, the guard of the transition labeled by b (resp. c) in $det(\mathcal{S})$ is strengthened by $x \leq 0$ (resp. $x \geq 0$).

2 Extended automata

Extended automata consist of a finite control structure and a finite set of typed variables V. Each variable $x \in V$ takes values in some domain dom_x. A *valuation* ν of the variables V is a function that associates to each variable $x \in V$ a value $\nu(x) \in dom_x$. The set of valuations of the variables V is denoted by $\mathcal{V}$. In the sequel, a predicate P over variables V is often identified with its set of "solutions", i.e., the set of valuations $\mathcal{V}' \subseteq \mathcal{V}$ of the variables V for which P is *true*.

Definition 1 (extended automaton). *An extended automaton (sometimes refered to simply as an* automaton*) is a tuple* $\mathcal{S} = \langle V, \Theta, L, l^0, \Sigma, T \rangle$*:*

[illegible] extended automaton S [illegible]

[illegible] assignments [illegible] form [illegible] which [illegible] [illegible] are simultaneously [illegible] assignments. [illegible] strengthened by [illegible]

[illegible] Extended Automata

[illegible] extended automaton [illegible] is a tuple $S = \langle V, \Theta, L, l^0, \Sigma, T \rangle$ [illegible]

The rule says that the transition $t : \langle l, G, a, A, l' \rangle$ is *fireable* in a state $\langle l, \nu \rangle$ if the guard G evaluates to $true$ when the variables evaluate according to ν; then the transition takes the system to the state $\langle l', \nu' \rangle$ where the assignment A of the transition maps the valuation ν to ν'.

We extend this notion to sequences of transitions $\sigma = t_1 \cdot t_2 \cdots t_n \in \mathcal{T}^*$, saying that σ is *fireable* in a state $q \in Q$ if there exists states $q_1 = q, q_2, \ldots q_n \in Q$ such that $\forall i = 1 \ldots n-1, q_i \xrightarrow{t_i} q_{i+1}$. We then write $q \xrightarrow{\sigma}$ to say that σ is fireable in q. The transition sequence σ is *initially fireable* if it is fireable in the initial state q_0. A state q is *reachable* if there exists an initially fireable transition sequence σ leading to it, i.e., $\exists \sigma \in \mathcal{T}^*, q_0 \xrightarrow{\sigma} q$. We denote by *Reach*($\mathcal{S}$) the set of reachable states. For a sequence $\sigma = t_1 \cdots t_n \in \mathcal{T}^n$ $(n \geq 1)$, we let *first*$(\sigma) \triangleq t_1$.

Definition 4 (trace). *The* trace *of a transition sequence $\sigma = t_1 \cdot t_2 \cdots t_n$ is the projection trace$(\sigma) = a_{t_1} \cdot a_{t_2} \cdots a_{t_n}$ of σ on the set Σ of actions. The* set of traces *of an extended automaton $\mathcal{S}$ is the set of traces of initially fireable transition sequences and is denoted by Traces$(\mathcal{S})$.*

3 Local Determinisation

Intuitively, an extended automaton is *deterministic* if in each location, the guards of the transitions labeled by the same action are mutually exclusive. *Determinising* an extended automaton $\mathcal{S}$ means computing a deterministic extended automaton *det*$(\mathcal{S})$ with the same traces as $\mathcal{S}$.

Definition 5 (deterministic extended automaton). *An extended automaton $\langle V, \Theta, L, l^0, \Sigma, \mathcal{T} \rangle$ is deterministic in a location $l \in L$ if for all actions $a \in \Sigma$ and each pair $t_1 : \langle l, G_1, a, A_1, l_1 \rangle$ and $t_2 : \langle l, G_2, a, A_2, l_2 \rangle$ of transitions with origin l and labeled by a, the conjunction of the guards $G_1 \wedge G_2$ is unsatisfiable. The automaton is deterministic if it is deterministic in all locations $l \in L$.*

It is assumed that the guards are written in a theory where satisfiability is decidable, such as, e.g., combinations of quantifier-free Presurger arithmetic formulas, arrays, and lists. Such formulas are expressive enough to encode the most common data structures, and their satisfiability is decidable using, e.g., the classical Nelson-Oppen combination of decision procedures [4]. Note that determinism does not take reachability of states into account. However, since extended automata have a unique initial state, the definition of determinism is equivalent to the fact that the semantics of a deterministic extended automaton is a deterministic LTS in the usual sense.

Exemple 1 shows that determinising two transitions consists in merging the two transitions into a new one, and propagating guards and assignments onto transitions following them (cf. Figure 1). Formally, *follow*$(t) \triangleq \{t' \in \mathcal{T} | \mathsf{o}_{t'} = \mathsf{d}_t\}$. We also denote by Id_V the *identity* assignments over variables V, i.e., $x := x$ for each $x \in V$.

[illegible] transition [illegible] is *enabled* in a state [illegible] the guard G evaluates to true when the variables evaluate according to [illegible] the transition takes the system to the state [illegible] where the assignment A of the transition [illegible] to [illegible].

We extend this notion to sequences of actions [illegible] [illegible] is *firable* in a state $q \in Q$ [illegible] [illegible]

Definition 4 (traces). The trace [illegible] *is the projection* [illegible] *of actions. The set of traces of* [illegible] *is* [illegible]

3 Local Determinisation

Intu[illegible] the [illegible] [illegible] [illegible]

Definition 5 [illegible] *and* [illegible] *origin* [illegible] *The* [illegible] *local* [illegible]

[illegible] [4]. [illegible] However, [illegible] extended [illegible] definition of determinism [illegible] the fact that the [illegible] extended automata [illegible]

Example [illegible] first merging the [illegible] assignments [illegible]

Definition 7 (Local determinisation in location). *The* local determinisation in location l *of an extended automaton* $\mathcal{S} = \langle V, \Theta, L, l^0, \Sigma, \mathcal{T} \rangle$, *where* $l \in L$, *is defined as follows. Let* $\mathcal{T}_l \subseteq \mathcal{T}$ *be the set of all transitions with origin* l, *then:*

- $det(\mathcal{S}, l) = \mathcal{S}$ *if for every pair of distinct transitions* $t_1, t_2 \in \mathcal{T}_l$ *such that* $\mathsf{a}_{t_1} = \mathsf{a}_{t_2}$, *the formula* $\mathsf{G}_{t_1} \wedge \mathsf{G}_{t_2}$ *is unsatisfiable;*
- *otherwise, choose two distinct transitions* $t_1, t_2 \in \mathcal{T}_l$ *such that* $\mathsf{a}_{t_1} = \mathsf{a}_{t_2}$, $\mathsf{G}_{t_1} \wedge \mathsf{G}_{t_2}$ *is satisfiable, and let* $det(\mathcal{S}, l) = det(det_2(\mathcal{S}, t_1, t_2), l)$.

The operation terminates, as the set of pairs of nondeterministic transitionsn decreases.

4 Bounded-Lookahead Extended Automata

We now know hot to eliminate nondeterminism from a location $l \in L_{\mathcal{S}}$. Then, to eliminate the nondeterminism globally from $\mathcal{S}$, one should iterate $det(\mathcal{S}, l)$ for all $l \in L_{\mathcal{S}}$. However, local determinisation creates new locations, which may themselves be nondeterministic and have to be determinised, which may give rise to yet another set of nondeterministic locations, etc. This raises the question of whether the global determinisation process ever terminates. In this section we define a global determinisation procedure that we show to terminate exactly for the class of *bounded lookahead* extended automata. Intuitively, an automaton is deterministic with lookahead n if any nondeterministic choice can be resolved by looking n actions ahead.

Definition 8 (bounded lookahead). *An automaton* $\mathcal{S} = \langle V, \Theta, L, q^0, \Sigma, \mathcal{T} \rangle$ *has lookahead* $n \in \mathbb{N}$ *in a state* $q \in Q_{[\mathcal{S}]}$ *if* $\forall \sigma_1, \sigma_2 \in \mathcal{T}^{n+1}.\ q \xrightarrow{\sigma_1} \wedge q \xrightarrow{\sigma_2} \wedge trace(\sigma_1) = trace(\sigma_2) \Rightarrow first(\sigma_1) = first(\sigma_2)$. *The automaton has lookahead* n *in a set* $Q' \subseteq Q_{[\mathcal{S}]}$ *of states if it has lookahead* n *in every* $q \in Q'$. *Finally,* $\mathcal{S}$ *has bounded lookahead if, for some* $n \in \mathbb{N}$, $\mathcal{S}$ *has lookahead* n *in the whole set* $Q_{[\mathcal{S}]}$.

We shall find it convenient to define the lookahead of a *location* of an automaton.

Definition 9 ((smallest) lookahead in location). *An automaton* $\mathcal{S}$ *has lookahead* n *in location* $l \in L$ *if* $\mathcal{S}$ *has lookahead* n *in the set* $\{\langle l, \nu \rangle | \nu \in \mathcal{V}\}$. $\mathcal{S}$ *has* smallest *lookahead* $n \in \mathbb{N}$ *in a given location* l *if it has lookahead* n *in* l, *and does not have lookahead* $n-1$ *in* l. *We denote by* $look(l, \mathcal{S}) \in \mathbb{N}$ *the smallest lookahead of location* l *in* $\mathcal{S}$ *(if it exists), otherwise,* $look(l, \mathcal{S}) \triangleq \infty$.

For example, the automaton depicted in the left-hand side of Figure 3 has $look = 1$ in l_0, because, when e occurs, the left-hand side a-labeled transition must have been fired, but when b occurs, the right-hand side a-labeled transition has been fired.

On the other hand, the automaton depicted in the left-hand side of Figure 4 does not have $look = 1$ in l_0, because the occurence of b does not reveal which of the a-labeled transitions was fired. However, the following action (either c or d) reveals all the past trace, hence, $look = 2$ in l_0 for the given automaton.

Definition 7 (Local determinisation [illegible]). *The local determinisation [illegible] of an extended automaton* [illegible] *is defined as follows* [illegible] *be the set of all [illegible] with origin* l*, then*

- $\det(S,l) =$ [illegible] *for every pair of distinct [illegible]* [illegible]
- [illegible]

[illegible]

4 Bounded Lookahead Extended Automata

We now [illegible] Then [illegible] $\det(S,l)$ [illegible] new locations, which [illegible] may [illegible] of whether the global determinisation [illegible] bounded lookahead [illegible] can [illegible]

Definition [illegible]

[illegible]

We shall find it convenient [illegible] automaton.

[illegible]

For example, the automaton [illegible] left-hand side of Figure [illegible] has [illegible] transition [illegible] labeled transition has been [illegible]

[illegible] side of Figure 4 does not have [illegible] not reveal which [illegible] following action [illegible] for the given automaton.

The difference between these situations is the following: in Figure 3, the determinisation step has merged the *nondeterministic* location l_2 into the *new* location $\langle l_0, \langle l_1, l_2 \rangle\rangle$, hence, the resulting automaton has *inherited* (in a sense that will be made precise below) the nondeterminism that l_2 had; because of that nondeterminism, the global lookahead has not decreased. On the other hand, the determinisation step in Fig. 4 does not have this problem: both l_1, l_2 are deterministic, and, even though the new location $\langle l_0, \langle l_1, l_2 \rangle\rangle$ is nondeterministic, the nondeterminism is *created* by the fact that l_1, l_2 bring one b-labeled transition each.

Definition 11 (created/inherited nondeterminism). *Let $\mathcal{S}$ be an extended automaton and t_1, t_2 be two transitions of $\mathcal{S}$ involved into a nondeterminism in $\mathsf{o}_{t_1} = \mathsf{o}_{t_2} = \mathsf{o}$. Let $\langle \mathsf{o}, \langle \mathsf{d}_{t_1}, \mathsf{d}_{t_2} \rangle\rangle$ be the new location resulting from the determinisation $det_2(\mathcal{S}, t_1, t_2)$, and assume that $\langle \mathsf{o}, \langle \mathsf{d}_{t_1}, \mathsf{d}_{t_2} \rangle\rangle$ is nondeterministic in $det_2(\mathcal{S}, t_1, t_2)$. We say that this nondeterminism is* created *if both d_{t_1}, d_{t_2} are deterministic in $\mathcal{S}$, otherwise, the nondeterminism is* inherited.

Now, consider a global determinisation procedure that performs local determinisation steps in a *breadth-first* order: the first iteration determinises the nondeterministic locations of the original automaton, and each subsequent iteration determinises the new nondeterministic locations, generated during the iteration that preceded it.

Figure 3 also illustrates the first iteration of such a *breadth-first* procedure on the automaton in the left-hand side. The resulting automaton is depicted on the right-hand side. Both automata have the same global lookahead =1. Hence, the lookahead cannot be used as a decreasing measure to ensure the termination of the procedure.

Even worse, applying local determinisations in a *depth-first* order (i.e., determinising new nondeterministic locations as soon as they are created) may not terminate, even when the automaton has bounded lookahead. An example is shown in Figure 5: the automaton in the left-hand side has global lookahead 1, and, by determinising in l_0, one obtains the automaton depicted in the right-hand side of the figure, which contains a sub-automaton isomorphic the automaton in the left-hand side, with global lookahead still 1. After determinising in the newly created location, the sub-automaton is still there, and remains present all through the process of *depth-first* determinisation, which, in this case, clearly does not terminate.

Hence, applying local determinisation steps in depth-first or in breadth-first order does not lead, in general, to a terminating global determinisation procedure.

However, Proposition 2 below shows that if an iteration of a breadth-first procedure only gives rise to *created* nondeterminism, the global lookahead does decrease.

Proposition 2 (Global lookahead decreases if all new nondeterminism is created). *Let $\mathcal{S}'$ be an automaton obtained by determinising all nondeterministic locations $\{l_1, \dots l_k\}$ of an automaton $\mathcal{S}$ in an arbitrary order, (i.e., $\mathcal{S}_0 = \mathcal{S}$,*

[illegible] is the following. In Figure 3, the [illegible] location l_2 into the new [illegible] the resulting automaton has [illegible] in a sense [illegible] the nondeterminism that [illegible] had, because of [illegible] determinism, the [illegible] has not decreased! On the other [illegible] does not [illegible] [illegible] is [illegible] [illegible] for each.

Definition [illegible] *local nondeterminism* [illegible]

[illegible] from the deter[illegible] is a local nondeterministic [illegible] [illegible] with [illegible] are [illegible]

Now [illegible] local deter[illegible] the first location [illegible] [illegible] that presented.

Figure [illegible] illustrates [illegible] depicted on [illegible] in Table 1. [illegible] the termination [illegible] procedure.

[illegible] [illegible] created [illegible] may [illegible] an example [illegible] global nondeterminism [illegible] [illegible] depth-first determinisation [illegible]

[illegible] depth-first or in breadth-first [illegible] in general non-terminating global determinisation procedure.

However, Proposition 2 below shows that [illegible] iteration of a breadth-first procedure [illegible] the global nondeterminism decreases.

Proposition 2 [illegible] all new nondeterministic [illegible] created [illegible] nondeterministic [illegible] order (see [illegible])

Lemma 1 says that cycles visiting l in $det(\mathcal{S}, l)$ are *not* nondeterministic, and cycles c' that do not visit l and that are *not* nondeterministic in $\mathcal{S}$ are still *not* nondeterministic cycles of $det(\mathcal{S}, l)$. *The consequences are that determinising one location per* elementary *nondeterministic cycle generates an automaton without* any *nondeterministic cycles, and determinisation does not add new nondeterministic cycles.*

We now introduce our global determinisation procedure (Fig. 6), which starts by "breaking" all elementary nondeterministic cycles, by determinising one location on each.

Procedure $det(\mathcal{S})$
while $\mathcal{C} := \{c \in \mathcal{N}(\mathcal{S}) | c \text{ elementary}\} \neq \emptyset$ **do**
  choose $c \in \mathcal{C}$; **choose** $l \in c$; $\mathcal{S} := det(\mathcal{S}, l)$
endwhile
$n := 0$; $\mathcal{S}_n := \mathcal{S}$
while $\mathcal{S}_n$ **is nondeterministic do**
  $\mathcal{S}'_n := \mathcal{S}_n$
  while $L' := \{l \in L_{\mathcal{S}_n} | \mathcal{S}'_n \textit{ is nondeterministic in } l\} \neq \emptyset$ **do**
    $L'' := \{l' \in L' | \mathcal{S}'_n \textit{ is deterministic in all direct successors of } l'\})$
    choose $l \in L''$
    $\mathcal{S}'_n := det(\mathcal{S}'_n, l)$
  endwhile
  $\mathcal{S}_n := \mathcal{S}'_n$; $n := n + 1$
endwhile
return $\mathcal{S}_n$.

Fig. 6. Global determinisation procedure $det(\mathcal{S})$

Theorem 1 (termination, sufficient condition). *$det(\mathcal{S})$ terminates if $look(\mathcal{S}) < \infty$.*

Proof. By Lemma 1 and Proposition 1, the elimination of nondeterministic cycles (first `while` loop in Figure 6) terminates and does not increase $look(\mathcal{S})$. Consider the sets $L'' \subseteq L'$ computed at each new iteration of the inner (third) `while` loop.

Note that $L' \neq \emptyset$ and $L'' = \emptyset$ implies that there exists a nondeterministic cycle in $\mathcal{S}_n$. Indeed, assume $l_1 \in L'$, then $L'' = \emptyset$ implies $l_1 \notin L''$, which implies that l_1 has a direct successor $l_2 \in L_{\mathcal{S}_n}$ where $\mathcal{S}'_n$ is also nondeterministic, which implies again $l_2 \in L'$. The process continues, and we eventually build a nondeterministic cycle in $\mathcal{S}_n$, which is impossible since all nondeterministic cycles were eliminated.

Inside the inner `while` loop, $L' \neq \emptyset$, and by the above reasoning, $L'' \neq \emptyset$. Hence, the `choose` l operation (from L'') inside the loop is always possible, and then determinising in location l decreases the cardinal of L' by one. Since L'

Then, the bounded lookahead condition for an extended automaton can be equivalently formulated as follows. Consider an extended automaton $\mathcal{S} = \langle V, \Theta, L, l^0, \Sigma, \mathcal{T} \rangle$, and let the *primed copy* $\mathcal{S}'$ of $\mathcal{S}$ be the automaton obtained by "priming" all the components of $\mathcal{S}$ except the alphabet Σ, i.e., $\mathcal{S}' = \langle V', \Theta', L', l'^0, \Sigma, \mathcal{T}' \rangle$, where $V' = \{v' | v \in V\}$, $L' = \{l' | l \in L\}$, and for states $q' = (\langle l, \nu \rangle)' = \langle l', \nu' \rangle$ where ν' is the same valuation as ν, but for variables V', i.e., $\forall x' \in V', \nu'(x') \triangleq \nu(x)$.

Proposition 4 (checking for bounded lookahead). *An extended automaton $\mathcal{S}$ has bounded lookahead iff, for all $q, q_1, q_2 \in Q_{[S]}$ and distinct transitions $t_1, t_2 \in \mathcal{T}_S$ with $\mathsf{a}_{t_1} = \mathsf{a}_{t_2}$, if $q \xrightarrow{t_1}_S q_1 \wedge q \xrightarrow{t_2}_S q_2$ then there exists no infinite execution in $\mathcal{S}||\mathcal{S}'$ starting from (q_1, q_2'), where $\mathcal{S}'$ denotes the primed copy of $\mathcal{S}$.*

The conditions of Proposition 4 are decidable if $\mathcal{S}$ is finite-state but are not decidable in general. For infinite-state extended automata $\mathcal{S}$, we can build finite-state abstractions $\mathcal{S}^\alpha$ that simulate the transition sequences σ of $\mathcal{S}$ (i.e., whenever $q \xrightarrow{\sigma} q'$ holds in $\mathcal{S}$, $\alpha(q) \xrightarrow{\alpha(\sigma)} \alpha(q')$ holds in $\mathcal{S}^\alpha$). The bounded lookahead conditions of Proposition 4 can be then automatically checked on $\mathcal{S}^\alpha$, and, if they hold, the simulation property guarantees that they also hold on $\mathcal{S}$. This gives a sufficient criterion for bounded lookahead, which is, in general, not necessary ($\mathcal{S}^\alpha$ may contain cycles not present in $\mathcal{S}$), and whose precision can be improved by taking more precise abstractions $\mathcal{S}^\alpha$.

5 Applications of Determinisation

Verification A standard verification problem is that of trace (or language) inclusion: given two systems $\mathcal{I}$ (the *implementation*) and $\mathcal{S}$ (the *specification*), decide whether *Traces*$(\mathcal{I}) \subseteq$ *Traces*$(\mathcal{S})$. When $\mathcal{I}$, $\mathcal{S}$ are extended automata and $\mathcal{S}$ is deterministic, the problem reduces to a reachability problem in the extended automaton $\mathcal{I}||\overline{\mathcal{S}}$, where $\overline{\mathcal{S}}$ is obtained from $\mathcal{S}$ by adding a new location *fail* $\notin L$, and for each $l \in L$ and $a \in \Sigma$, a new transition with origin l, destination *fail*, action a, identity assignments, and guard $\bigwedge_{t:\langle l,a,G_t,A_t,l'_t \rangle \in \mathcal{T}} \neg G_t$. The new transitions allow actions in $\overline{\mathcal{S}}$ whenever they are not allowed in $\mathcal{S}$. Hence, when $\mathcal{S}$ is deterministic, *Traces*$(\mathcal{I}) \subseteq$ *Traces*$(\mathcal{S})$ iff no location in the set $\{\langle l, \mathit{fail} \rangle | l \in L_{\mathcal{I}} \rangle\}$ is reachable in $\mathcal{I}||\overline{\mathcal{S}}$.

When $\mathcal{S}$ is *not* deterministic, the above statement is incorrect. Let $\mathcal{S}$ be the nondeterministic automaton in the left-hand side of Figure 3. A naive application of the completion operation on $\mathcal{S}$ builds a transition labeled b from l_1 to *fail*, suggesting that $a \cdot b$ is not a trace of $\mathcal{S}$, which is obviously false. In particular, verification would wrongly declare erroneous an implementation that exhibits the trace $a \cdot b$. Hence, to be adequate for verification, $\mathcal{S}$ has to be *determinised* before being completed.

Thus, the completed lookahead condition for an extended automaton can be equivalently formulated as follows. Consider an extended automaton $S =$ [illegible] and let the [illegible] of S be the automaton obtained by "pruning" all the components of S except the alphabet [illegible] [illegible] and [illegible]

[illegible]

[illegible] where S denotes the [illegible] of S.

The conditions of Proposition [illegible] are decidable if S is finite state but are not decidable in general. For infinite-state extended automata S, we can build finite-state abstractions S' [illegible] when [illegible]. The notion of lookahead conditions of Proposition [illegible] can be automatically checked [illegible], and, if they hold, [illegible] that they also hold [illegible]. This gives a sufficient criterion [illegible], which is, in general, not necessary [illegible] whose precision can be improved by using a more precise [illegible].

[illegible] of Determinisation

We illustrate [illegible] a determinisation [illegible] (or language) [illegible] given [illegible] [illegible] automata and S [illegible] in the extended automaton [illegible], where S [illegible]

[illegible]

[illegible] but S be [illegible] have [illegible] S builds a transition labeled [illegible] from [illegible] which is obviously false. In particular, [illegible] would [illegible] declare [illegible] in implementation [illegible]. S has to be [illegible] consistent.

In this case, determinisation first consists in an extended ϵ-*closure* generalising that of finite automata. The extended ϵ-closure algorithm is then based on the propagation of guards and actions onto the next transitons labeled by observable actions [9], and terminates iff there are no cycles of transitions labeled by internal actions.

The present work was initially motivated by *conformance testing*, more specifically, model-based testing based on the **ioco** theory [6]. In this framework, off-line test generation (computation of test cases from specifications) involves *determinising* the specification in order to compute the next possible observable actions after each trace, and, therefore, to obtain *deterministic* test cases [10]. In that work, we consider an extension of the model presented here (actions are either inputs or outputs and may carry communication parameters), which can be handled by a small modification of our determinisation procedure. The procedure also has potentially interesting application in the verification and diagnosis of infinite-state systems.

An alternative approach, which is also used in conformance testing and in fault diagnosis, is on-the-fly determinisation of a bounded number of transitions of a (basic, symbolic, or timed) automaton, starting from the initial state [6, 11, 12]. In this case, the problems related to termination disappear, because the number of determinisation steps is finite and defined in advance by the bounded exploration depth. However, this approach cannot be used for constructing canonical testers, which we found to be a useful object, and cannot be used for proving trace inclusion.

References

1. John E. Hopcroft, Rajeev Motwani, and Jeffrey D. Ullman. *Introduction to Automata Theory, Languages and Computability*. Addison-Wesley Longman Publishing Co., Inc., Boston, MA, USA, 2000.
2. Rajeev Alur and David L. Dill. A theory of timed automata. *Theoretical Computer Science*, 126(2):183–235, 1994.
3. T. Jéron, H. Marchand, and V. Rusu. Symbolic determinisation of extended automata. Technical Report 1176, IRISA, February 2006.
4. Greg Nelson and Derek C. Oppen. Simplification by cooperating decision procedures. *ACM Trans. Program. Lang. Syst.*, 1(2):245–257, 1979.
5. Vlad Rusu, Hervé Marchand, and Thierry Jéron. Automatic verification and conformance testing for validating safety properties of reactive systems. In *Formal Methods 2005 (FM'05)*, volume 2805 of *LNCS*, pages 223–243, 2005.
6. Jan Tretmans. Test generation with inputs, outputs and repetitive quiescence. *Software - Concepts and Tools*, 17(3):103–120, 1996.
7. M. Sampath, R. Sengupta, S. Lafortune, K. Sinnamohideen, and D. Teneketzis. Failure diagnosis using discrete event models. *Proceedings of the IEEE Transactions on Automatic Control*, 4(2):105–124, 1996.
8. S. Jiang, Z. Huang, V. Chandra, and R. Kumar. A polynomial time algorithm for diagnosability of discrete event systems. *IEEE Transactions on Automatic Control*, 46(8):1318–1321, August 2001.

In this [illegible] extended [illegible] are generalising [illegible] algorithm is then based on the [illegible] of [illegible] transitions labeled by observ- [illegible] of transitions labeled by [illegible]

[illegible] more [illegible] theory [6]. In this frame- [illegible] the [illegible] work, [illegible] here [illegible] of our [illegible] the [illegible]

[illegible] the [illegible] defined [illegible] cannot be used for [illegible] object, and cannot [illegible]

References

[illegible] Addison-Wesley [illegible]

[illegible] automata. *Theoretical Comput. Science* [illegible]

[illegible] determinization [illegible]

[illegible] and negative [illegible]

[illegible] and D. Teneketzis. [illegible] *IEEE Transac-* [illegible]

[illegible] polynomial time algorithm [illegible] *IEEE Transactions on Automatic Control* [illegible] 2001.

Regular Hedge Model Checking

Julien d'Orso[1] and Tayssir Touili[2]

[1] University of Illinois at Chicago. dorso@liafa.jussieu.fr
[2] LIAFA, CNRS & Univ. of Paris 7. touili@liafa.jussieu.fr

Abstract. We extend the regular model checking framework so that it can handle systems with arbitrary width tree-like structures. Configurations of a system are represented by trees of arbitrary arities, sets of configurations are represented by regular hedge automata, and the dynamics of a system is modeled by a regular hedge transducer. We consider the problem of computing the transitive closure $\mathcal{T}^+$ of a regular hedge transducer $\mathcal{T}$. This construction is not possible in general. Therefore, we present a *general acceleration* technique for computing $\mathcal{T}^+$. Our method consists of enhancing the termination of the iterative computation of the different compositions $\mathcal{T}^i$ by merging the states of the hedge transducers according to an *appropriate* equivalence relation that preserves the traces of the transducers. We provide a methodology for *effectively* deriving equivalence relations that are appropriate. We have successfully applied our technique to compute transitive closures for some mutual exclusion protocols defined on arbitrary width tree topologies, as well as for an XML application.

1 Introduction

Regular Model Checking has been proposed as a general and uniform framework to analyse infinite-state systems [21, 28, 12, 7]. In this framework, configurations are represented by words or trees, sets of configurations by regular finite word/tree automata, and the transitions of the system by a regular relation described by a word/tree transducer. A central problem in regular model checking is to compute the transitive closure of a regular relation given by a finite-state transducer. Such a representation allows to compute the set of reachable configurations of a system (thus enabling verification of safety properties) as well as to detect loops between configurations if the transformations are structure preserving (thus enabling verification of liveness properties) [12, 6]. However, computing the transitive closure of a transducer is not possible in general since the transition relation of any Turing machine can be represented by a regular word transducer. In fact, the major problem in regular model checking is that a naive computation that consists in iteratively computing the different compositions $\mathcal{T}^i$ of a transducer $\mathcal{T}$ does not terminate in general. Therefore, a main issue in regular model checking is to define *general acceleration* techniques that will force the above iterative procedure to terminate for many practical applications.

Please use the following format when citing this chapter:

d'Orso, J., Touili, T., 2006, in International Federation for Information Processing, Volume 209, Fourth IFIP International Conference on Theoretical Computer Science-TCS 2006, eds. Navarro, G., Bertossi, L., Kohayakwa, Y., (Boston: Springer), pp. 213–230.

Regular Hedge Model Checking

[illegible]

[illegible]

1 Introduction

[illegible]

[illegible]

We use *hedge automata* [18] to symbolically represent infinite sets of unranked trees, and *hedge transducers* to model transformations on these trees. Then, as in the case of regular *word* and *tree* model checking, the central problem is to compute the transitive closure of a hedge transducer $\mathcal{T}$. Our aim is then to define *general* techniques which can deal with different classes of relations, and which can be applied *uniformly* in many verification and analysis contexts such as those mentioned above.

The main contribution of this work is the definition of a *general acceleration* technique on relabeling hedge transducers (tranducers that preserve the structure of the trees). Our technique works as follows: To enhance the termination of the iterative computation of the different compositions $\mathcal{T}^i$, we merge equivalent states using an *appropriate* equivalence relation, i.e., an equivalence relation that preserves the traces of the transducers (for which collapsing two states does not add new traces to the transducers). The main problem amounts then to defining and computing appropriate equivalences. We provide a methodology for deriving such equivalence relations. More precisely, we consider equivalence relations induced by two simulation relations, namely a *downward* and an *upward* simulation, both defined on hedge automata. We give sufficent conditions on the simulations that guarantee appropriateness of the induced equivalence. Furthermore, we define *effectively computable downward* and *upward* simulations for which the induced relation is guaranteed to be appropriate. We have successfully applied our technique to compute transitive closures of some mutual exclusion protocols defined on arbitrary width tree topologies. We were also able to handle an XML application. This effort is reported in Section 6.

Related work. There are several works on efficient computation of transitive closures for *word* transducers [12, 19, 25, 5, 11, 6, 4] and *tree* transducers [17, 2, 1]. However, these works only consider trees where the arities are fixed, whereas our framework allows to consider ranked *as well as* unranked trees. In fact, our technique can be seen as an extension of the approach used in [1] to hedge transducers. Note that arbitrary arities make this extension non-trivial. In particular, the transition rules of the collapsed hedge transducer under construction make use of regular languages over classes of tuples, these classes themselves being potentially regular languages. This nesting of languages is delicate to manipulate.

More recently, *hedge automata* have been used to compute reachability sets of some classes of transformations, namely *Process Rewrite Systems* (PRS) [15] and *Dynamic Pushdown Networks* (DPN) [16]. Compared to our work, these algorithms compute the sets of the reachable states of the systems, whereas we consider the more general problem of computing the transitive closure of the system's transducer. Moreover, our technique is *general* and can be *uniformly* applied to all the classes of relabeling transformations, whereas the algorithms of [15, 16] can only be applied to the specific class of PRS or DPN.

Outline. In Section 2, we give the definitions of hedge automata and transducers, and show how the ith iterations for a relabeling hedge transducer can be

The language of $\mathcal{A}$, denoted by $L(\mathcal{A})$, is the set of all ground terms accepted by $\mathcal{A}$. A set of terms $\mathcal{L}$ over Σ is *hedge regular* if there exists a hedge automaton $\mathcal{A}$ such that $\mathcal{L} = L(\mathcal{A})$.

Intuitively, given an input term t, a run of $\mathcal{A}$ on t according to the move relation $\rightarrow_\delta$ can be done in a bottom-up manner as follows: first, we assign nondeterministically a state q to each leaf labeled with symbol f if there is in δ a rule of the form $f(L) \rightarrow q$ s.t. $\epsilon \in L$. Then, for each node labeled with a symbol g, and having the terms $t_1, \ldots, t_n$ as children, we must collect the states $q_1, \ldots, q_n$ assigned to all its children, i.e., such that $t_i \xrightarrow{*}_\delta q_i(t_i)$, for $1 \leq i \leq n$, and then associate a state q to the node itself if there exists in δ a rule $r = g(L) \rightarrow q$ such that $q_1 \cdots q_n \in L$. A term t is accepted if $\mathcal{A}$ reaches the root of t in a final state.

Theorem 1. *[18] The class of Hedge automata is effectively closed under determinization and under boolean operations. Moreover, the emptiness problem for Hedge automata is decidable.*

2.3 Relabeling hedge transducers and relations

Definition 2. *A* **Relabeling Hedge Transducer** *is a tuple $\mathcal{T} = (Q, \Sigma, F, \Delta)$ where Q is a finite set of states, Σ is an unranked alphabet, $F \subseteq Q$ is a set of final states, and Δ is a set of rules of the form $f(L) \rightarrow q(g)$, where $f, g \in \Sigma$, $q \in Q$, and $L \subseteq Q^*$ is a regular* word *language over Q.*

As for hedge automata, a *relabeling hedge transducer* defines a *move relation* $\rightarrow_\Delta$ between ground terms in $T_{\Sigma \cup Q}$ as follows: for every two terms t and t', we have $t \rightarrow_\Delta t'$ iff there exist a context C and a rule $r = f(L) \rightarrow q(g) \in \Delta$ such that $t = C\Big[f\big(q_1(t_1), \ldots, q_n(t_n)\big)\Big]$, $q_1 \cdots q_n \in L$, and $t' = C\Big[q\big(g(t_1, \ldots, t_n)\big)\Big]$.

Let $\xrightarrow{*}_\Delta$ denote the reflexive-transitive closure of $\rightarrow_\Delta$. The transducer $\mathcal{T}$ defines the following relation between unbounded width trees: $R_\mathcal{T} = \{(t, t') \in T_\Sigma \times T_\Sigma \mid t \xrightarrow{*}_\Delta q(t'), \text{ for some } q \in F\}$. Note that $R_\mathcal{T}$ is structure preserving, i.e., if $(t, t') \in R_\mathcal{T}$, then t and t' correspond to two different labelings of the same skeleton tree.

Remark 1. Let f and g be two letters in Σ. We represent the pair (f, g) by f/g. Let t and t' be two terms corresponding to different labelings λ_1 and λ_2 of the same underlying tree u. We define the term t/t' as the labeling λ_3 of u such that for every node N of u, $\lambda_3(N) = \lambda_1(N)/\lambda_2(N)$.

A relabeling hedge transducer $\mathcal{T} = (Q, \Sigma, F, \Delta)$ can be seen as a hedge automaton $\mathcal{A} = (Q, \Sigma \times \Sigma, F, \delta)$ over the alphabet $\Sigma \times \Sigma$, where δ is the set of rules $f/g(L) \rightarrow q$ s.t. $f(L) \rightarrow q(g) \in \Delta$. Then it is easy to see that $L(\mathcal{A}) = \{t/t' \mid (t, t') \in R_\mathcal{T}\}$.

A relation R over T_Σ is hedge regular if there exists a relabeling hedge transducer $\mathcal{T}$ such that $R = R_\mathcal{T}$. We denote by $R_\mathcal{T}^n$ the composition of $R_\mathcal{T}$,

case of termination, computes a relabeling hedge transducer that recognizes the transitive closure $R^+_{\mathcal{T}}$.

More precisely, starting from a relabeling hedge transducer $\mathcal{T}$, we derive a transducer, called the *history hedge transducer* that characterizes the transitive closure $R^+_{\mathcal{T}}$. The set of states of the history transducer is infinite. To tackle this issue, we present a method (that is not guaranteed to terminate) for computing a finite-state transducer which is an abstraction of the history transducer, based on a notion of an equivalence relation on the states of the history transducer. The abstract transducer can be generated on-the-fly by a procedure which starts from the original transducer $\mathcal{T}$, and then incrementally adds new states and transition rules, merging equivalent states.

Let us first give the formal definition of the history hedge transducer:

Definition 4. *The* history hedge transducer *of a relabeling hedge transducer* $\mathcal{T} = (Q, \Sigma, F, \Delta)$ *is the (infinite) transducer given by the tuple* $\mathcal{H} = (Q_H, \Sigma, F_H, \Delta_H)$ *such that:* $Q_H = \bigcup_{n\geq 1} Q_n$, $F_H = \bigcup_{n\geq 1} F_n$, *and* $\Delta_H = \bigcup_{n\geq 1} \Delta_n$.

Since $R^n_{\mathcal{T}} = R_{\mathcal{T}_n}$ (Lemma 2), and by definition $R_{\mathcal{H}} = \bigcup_{n\geq 1} R_{\mathcal{T}_n}$, it follows that:

Theorem 2. $R^+_{\mathcal{T}} = R_{\mathcal{H}}$.

As mentioned previously, $\mathcal{H}$ cannot be computed in general since it has an infinite number of states. To sidestep this problem, we will compute an equivalent smaller transducer $\mathcal{H}_\sim$ (that might be finite), obtained by merging the states of $\mathcal{H}$ according to an equivalence $\sim$ on Q_H. This transducer is defined as $\mathcal{H}_\sim = (Q_\sim, \Sigma, F_\sim, \Delta_\sim)$ such that:

- $Q_\sim = \{q_\sim \mid q \in Q_H\}$, where $q_\sim$ denotes the equivalence class of the state q w.r.t. $\sim$;
- $F_\sim = \{q_\sim \mid q \in F_H\}$ is the set of equivalence classes of F_H w.r.t. $\sim$;
- $\Delta_\sim$ is the set of rules $f(L_\sim) \to s_\sim(g)$ such that $f(L) \to s(g)$ is a rule in Δ_H, where $L_\sim$ is obtained from L by substituting each state q by its equivalence class $q_\sim$.

We compute $\mathcal{H}_\sim$ iteratively according to the following *procedure*:

1. We compute successive powers of $\mathcal{T}$: $\mathcal{H}^{\leq 1}$, $\mathcal{H}^{\leq 2}$, $\mathcal{H}^{\leq 3}$,... (where $\mathcal{H}^{\leq i} = \bigcup_{j=1}^{i} \mathcal{T}_j$) while collapsing states according to $\sim$. We obtain the sequence of transducers $\mathcal{H}^{\leq 1}_\sim$, $\mathcal{H}^{\leq 2}_\sim$, $\mathcal{H}^{\leq 3}_\sim$,...
2. If at step i we obtain that $R_{\mathcal{H}^{\leq i-1}_\sim} = R_{\mathcal{H}^{\leq i}_\sim}$, the procedure terminates.

This procedure is not guaranteed to terminate, but if it does, it is clear that the obtained transducer $\mathcal{H}^{\leq i}_\sim$ is equivalent to $\mathcal{H}_\sim$ (i.e. $R_{\mathcal{H}^{\leq i}_\sim} = R_{\mathcal{H}_\sim}$). The problem then amounts to *defining an appropriate equivalence relation* $\sim$ for which $R_{\mathcal{H}_\sim} = R_{\mathcal{H}}$. More generally, since a relabeling hedge transducer can be seen as a hedge automaton (Remark 1), in the next section, we define for every hedge automaton $\mathcal{A}$ an equivalence $\sim$ such that $L(\mathcal{A}_\sim) = L(\mathcal{A})$.

[illegible] of [illegible] comp[illegible] a [illegible] before [illegible] transducer that recognizes the [illegible] R^+_T.

More precisely [illegible] a length-preserving [illegible] transducer T, we derive a transducer, called the *history transducer*, [illegible] characterizes the transitive closure R^+_T [illegible] the history transducer is infinite. To tackle this [illegible] compute [illegible] we must [illegible] to terminate [illegible] for computing [illegible] of history transducer, based [illegible] equivalence [illegible] the states of the history transducer [illegible] a procedure which [illegible] of the [illegible] transducer [illegible] and [illegible] states and [illegible] state.

[illegible]

Definition [illegible] *The history transducer* [illegible] *of a transducer* [illegible] $T = (Q, q_0, \delta, F)$ [illegible] $H = (Q^+, \dots, F^+)$ [illegible]

[illegible] $\bigcup_{i \geq 1} R^i_T$ [illegible]

Theorem [illegible]

[illegible] in general since it has [illegible] we will compute an [illegible] merging [illegible] the [illegible] states of [illegible] such that

[illegible]

[illegible] equivalence [illegible] is a rule in [illegible] equivalence [illegible]

[illegible]

[illegible] history states [illegible] sequence [illegible] letters [illegible]

[illegible] terminates.

This procedure [illegible] if it does, it is clear [illegible] $R_{H} = R_{H_{\simeq}}$). The [illegible] relation [illegible] transducer can be [illegible] as [illegible] In the next section, we define for every [illegible] (4.1).

4.2 Induced equivalence

We define an equivalence relation derived from two binary relations:

Definition 7. *Two binary relations $\preceq_1$ and $\preceq_2$ are said to be* independent *iff whenever $q \preceq_1 r$ and $q \preceq_2 r'$, there exists s such that $r \preceq_2 s$ and $r' \preceq_1 s$. Moreover, the relation $\sim$* induced *by $\preceq_1$ and $\preceq_2$ is defined as:*

$$\preceq_1 \circ \preceq_2^{-1} \cap \preceq_2 \circ \preceq_1^{-1} .$$

In [4], Abdulla et al. have shown the following fact:

Lemma 5. *Let $\preceq_1$ and $\preceq_2$ be two binary relations. If $\preceq_1$ and $\preceq_2$ are reflexive, transitive, and independent, then their induced relation $\sim$ is an* equivalence relation. *Moreover, whenever $x \sim y$ and $x \preceq_1 z$, there exists t such that $y \preceq_1 t$ and $z \preceq_2 t$.*

4.3 Defining an appropriate equivalence

Let $\mathcal{A} = (Q, \Sigma, F, \delta)$ be a hedge automaton. Let $\preccurlyeq_{down}$ be a downward simulation, and let $\preccurlyeq_{up}$ be an upward simulation w.r.t. $\preccurlyeq_{down}$. Thanks to Lemmas 3 and 4, we suppose without loss of generality that $\preccurlyeq_{down}$ and $\preccurlyeq_{up}$ are reflexive and transitive. Let $\preceq$ be a reflexive and transitive relation included in $\preccurlyeq_{up}$ such that $\preccurlyeq_{down}$ and $\preceq$ are independent, and let $\sim$ be the relation induced by $\preccurlyeq_{down}$ and $\preceq$. It follows from Lemma 5 that $\sim$ defines an equivalence relation on states of $\mathcal{A}$. Suppose in addition that:

- whenever $x \in F$ and $x \preccurlyeq_{up} y$, then $y \in F$; and that
- if $X \in F_\sim$ and $x \in X$, then $x \in F$.

In this case, we show that $\sim$ is an appropriate equivalence.

Theorem 3. $L(\mathcal{A}_\sim) = L(\mathcal{A})$.

5 An instance of an appropriate equivalence

Let us now come back to our relabeling hedge transducer $\mathcal{T} = (Q, \Sigma, F, \Delta)$ and its corresponding history transducer $\mathcal{H} = (Q_H, \Sigma, F_H, \Delta_H)$. We suppose that $\mathcal{T}$ is deterministic (this is not a restriction thanks to Theorem 1 and Remark 1). Recall that our purpose is to *effectively* compute an appropriate equivalence relation $\sim$ on Q_H such that $L(\mathcal{H}_\sim) = L(\mathcal{H})$. We give in this section an example of a *computable* equivalence $\sim$ on Q_H induced by a downward simulation $\preccurlyeq_{down}$, an upward simulation w.r.t. $\preccurlyeq_{down}$, and a relation $\preceq$ satisfying the conditions required in the previous section.

First, we need to introduce the notion of *copying* states:

Definition 8 (Copying States). *Let $q \in Q$ be a state:*

1.2 [illegible] equivalence

We define an [illegible] relation [illegible] from two binary relations.

Definition [illegible] are said to be independent [illegible] [illegible]

[illegible]

[illegible] first.

[illegible] reflexive, [illegible] an equivalence [illegible]

1.3 [illegible] equivalence

[illegible] Lemma [illegible] reflexive [illegible] included [illegible] induced by [illegible] relation on states [illegible]

[illegible]

[illegible] equivalence.

Theorem [illegible]

[illegible] equivalence

[illegible] Theorem 1 and Remark [illegible] compute [illegible] equivalence [illegible] We give in this section an example [illegible] deletion [illegible] the conditions [illegible]

[illegible]

Definition [illegible] States [illegible]

Input:
  Hedge transducer $\mathcal{T} = (Q, \Sigma, F, \Delta)$, and a state q.
Begin
  $d \; := \; \{q\}$
Repeat
  for each $q_1 \in d$, and for each rule $r = f(L) \to g(q_1)$,
    add $\{q_2 \mid L \cap (Q^* q_2 Q^*) \neq \emptyset\}$ to d.
Until No more additions can be made
End
Output:
  "Yes" if all rules r encountered were copying (i.e. such that $f = g$).
  "No" otherwise.

Fig. 1. Determining whether a state is prefix copying.

5.1 Computing copying states

The algorithm for checking whether a state q is prefix copying is shown in Figure 1. Intuitively, the algorithm works as follows: it tries to explore all rules r useful for computing the language of $\mathcal{T}$ with q as the only accepting state. If all such rules r are of the form $f(L_1) \to f(q_1)$, then q is indeed prefix-copying.

Input:
  Hedge transducer $\mathcal{T} = (Q, \Sigma, F, \Delta)$, and a state q.
Begin
  $up \; := \; \{q\}$, $side \; := \; \emptyset$
Repeat
  for each $q_1 \in up$, and for each rule $r = f(L) \to g(q_2)$
  such that $L \cap (Q^* q_2 Q^*) \neq \emptyset$, then
    add q_2 to up, and add $\{q' \mid L \cap (Q^* q' Q^*) \neq \emptyset \wedge q' \neq q\}$ to *side*.
Until No more additions can be made
End
Output:
  "Yes" if all rules r encountered were copying (i.e. such that $f = g$)
  and all states in *side* are prefix-copying and there is a final state in *up*.
  "No" otherwise.

Fig. 2. Determining whether a state is suffix copying.

The algorithm for checking whether a state q is suffix copying is shown in Figure 2. Intuitively, the algorithm explores all rules r leading from state q to a final state according to the move relation for $\mathcal{T}$. We must first check that all rules r encountered are copying rules. However, the test performed until now only checks what lies on the path from q up to the root of an accepted context. Therefore, we need to also check what's happening to the child nodes along this root path. This is the purpose of the variable *side*. Any subtree attached to a

[illegible]

[illegible] Computing [illegible] states

[illegible]

[illegible]

The algorithm [illegible] is shown in [illegible] from state q to [illegible] first check that all [illegible] performed until now [illegible] good contexts [illegible] the child nodes along this [illegible] attached to a [illegible]

For example, rule (5) is obtained by composing rules (2) and (1). The resulting product is the rule $t((q_0, q_0)^*) \to (q_1, q_0)(n)$ (denoted (2)⊗(1) above). Since $(q_0, q_0) \preccurlyeq_{down} q_0$ ($q_0 \in Q_{pref}$) and $\preccurlyeq_{down} \subseteq \sim$ (Remark 2), we get that $(q_0, q_0) \sim q_0$. Therefore, merging w.r.t. $\sim$, we get rule (5).

Note that rule (7) has been simplified. Indeed, performing the product of the rules (4) and (3) yields the rule $n(L) \to q_{2\sim}(t)$, where L is the following regular word language: $(q_0, q_0)^*(q_2, q_0)(q_0, q_0)^*(q_0, q_1)(q_0, q_0)^* + (q_0, q_0)^*(q_0, q_1)$ $(q_0, q_0)^*(q_2, q_0)(q_0, q_0)^* + (q_0, q_0)^*(q_2, q_1)(q_0, q_0)^*$. For the sake of brevity, We omit the first part of L since the states (q_2, q_0) and (q_0, q_1) are not reachable.

Computing $\mathcal{H}_{\approx}^{\leq 3}$: Take $\mathcal{H}_{\approx}^{\leq 2}$ and add the following rules obtained as described previously:

$$n(q_{0\sim}^*(q_1, q_0)_{\sim} q_{0\sim}^*) \to (q_2, q_1, q_0)_{\sim}(n) \quad (8) = (3)\otimes(5) = (6)\otimes(1)$$
$$n(q_{0\sim}^*(q_2, q_1, q_0)_{\sim} q_{0\sim}^*) \to (q_2, q_1)_{\sim}(n) \quad (9) = (7)\otimes(2) = (4)\otimes(6)$$

Computing $\mathcal{H}_{\approx}^{\leq 4}$: Take $\mathcal{H}_{\approx}^{\leq 3}$ and add the following rule:

$$n(q_{0\sim}^*(q_2, q_1, q_0)_{\sim} q_{0\sim}^*) \to (q_2, q_1, q_0)_{\sim}(n) \quad (10) = (9)\otimes(1) = (4)\otimes(8)$$

The procedure terminates at step 4, since subsequent iterations do not change the accepted language.

6.2 The unranked two-way token protocol

This mutual exclusion protocol is similar to the *Simple Token Protocol* above, with the following difference: the node that currently owns the token can release it to its parent neighbor, or it can release it to one of its child neighbors. Thus, the token can move upward, as well as downward inside the tree of processes.

Formally, these transformations can be represented by the following relabeling hedge transducer $\mathcal{T} = (Q, \Sigma, F, \Delta)$, where $Q = \{q_0, q_1, q_2, q_3\}$, $\Sigma = \{n, t\}$, $F = \{q_3\}$, and Δ contains the rules:

$$n(q_0^*) \to q_0(n) \ (1) \qquad n(q_0^*) \to q_1(t) \ (2) \qquad t(q_0^*) \to q_2(n) \ (3)$$
$$t(q_0^* q_1 q_0^*) \to q_3(n) \ (4) \qquad n(q_0^* q_2 q_0^*) \to q_3(t) \ (5) \qquad n(q_0^* q_3 q_0^*) \to q_3(n) \ (6)$$

The intuition behind the states of the transducer is as follows:

- State q_0 accepts all "pairs" of identical trees where the token never appears. This state is prefix-copying.
- State q_1 is the intermediate state denoting that the current node just acquired the token. Its parent neighbor releases the token.
- State q_2 is also an intermediate state. It means that the current node releases the token. The parent node acquires the token.
- State q_3 is the final state. It accepts all "pairs" of trees in which the token has moved one step upward or downward. This state is suffix-copying.

Computing $\mathcal{H}_{\approx}^{\leq 1}$: Take $\mathcal{T}$ and replace occurences of a state in a rule of Δ with its equivalence class w.r.t. $\sim$.

$$n(q_{0\sim}^*) \to q_{0\sim}(n) \ (1) \qquad n(q_{0\sim}^*) \to q_{1\sim}(t) \ (2)$$
$$t(q_{0\sim}^*) \to q_{2\sim}(n) \ (3) \quad t(q_{0\sim}^* q_{1\sim} q_{0\sim}^*) \to q_{3\sim}(n) \ (4)$$
$$n(q_{0\sim}^* q_{2\sim} q_{0\sim}^*) \to q_{3\sim}(t) \ (5) \quad n(q_{0\sim}^* q_{3\sim} q_{0\sim}^*) \to q_{3\sim}(n) \ (6)$$

[illegible] rule (5) is obtained by composing rules (2) and (1). The [illegible] product of the rule [illegible] (denoted (2)⊗(1) above) [illegible] (Remark 2), we get that [illegible]. Therefore, merging with [illegible], we get rule (5).

Note that rule (2) has been [illegible] performing the product of [illegible] the rule [illegible], where [illegible] for the [illegible] of [illegible] [illegible] not reachable.

[illegible] rules [illegible] previously:

[illegible] (4)

[illegible] (5)

Computing [illegible] ended [illegible] following rules:

[illegible] (7) = [illegible]

[illegible] do not change the accepted language.

[illegible] The [illegible] two-way token protocol

[illegible]

[illegible] (2) [illegible] (3)

[illegible] is as follows:

[illegible]

[illegible] is the first [illegible] in which the token [illegible] This state has suffix copying.

Computing [illegible] of a state [illegible] with [illegible]

[illegible] (2) [illegible]

[illegible] (1) [illegible]

[illegible] (3)

```
<clients>
   <client>
         <name> Philipp </name>
         <address> ··· </address>
         <status> 1 </status>
         <items>
            <item> bed </item>
            <item> chair </item>
            ...
            <item> fridge </item>
         </items>
   </client>
   <client>
         <name>Maria </name>
         <address> ··· </address>
         <status> 0 </status>
         <items>
            <item> TV </item>
            <item> radio </item>
            ...
            <item> closet </item>
         </items>
   </client>
   ...
</clients>
```

Fig. 3. Part of a document containing information about the clients of a store

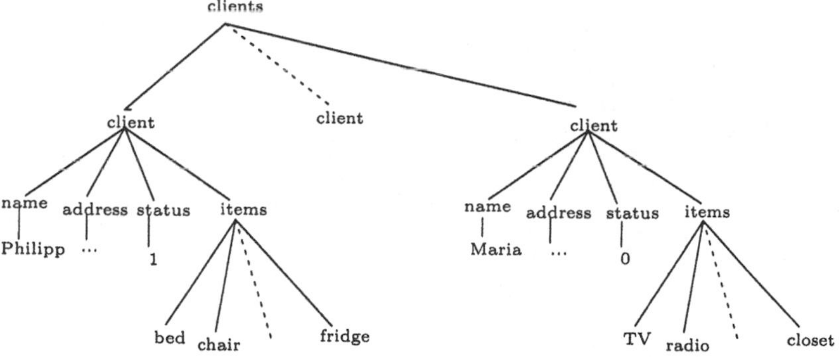

Fig. 4. The previous XML document as a tree

The store has a software that treats the clients in the order they appear in the XML document. The effect of one action of the software consists in changing the status of the current client (resp. the next one) to 2 (resp. to 1) to

2. Parosh Aziz Abdulla, Bengt Jonsson, Pritha Mahata, and Julien d'Orso. Regular tree model checking. In *Proc.* 14th *Int. Conf. on Computer Aided Verification*, volume 2404 of *Lecture Notes in Computer Science*, pages 555–568, 2002.
3. Parosh Aziz Abdulla, Bengt Jonsson, Marcus Nilsson, and Julien d'Orso. Regular model checking made simple and efficient. In *Proc. CONCUR 2002,* 13th *Int. Conf. on Concurrency Theory*, volume 2421 of *Lecture Notes in Computer Science*, pages 116–130, 2002.
4. Parosh Aziz Abdulla, Bengt Jonsson, Marcus Nilsson, and Julien d'Orso. Algorithmic improvements in regular model checking. In *Proc.* 15th *Int. Conf. on Computer Aided Verification*, volume 2725 of *Lecture Notes in Computer Science*, pages 236–248, 2003.
5. Bernard Boigelot, Axel Legay, and Pierre Wolper. Iterating transducers in the large. In *Proc.* 15th *Int. Conf. on Computer Aided Verification*, volume 2725 of *Lecture Notes in Computer Science*, pages 223–235, 2003.
6. Bernard Boigelot, Axel Legay, and Pierre Wolper. Omega regular model checking. In *Proc. TACAS '04,* 10th *Int. Conf. on Tools and Algorithms for the Construction and Analysis of Systems*, Lecture Notes in Computer Science, pages 561–575, 2004.
7. A. Bouajjani. Languages, Rewriting systems, and Verification of Infinte-State Systems. In *ICALP'01*. LNCS 2076, 2001. invited paper.
8. A. Bouajjani, J. Esparza, and T. Touili. Reachability Analysis of Synchronised PA systems. In *INFINITY'04*. ENTCS, 2004.
9. A. Bouajjani, P. Habermehl, P. Moro, and T. Vojnar. Verifying programs with dynamic 1-selector-linked structures in regular model checking. *Proceedings of TACAS'05*, 2005.
10. A. Bouajjani, P. Habermehl, P. Moro, and T. Vojnar. Verifying programs with dynamic 1-selector-linked structures in regular model checking. In *TACAS05*, Lecture Notes in Computer Science, pages 13–29. Springer, 2005.
11. A. Bouajjani, P. Habermehl, and T. Vojnar. Abstract regular model checking. In *CAV04*, Lecture Notes in Computer Science, pages 372–386, Boston, July 2004. Springer-Verlag.
12. A. Bouajjani, B. Jonsson, M. Nilsson, and T. Touili. Regular model checking. In Emerson and Sistla, editors, *Proc.* 12th *Int. Conf. on Computer Aided Verification*, volume 1855 of *Lecture Notes in Computer Science*, pages 403–418. Springer Verlag, 2000.
13. A. Bouajjani, A. Muscholl, and T. Touili. Permutation rewriting and algorithmic verification. In *Proc. LICS' 01* 17th *IEEE Int. Symp. on Logic in Computer Science.* IEEE, 2001.
14. A. Bouajjani and T. Touili. Reachability analysis of process rewrite systems. In *FSTTCS03*, Lecture Notes in Computer Science, pages 73–87, 2003.
15. A. Bouajjani and T. Touili. On computing reachability sets of process rewrite systems. In *Proc.* 16th *Int. Conf. on Rewriting Techniques and Applications (RTA'05)*, volume 3467 of *Lecture Notes in Computer Science*, April 2005.
16. Ahmed Bouajjani, Markus Müller-Olm, and Tayssir Touili. Regular symbolic analysis of dynamic networks of pushdown systems. In *CONCUR'05*, LNCS, 2005.
17. Ahmed Bouajjani and Tayssir Touili. Extrapolating Tree Transformations. In *Proc.* 14th *Int. Conf. on Computer Aided Verification*, volume 2404 of *Lecture Notes in Computer Science*, pages 539–554, 2002.
18. A. Bruggemann-Klein, M. Murata, and D. Wood. Regular tree and regular hedge languages over unranked alphabets. Research report, 2001.

Completing Categorical Algebras
(Extended Abstract)

Stephen L. Bloom[1] and Zoltán Ésik[2*]

[1] Department of Computer Science
Stevens Institute of Technology
Hoboken, NJ 07030
[2] Institute for Informatics
University of Szeged
Szeged, Hungary, and
GRLMC
Rovira i Virgili University
Tarragona, Spain

Abstract. Let Σ be a ranked set. A categorical Σ-algebra, cΣa for short, is a small category C equipped with a functor $\sigma_C : C^n \longrightarrow C$, for each $\sigma \in \Sigma_n$, $n \geq 0$. A continuous categorical Σ-algebra is a cΣa which has an initial object and all colimits of ω-chains, i.e., functors $\mathbb{N} \longrightarrow C$; each functor σ_C preserves colimits of ω-chains. ($\mathbb{N}$ is the linearly ordered set of the nonnegative integers considered as a category as usual.)
We prove that for any cΣa C there is an ω-continuous cΣa C^ω, unique up to equivalence, which forms a "free continuous completion" of C. We generalize the notion of inequation (and equation) and show the inequations or equations that hold in C also hold in C^ω. We then find examples of this completion when
- C is a cΣa of finite Σ-trees
- C is an ordered Σ algebra
- C is a cΣa of finite A-sychronization trees
- C is a cΣa of finite words on A.

1 Introduction

Computer science is necessarily concerned with fixed point equations, and in finding settings in which fixed point equations may be solved. Such equations arise in well known ways, for example, in specifying both the syntax and semantics of programming languages. In many examples, the setting is some kind of ordered algebra A with the properties that A contains a least element $\perp$, and ω-chains, i.e., increasing sequences $a_0 \leq a_1 \leq \ldots$ have least upper bounds. In this setting, the least solution of an equation

$$x = f(x),$$

* Partially supported by the National Foundation of Hungary for Scientific Research.

Please use the following format when citing this chapter:

Bloom, S.L., Ésik, Z., 2006, in International Federation for Information Processing, Volume 209, Fourth IFIP International Conference on Theoretical Computer Science-TCS 2006, eds. Navarro, G., Bertossi, L., Kohayakwa, Y., (Boston: Springer), pp. 231–249.

$$\bot \xrightarrow{!} F(\bot) \xrightarrow{F(!)} F^2(\bot) \xrightarrow{F^2(!)} \ldots.$$

Thus, $\mathcal{ST}_A$ is an example of a continuous cΣa defined in the abstract (and immediately below). There are other examples which we will mention after stating our main results.

Although there are many kinds of completions in the category-theory literature, we were not able to find this particular completion, except for the case of linear orders. In volume 2 of [Ele02], Johnstone describes an "Ind-completion" of a category, which is certainly related to this one. However, Johnstone does not study algebraic structures on the category and thus does not consider (in)equations.

The notion of a cΣa probably occurs to all those familiar with both universal algebra and category theory, and the outline of an ω-completion result is probably obvious to many. Perhaps the "right" notion of the truth of an inequation in a cΣa is not obvious, and the details of the construction have turned out to be more delicate than expected. We think they merit exposition in this paper.

In this extended abstract, only a few proofs will be given. A version of this paper with full proofs may be found at
`www.cs.stevens.edu/~bloom/research/pubs2/ccafull.pdf`.

2 Some notation

$\mathbb{N}$ is the category whose objects are the nonnegative integers, in which there is a morphism $n \longrightarrow p$ exactly when $n \leq p$. If $f : X \longrightarrow Y$ is either a function or functor, we write

$$i\,f,\ f_i,\ f(i)$$

for the value of f on the argument i. The composite of $f : x \longrightarrow y$ and $g : y \longrightarrow z$ is written $fg : x \longrightarrow z$, where f, g are functions or functors.

3 The completion and characterization theorems

Let Σ be a ranked alphabet. A **categorical Σ-algebra** C consists of a small category C, and, for each letter $\sigma \in \Sigma_n$, a functor $\sigma_C : C^n \longrightarrow C$. A **morphism**

$$h : C \longrightarrow C'$$

of categorical Σ-algebras is a functor $h : C \longrightarrow C'$ such that for each $n \geq 0$ and each $\sigma \in \Sigma_n$, $C^n \xrightarrow{\sigma} C \xrightarrow{h} D$ and $C^n \xrightarrow{h^n} D^p \xrightarrow{\sigma} D$ are naturally isomorphic. A cΣa-morphism h is **strict** if the functors $\sigma \cdot h$ and $h^n \cdot \sigma$ are the same for all $\sigma \in \Sigma_n$.

Recall that a functor $h : D \longrightarrow D'$ is **ω-continuous**, or just "continuous", for short, if whenever a functor $f : \mathbb{N} \longrightarrow D$ has a colimit $(\nu_n : f_n \longrightarrow d)_n$ in D, then $(\nu_n h : f_n h \longrightarrow dh)_n$ is a colimit of $f \cdot h : \mathbb{N} \longrightarrow D'$.

A cΣa C is **(ω-)continuous** if

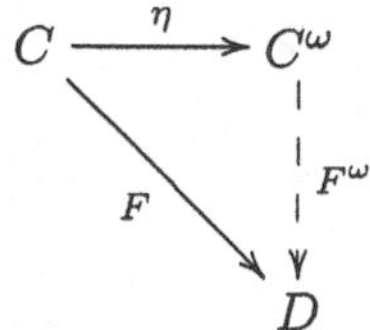

It then follows that

- C^ω *is unique up to categorical equivalence.*
- η *is a full and faithful functor which is injective on objects, and which preserves initial objects.*
- *Any* $c\Sigma a$ *inequality or equality which holds in* C*, also holds in* C^ω*.*

Our characterization of C^ω involves the following notion.

Definition 1. *Suppose that* K *is a full subcategory of the category* D*.*

- K *is* **compact in** D *if for each object* c *in* K*, and each object* d *of* D*, if there is a colimiting cone*

$$(\tau_i^d : f_i \longrightarrow d)_i \tag{1}$$

where $f : \mathbb{N} \longrightarrow K$*, then any map* $c \longrightarrow d$ *factors through some* τ_i^d*.*
- D *is* **compactly generated by** K *if* K *is compact in* D *and for every object* d *of* D*, there is a functor* $f : \mathbb{N} \longrightarrow K$ *and a colimiting cone as in (1) in which each colimit morphism* $\tau_i^d : f_i \longrightarrow d$ *is monic.*

Using this notion, we describe those situations in which the induced functor F^ω in Theorem 1 is an equivalence.

Theorem 2 (Characterization theorem). *Suppose that* D *is a continuous* $c\Sigma a$ *and* $F : C \longrightarrow D$ *is a* $c\Sigma a$ *morphism which preserves initial objects. Then the induced functor* $F^\omega : C^\omega \longrightarrow D$ *is an equivalence iff* F *is full, faithful, and* D *is compactly generated by the image of* F*.*

We will outline the proofs after discussing some examples.

3.1 Ordered Σ-algebras

When Σ is a ranked set, an **ordered Σ-algebra** consists of a partially ordered set $(A, \leq)$ equipped with a function

$$\sigma : A^n \longrightarrow A$$

which is order preserving. Such algebras are categorical Σ-algebras, in which the objects are the elements of A and in which there is a morphism $a \longrightarrow b$ exactly when $a \leq b$. Also, when s, t are in $\mathbf{Tm}_\Sigma(p)$, an inequation $s \leq t$ holds in A exactly when there is a natural transformation $s \longrightarrow t$.

In [Blo76], varieties of ordered algebras were considered, and it was shown that each variety V was closed under the free ω-completion of any algebra in V. Our main theorem is a significant generalization of this result.

[illegible] as follows that:

[illegible]

[illegible]

[illegible] characterization of C^* involves the following notion.

Definition [illegible] Suppose that K is a [illegible] subcategory of the category D.

K is cofinal in D [illegible] and each object [illegible] of D [illegible]

[illegible]

where [illegible] generated by [illegible]

[illegible]

Theorem 3 (Characterization theorem) [illegible] Suppose that D is a [illegible]

We will [illegible]

[illegible] Ordered Algebras

[illegible]

[illegible] such algebras are categorical [illegible] in which the objects [illegible] and in which there is a morphism [illegible] exactly [illegible] in equation $s < t$ holds [illegible] exactly [illegible] the notation [illegible]

In [20] [illegible] of ordered [illegible] were considered, and it was shown that such [illegible] completion of any algebra in [illegible] Our main theorem is a significant generalization of this result.

Proposition 2. *$\mathcal{ST}_A$ is the completion of $\mathcal{FST}_A$.* □

Let $\mathcal{V}$ be the collection of all cΣa's D in which 0 is an initial object which satisfy the following:

$$x + 0 \cong x$$
$$x + y \cong y + x$$
$$x + (y + z) \cong (x + y) + z$$

Then it is not hard to show that the subcategory $\mathcal{FST}_A(\text{mon})$ of $\mathcal{FST}_A$ with the same objects having only monics as morphisms is the initial cΣa in $\mathcal{V}$, in the following sense: for any cΣa in $\mathcal{V}$ there is a cΣa-morphism $F : \mathcal{FST}_A(\text{monics}) \longrightarrow D$, unique up to a natural isomorphism.

Corollary 2. *$\mathcal{FST}_A(mon)^\omega$ is initial in the category of all continuous cΣa's in $\mathcal{V}$.*

Proof. Let D be a continuous cΣa in $\mathcal{V}$. Then there is a cΣa morphism $F : \mathcal{FST}_A(\text{mon}) \longrightarrow D$, since $\mathcal{FST}_A(\text{mon})$ is initial in D. But then there is a continuous $F^\omega : \mathcal{FST}_A(\text{mon})^\omega \longrightarrow D$, unique up to natural isomorphism, by the completion theorem. □

3.4 Words

We recall from [Cou78, BE05] that when A is a finite or countable set, a **word over** A (called an *arrangement* in [Cou78]) is a triple $u = (L_u, \leq_u, \lambda_u)$ consisting of a finite or countable linearly ordered set $(L_u, \leq_u)$ and a labeling function $\lambda : L_u \longrightarrow A$. A word u is finite if the set L_u is finite. A morphism between words $u = (L_u, \leq, \lambda_u)$ and $v = (L_v, \leq, \lambda_v)$ is an order and label preserving map $h : L_u \longrightarrow L_v$. It is clear that words over A and their morphisms form a category that we denote $\mathcal{W}_A$. The finite words over A determine a full subcategory of $\mathcal{W}_A$ denoted $\mathcal{FW}_A$.

The basic operation on words is **concatenation** $u, v \mapsto u; v$ defined as follows. Without loss of generality we may assume that L_u and L_v are disjoint. Then the *concatenation* $u \cdot v$ is the word whose underlying linear order is $(L_u \cup L_v, \leq)$ where $x \leq y$ for all $x \in L_u$ and $y \in L_v$ and such that the restriction of $\leq$ to L_u agrees with $\leq_u$ and the restriction of $\leq$ to L_v agrees with $\leq_v$. The labeling function λ is given by

$$\lambda(x) = \begin{cases} \lambda_u(x) \text{ if } x \in L_u \\ \lambda_v(x) \text{ if } x \in L_u. \end{cases}$$

We extend concatenation to a functor. Given $f : u \longrightarrow u'$ and $g : v \longrightarrow v'$, we define the morphism $f \cdot g : u \cdot v \longrightarrow u' \cdot v'$ so that it agrees with f on the elements of L_u and with g on the elements of L_v.

Let Σ be the signature with a constant symbol a, for each $a \in A$, denoting the constant functor $\mathcal{W}_A^0 \longrightarrow \mathcal{W}_A$ whose value is the singleton word labeled

Proposition [illegible] T is the [illegible] of FST [illegible] □

[illegible] which has an initial object which satisfy the following [illegible]

[illegible]

[illegible] hard to show that the [illegible] T [illegible] the [illegible] is the [illegible] FST [illegible]

Corollary [illegible] of all [illegible]

[illegible] there is a continuous [illegible] FST [illegible] natural isomorphism [illegible] the [illegible]

[illegible] Words

We [illegible] the [illegible] of [illegible] word [illegible] consists [illegible] labeling function [illegible] between words [illegible] then [illegible] form a category [illegible] full subcategory [illegible]

The [illegible] defined as follows. [illegible] the [illegible] elements [illegible] The [illegible]

$$[illegible]$$

[illegible] and [illegible] define the [illegible] on the [illegible]

To [illegible] the signature with a constant symbol [illegible] for each [illegible], denoting the constant [illegible] whose [illegible] is the singleton word labeled

Definition 2. *For weak maps $\alpha : f \longrightarrow m_\alpha g$ and $\beta : f \longrightarrow m_\beta g$, define $\alpha \simeq \beta$ by: for all $i \geq 0$ there is some $j \geq im_\alpha, im_\beta$ such that*

$$\alpha_i \cdot g(im_\alpha, j) = \beta_i \cdot g(im_\beta, j). \tag{2}$$

It is clear that $\simeq$ is an equivalence relation on the weak maps with the same source and target. Let $[\alpha] : f \longrightarrow g$ denote the $\simeq$-equivalence class of the weak map $\alpha : f \longrightarrow g$. This equivalence relation is compatible with composition.

Proposition 5. *If $\alpha \simeq \alpha' : f \longrightarrow g$ and $\beta \simeq \beta' : g \longrightarrow h$, then $\alpha \circ \beta \simeq \alpha' \circ \beta'$.* □

We will need the following fact about $\alpha \simeq \beta$.

Lemma 1 (Inflation Lemma). *Suppose that $\alpha : f \longrightarrow mg$ and that $m' : \mathbb{N} \longrightarrow \mathbb{N}$ is any functor satisfying*

$$k\,m \leq km',$$

for all $k \geq 0$. Define the natural transformation

$$\alpha' : f \longrightarrow m'g$$

by

$$\alpha'_i := f_i \xrightarrow{\alpha_i} g_{im} \xrightarrow{g(im,\ im')} g_{im'}.$$

Then

$$\alpha \simeq \alpha'.$$

4.1 Compact generation

Recall Definition 1. Note the similarity of this notion to that of the definition in [CCL80] of a continuous lattice.

The following lemma indicates where compact generation arises.

Lemma 2. *Let C be a full subcategory of D. Suppose that $f, f' : \mathbb{N} \longrightarrow C$ and that $(\tau_i^d : f_i \longrightarrow d)_i$ and $(\tau_i^{d'} : f'_i \longrightarrow d')_i$ are colimiting cones in D. Then*

1. *A weak map $\gamma : f \longrightarrow mf'$ determines the map*

$$\kappa(\gamma) : d \longrightarrow d'$$

as the unique morphism $d \longrightarrow d'$ such that

$$\tau_i^d \cdot \kappa(\gamma) = \gamma_i \cdot \tau_{im}^{d'}$$

for all $i \geq 0$.

The following Proposition is quite useful.

Proposition 6. *Suppose that D is compactly generated by the full subcategory C. Then:*

1. *C has initial object iff D has.*
2. *D has colimits of all ω-diagrams iff each functor $\mathbb{N} \longrightarrow C$ has a colimit in D.*
3. *A functor $F : D \longrightarrow D'$ is continuous iff it preserves colimits of all functors $\mathbb{N} \longrightarrow C$.*

Proof. We prove only the second two statements.

Proof of 2. Suppose that each functor $\mathbb{N} \longrightarrow C$ has a colimit in D. We show that if $G : \mathbb{N} \longrightarrow D$ is a functor, G has a colimit in D.

For each $n \geq 0$, let $f^n : \mathbb{N} \longrightarrow C$ be a functor such that $(\tau_i^n : f_i^n \longrightarrow G_n)_i$ is a colimiting cone in D.

By Lemma 2, each $0 \leq i \leq j$, each morphism $G(i,j) : G_i \longrightarrow G_j$ is determined by a weak map

$$\beta^{i,j} : f^i \longrightarrow m_{i,j} f^j.$$

For ease of notation, let's assume that all functors $m_{i,j}$ are the identity, so that for each $0 \leq i \leq j$, $\beta^{i,j} : f^i \longrightarrow f^j$ is a natural transformation.

Define $g : \mathbb{N} \longrightarrow C$ by:

$$\begin{aligned} g_i &:= f_i^i \\ g(i,j) &:= f^i(i,j) \cdot \beta_j^{i,j} \\ &= \beta_i^{i,j} \cdot f^j(i,j). \end{aligned}$$

Since every functor $\mathbb{N} \longrightarrow C$ has a colimit in D, let $(\tau_i^g : g_i \longrightarrow d)_i$ be a colimit in D.

For each $i \geq 0$, there is a weak map $\delta^i : f^i \longrightarrow \mu_i g$ defined by

$$\delta_j^i := \begin{cases} f^i(j,i) & j \leq i \\ \beta_j^{i,j} & i < j. \end{cases}$$

(As above, $\mu_i(j) = \max(i,j)$.) Thus, there is a unique map $\kappa(\delta^i) : G_i \longrightarrow d$ such that for all $j \geq 0$, (3) holds. In particular, letting $j = i$,

$$\begin{aligned} \tau_i^g &= \delta_i^i \cdot \tau_i^g \\ &= \tau_i^i \cdot \kappa(\delta^i). \end{aligned} \tag{4}$$

Claim. $(\kappa(\delta^i) : G_i \longrightarrow d)_i$ is a colimiting cone. Indeed, any cone $(\nu_i : G_i \longrightarrow e)_i$ over G determines the cone

$$(\tau_i^i \cdot \nu_i : g_i \longrightarrow e)_i$$

over g, and hence, there is a unique map

The following [illegible] is quite useful.

[illegible] is complete [illegible] generated by the full subcategory [illegible]

1. [illegible]
2. D [illegible]

[illegible]

[illegible] has a colimit in D. We [illegible] has a colimit in D [illegible]

[illegible] is determined [illegible]

[illegible]

[illegible] is a natural transformation.

[illegible]

[illegible] there is a [illegible] map [illegible] defined by

[illegible]

[illegible] Indeed, any [illegible]

[illegible]

[illegible] then [illegible]

But now, applying F, the assumptions imply that

$$(\tau_j^i F : f_j^i F \longrightarrow G_i F)_j$$

is a colimiting cone, as is

$$(\tau_i^g F : g_i F \longrightarrow gF)_i.$$

It then follows from Lemma 3 that

$$([\kappa(\delta^i)F] : G_i F \longrightarrow gF)_i$$

is a colimiting cone in D'. □

5 Construction of C^ω

We now describe the cΣa C^ω as a quotient of the functor category $C^{\mathbb{N}}$.

5.1 Step 1.

We assume C has an initial object (if necessary, we adjoin one freely.)

Let $C^{\mathbb{N}}$ be the category whose objects are all functors $f : \mathbb{N} \longrightarrow C$; a morphism $\alpha : f \longrightarrow g$ is a natural transformation. We usually denote the components of a natural transformation $\alpha : f \longrightarrow g$ by

$$\alpha_n : f_n \longrightarrow g_n,$$

for $n \geq 0$.

We impose the structure of a cΣa on $C^{\mathbb{N}}$ by 'lifting' the functors $\sigma : C^p \longrightarrow C$ to $\mathbb{N}$.

For example, if $\sigma \in \Sigma_2$, and $f, g : \mathbb{N} \longrightarrow C$, $\sigma_{C^{\mathbb{N}}}(f, g) : \mathbb{N} \longrightarrow C$ is the functor whose value on n is

$$\sigma_C(f_n, g_n).$$

The value on the arrow $n \leq p$ in $\mathbb{N}$ is:

$$\sigma_C(f(n,p), g(n,p)) : \sigma_C(f_n, g_n) \longrightarrow \sigma_C(f_p, g_p).$$

So, now, for every term s in $\mathbf{Tm}_\Sigma(p)$, $s_{C^{\mathbb{N}}}$ is defined. (We usually will drop subscripts.) For example, if $p = 2$, and $\alpha : f \longrightarrow f'$ and $\beta : g \longrightarrow g'$ are arrows in $C^{\mathbb{N}}$ (i.e., natural transformations),

$$s(\alpha, \beta) : s(f, g) \longrightarrow s(f', g')$$

is the natural transformation with components

$$(s(\alpha, \beta))_n = s(\alpha_n, \beta_n) : s(f_n, g_n) \longrightarrow s(f'_n, g'_n).$$

Definition 6 **(C^ω as cΣa).** *Suppose $\sigma \in \Sigma_n$ and $n \geq 0$. For any n-tuple $[\alpha_1], \ldots, [\alpha_n]$, where $[\alpha_i]$ is an equivalence class of a weak map $\alpha_i : f_i \longrightarrow g_i$, $i = 1, \ldots, n$, choose some $m : \mathbb{N} \longrightarrow \mathbb{N}$ and some $\beta_i : f_i \longrightarrow mg_i$, for $i = 1, \ldots, n$ such that*

- *$\alpha_i \simeq \beta_i$, for each i;*
- *$\beta_i : f_i \longrightarrow mg_i$, for each i.*

The existence of such β_i and m follows by the Inflation Lemma. Now **define**

$$\sigma_{C^\omega}([\alpha_1], \ldots, [\alpha_n]) : \sigma(f_1, \ldots, f_n) \longrightarrow \sigma(g_1, \ldots, g_n)$$

as

$$[\sigma(\beta_1, \ldots, \beta_n)],$$

the equivalence class of the weak map $\sigma(\beta_1, \ldots, \beta_n)$. (We write just σ for $\sigma_{C^{\mathbb{N}}}$.)

The fact that $\sigma([\alpha_1], \ldots, [\alpha_n])$ is independent of the choice of m follows Lemma 4.

It should be checked that with this definition, σ is indeed a functor $C^\omega \times \ldots \times C^\omega \longrightarrow C^\omega$. But this is easy. We have thus constructed the cΣa C^ω.

We omit the proof of the following fact.

Proposition 8. *The functor η is a strict cΣa morphism which preserves the initial object, and is full, faithful and injective on objects.* □

In the next section we will prove that C^ω is an ω-continuous cΣa.

6 C^ω has the required properties

In the previous section we defined the categorical Σ-algebra C^ω and the embedding $\eta : C \longrightarrow C^\omega$. In this section, we prove that the construction satisfies all properties required in Theorem 1.

We will show that C^ω is compactly generated by $\eta(C)$, and then apply Proposition 6.

Lemma 5. *If $f : \mathbb{N} \longrightarrow C$ is any functor, then f is the colimit object in C^ω of the diagram*

$$f \cdot \eta = \eta(f_0) \xrightarrow{\eta(f(0,1))} \eta(f_1) \xrightarrow{\eta(f(1,2))} \ldots$$

via the colimit morphisms

$$[\tau_n^f] : \eta(f_n) \longrightarrow f$$

where, for each n, τ_n^f has the components

$$\tau_n^f(i) := f(n, \max\{i, n\}). \tag{6}$$

Further, each morphism $[\tau_n^f]$ is monic.

Proof. If $\alpha : c\eta \longrightarrow mf$ is any weak map, then, for any i, since $(c\eta)(0,i) = \mathbf{1}_c$,

$$\alpha_i = c \xrightarrow{\alpha_0} f_{0m} \xrightarrow{f(0m,\,im)} f_{im}.$$

If $g = \alpha_0 : f_0 \longrightarrow f_{0m}$ in C, we have

$$[\alpha] = [g] \cdot [\tau^f_{0m}]. \quad \square$$

Proposition 9. *C^ω is compactly generated by $\eta(C)$.*

Proof. By Lemmas 5 and 6.

Corollary 4. *C^ω is ω-complete.*

Proof. By Proposition 6 and Proposition 9. $\square$

We now show C^ω is a continuous cΣa.

Proposition 10. *For each $\sigma \in \Sigma$, the functor σ_{C^ω} is continuous.*

Proof. For ease of notation, assume that $\sigma \in \Sigma_1$. We have to show that if $([\tau^i] : f^i \longrightarrow g)_i$ is a colimit of the ω-diagram Δ, then $([\sigma(\tau^i)] : \sigma(f^i) \longrightarrow \sigma(g))_i$ is a colimit of $\sigma(\Delta)$, i.e., the diagram

$$\sigma(f^0) \xrightarrow{[\sigma(\beta^0)]} \sigma(f^1) \xrightarrow{[\sigma(\beta^1)]} \sigma(f^2) \longrightarrow \ldots$$

But this fact follows just as above, since the colimit of this diagram is the diagonal, which is $\sigma(g)$.

There is an alternative argument using the fact that for each $n \geq 1$, $(C^\omega)^n$ is compactly generated by C^n. Then, by Proposition 6, we need show only that σ preserves colimits of functors $\mathbb{N} \longrightarrow C^n$. $\square$

Proposition 11. *If s, t are Σ-terms in $\boldsymbol{Tm}_\Sigma(p)$, then $C \models s \preceq t$ iff $C^\omega \models s \preceq t$.* $\square$

We turn now to showing that $\eta : C \longrightarrow C^\omega$ has the universal property stated in Theorem 1.

Suppose that D is an ω-continuous cΣa, and $F : C \longrightarrow D$ is a cΣa-morphism. We want to define $F^\omega : C^\omega \longrightarrow D$. We use Proposition 6.

For each chain $f : \mathbb{N} \longrightarrow C$ be an object of C^ω, choose a colimit cone

$$(\lambda^f_i : f_i F \longrightarrow \kappa(fF))_i \tag{7}$$

in D.

On the object f in C^ω, we define fF^ω as the colimit object $\kappa(fF)$.

Suppose $f, g : \mathbb{N} \longrightarrow C$ are objects in C^ω and $\alpha : f \longrightarrow m_\alpha g$ is any weak map.

Then α determines the weak map $\alpha F : fF \longrightarrow m(gF)$, which in turn determines the map

$$\alpha^\# : \kappa(fF) \longrightarrow \kappa(gF)$$

by the property that for each $i \geq 0$,

$$\lambda^f_i \cdot \alpha^\# = \alpha_i \cdot \lambda^g_{im_\alpha}.$$

[illegible] f is any weak [illegible], then, for any x, since [illegible] $= 1$, [illegible]

[illegible]

Proof. By Propositions 5 and Proposition 6 [illegible]

We [illegible] now [illegible]

Proposition 10. [illegible]

Proof. [illegible] We have to show that [illegible]

[illegible]

but this [illegible] of this diagram is the [illegible]

[illegible] for each $n \geq$ [illegible] we need show only that [illegible]

Proposition 11. [illegible]

[illegible] Theorem [illegible]

[illegible]

[illegible] which in turn [illegible]

[illegible]

References

[Blo76] S.L. Bloom. Varieties of ordered algebras. *J. Computer and System Sci.*, vol. 13, no. 2 (1976) 200-212

[BE93] S.L. Bloom and Z. Ésik. *Iteration Theories.* Springer, 1993.

[BE05] S.L. Bloom and Z. Ésik. The equational theory of regular words. *Information and Computation*, 197/1-2 (2005) 55-89.

[BET93] S.L. Bloom, Z. Ésik and D. Taubner. Iteration theories of synchronization trees. *Information and Computation*, 102/1 (1993) 1–55.

[Cou78] B. Courcelle. Frontiers of infinite trees. *RAIRO Inform. Théor.*, 12/4 (1978), 319–337.

[EBT78] C. Elgot, S.L. Bloom, R. Tindell. The algebraic structure of rooted trees. *J. Computer and System Sci.*, vol. 16, no. 3 (1978) 362-399.

[CCL80] G. Gierz, K.H. Hofmann, K.Keimel, J.D. Lawson, M.Mislove, D.S. Scott. *A compendium of continuous lattices.* Springer-Verlag 1980.

[GTWW77] J.A. Goguen, J.W. Thatcher, E.G. Wagner and J.B. Wright. Initial algebra semantics and continuous algebras. *J. Assoc. Comput. Mach.*, 24/1 (1977), 68–95.

[Gue81] I. Guessarian. *Algebraic Semantics.* Lecture Notes in Computer Science, 99. Springer-Verlag, Berlin-New York, 1981.

[Ele02] P.T. Johnstone. *Sketches of an Elephant: A topos theory compendium* Oxford University Press, 2002.

[LW00] K. Lodaya and P. Weil. Series-parallel languages and the bounded-width property. *Theoret. Comput. Sci.* 237 (2000), 347–380.

[Mil89] R. Milner. *Communication and Concurrency.* Prentice-Hall, Englewood Cliffs, NJ., 1989.

[Pra86] V. Pratt. Modeling concurrency with partial orders. *Internat. J. Parallel Programming*, 15/1 (1986), 33–71.

[Ren96] A. Rensink. Algebra and theory of order-deterministic pomsets. Combining logics. *Notre Dame J. Formal Logic* 37/2 (1996), 283–320.

[Win84] G. Winskel. Synchronization trees. *Theoretical Computer Science*, 34 (1984), 33-82.

[WN95] G. Winskel and M. Nielsen. Models for concurrency. in: *Handbook of Logic in Computer Science*, Vol. 4, Oxford University Press, 1995, 1–148.

Reusing Optimal TSP Solutions for Locally Modified Input Instances*
(Extended Abstract)

Hans-Joachim Böckenhauer[1], Luca Forlizzi[2], Juraj Hromkovič[1], Joachim Kneis[3**], Joachim Kupke[1], Guido Proietti[2,4], and Peter Widmayer[1]

[1] Department of Computer Science, ETH Zurich, Switzerland,
{hjb,juraj.hromkovic,jkupke,widmayer}@inf.ethz.ch
[2] Department of Computer Science, Università di L'Aquila, Italy,
{forlizzi,proietti}@di.univaq.it
[3] Department of Computer Science, RWTH Aachen University, Germany,
joachim.kneis@cs.rwth-aachen.de
[4] Istituto di Analisi dei Sistemi ed Informatica "A. Ruberti", CNR, Roma, Italy

Abstract. Given an instance of an optimization problem together with an optimal solution, we consider the scenario in which this instance is modified locally. In graph problems, e. g., a singular edge might be removed or added, or an edge weight might be varied, etc. For a problem U and such a local modification operation, let LM-U (local-modification-U) denote the resulting problem. The question is whether it is possible to exploit the additional knowledge of an optimal solution to the original instance or not, i. e., whether LM-U is computationally more tractable than U. Here, we give non-trivial examples both of problems where this is and problems where this is not the case. Our main results are these:

1. The local modification to change the cost of a singular edge turns the traveling salesperson problem (TSP) into a problem LM-TSP which is as hard as TSP itself, i. e., unless $P = NP$, there is no polynomial-time $p(n)$-approximation algorithm for LM-TSP for any polynomial p. Moreover, LM-TSP where inputs must satisfy the β-triangle inequality (LM-Δ_β-TSP) remains NP-hard for all $\beta > \frac{1}{2}$.
2. For LM-Δ-TSP (i. e., metric LM-TSP), an efficient 1.4-approximation algorithm is presented. In other words, the additional information enables us to do better than if we simply used Christofides' algorithm for the modified input.
3. Similarly, for all $1 < \beta < 3.34899$, we achieve a better approximation ratio for LM-Δ_β-TSP than for Δ_β-TSP.
4. Metric TSP with deadlines (time windows), if a single deadline or the cost of a single edge is modified, exhibits the same lower bounds on the approximability in these local-modification versions as those currently known for the original problem.

* This work was partially supported by SNF grant 200021-109252/1, by the research project GRID.IT, funded by the Italian Ministry of Education, University and Research, and by the COST 293 (GRAAL) project funded by the European Union.
** This author was staying at ETH Zurich when this work was done.

Please use the following format when citing this chapter:

Böckenhauer, H.-J., Forlizzi, L., Hromkovič, J., Kneis, J., Kupke, J., Proietti, G., Widmayer, P., 2006, in International Federation for Information Processing, Volume 209, Fourth IFIP International Conference on Theoretical Computer Science-TCS 2006, eds. Navarro, G., Bertossi, L., Kohayakwa, Y., (Boston: Springer), pp. 251–270.

holds for LM-TSP, too. Thus, in terms of a worst-case analysis, LM-TSP is as hard as TSP, and we do not have anything to gain from knowing an optimal solution to a close problem instance. By parameterizing TSP with respect to the β-triangle inequality [1, 2, 3, 4, 5] and by introducing the concept of stability of approximation [15, 5], it was shown that TSP is not as hard as it may look like in the light of worst-case analyses. For any $\beta > \frac{1}{2}$, we have a constant polynomial-time approximation ratio, depending on β only. Böckenhauer and Seibert [8] proved that Δ_β-TSP is APX-hard for every $\beta > \frac{1}{2}$ (note that for $\beta = \frac{1}{2}$, the problem becomes trivially solvable in polynomial time). Here, we prove that LM-Δ_β-TSP is NP-hard for every $\beta > \frac{1}{2}$. This implies in particular that LM-Δ-TSP, too, is NP-hard. We conjecture that this problem is also APX-hard, which, so far, we have been unable to prove and thus leave as an open research problem.

(ii) For many years, Christofides' algorithm [9] with its approximation ratio of 1.5 has been the best known approximation algorithm for attacking Δ-TSP. It remains a grand challenge to improve on Christofides' algorithm. We will show that, intriguingly enough, LM-Δ-TSP admits an efficient 1.4-approximation algorithm. This result can be generalized to LM-Δ_β-TSP, and the resulting approximation guarantee beats all previously-known approximation algorithms for Δ_β-TSP for all $1 < \beta < 3.34899$, which includes the practically most relevant TSP instances.

(iii) TSP with time windows is one of the fundamental problems in operations research [10]. Usually, only heuristic algorithms are used to attack it although the question how hard it is w. r. t. approximability has only been resolved in [6, 7], where even an $\Omega(n)$ lower bound on the polynomial-time approximability of Δ-TSP with time windows was shown, in contrast to the constant approximability of Δ-TSP. This lower bound already holds for the special case of this problem where all time windows are immediately open, a special case of the problem which we will call TSP with deadlines, or Δ-DLTSP for short. Here, we consider local-modification versions of Δ-TSP with deadlines. We show that already if we only allow a single deadline to be changed, and only by an amount of one time unit, the resulting problem, LM-Δ-DLTSP, has the same lower bound of $\Omega(n)$ on the approximation ratio as Δ-DLTSP. Let us underscore the importance of this negative result: Not only does TSP with deadlines remain an intractable problem in its LM version, but the extra knowledge of an optimal solution to a related instance does not even help a single bit. Likewise, we will establish the lower bound of $(2 - \varepsilon)$, for any $\varepsilon > 0$, for LM-Δ-DLTSP with a constant number of deadlines, the same as is known for Δ-DLTSP with a constant number of deadlines [6, 7]. These results can also be obtained if, again, we modify the cost of an edge rather than a deadline.

So, on the one hand, additional information about an optimal solution to a related input instance may be useful to some extent, and on the other hand, the local-modification problem variant may remain exactly as hard as the original problem. Yet, the final aim of our paper is to call forth the investigation of

2.1 Hardness Results

Before presenting approximation algorithms for LM-Δ-TSP, we start by proving some hardness results.

First, we will show that LM-TSP is as hard to approximate as "normal" (i. e., unaltered) TSP.

Theorem 1. *There is no polynomial-time $p(n)$-approximation algorithm for* LM-TSP *for any polynomial p (unless $P = NP$).*

Proof idea. We will give a reduction from the Hamiltonian cycle problem (HC): Given an undirected, unweighted graph G, decide whether G contains a Hamiltonian cycle or not. Let $G = (V, E)$ be an input instance for HC where $V = \{v_1, \ldots, v_n\}$.

In order to construct an input instance $(G_O, G_N, \overline{C})$ for LM-TSP, we employ a graph construction due to Papadimitriou and Steiglitz [19], who used the same construction in order to give examples of TSP instances which are hard for local search strategies. For each vertex v_i, we construct a so-called diamond graph D_i as shown in Figure 1 (a). These diamonds are connected as shown in Figure 1 (b).

The edge costs in G_O are set as follows. Let $M := n \cdot 2^n + 1$. All diamond edges shown in Figure 1 (a) and the connections from E_i to W_{i+1} and from E_n to W_1 as shown in Figure 1 (b) are assigned a cost of 1 each. Edges $\{N_i, S_j\}$ are assigned a cost of 1 whenever $\{v_i, v_j\} \in E$ and a cost of M otherwise. All other edges receive a cost of M each. In G_N, the cost of the edge $\{E_n, W_1\}$ is changed from 1 to M. The given optimal Hamiltonian cycle $\overline{C}$ is the one shown in Figure 1 (b). This optimal solution for G_O has a cost of $8n$.

It is easy to see that if there is a Hamiltonian cycle H' in G, a corresponding Hamiltonian cycle H in G can traverse all diamonds from N_i via W_i via E_i to S_i. Hence, $c_N(H) = 8n$. All Hamiltonian cycles in G_N that do not correspond (in this way) to Hamiltonian cycles in G cost at least $M + 8n - 1$. Thus, the approximation ratio of any non-optimal solution is at least as bad as $1 + 2^{n-3}$. For a more detailed description of diamond graph constructions, also see, for example, [16]. □

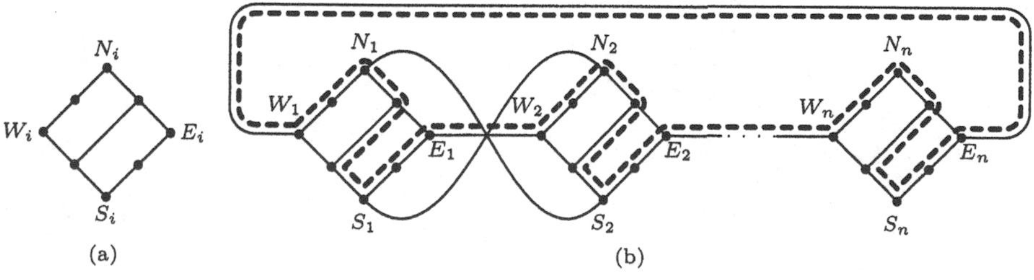

Fig. 1. The diamond construction in the proof of Theorem 1.

Lemma 2. *Let* $(G_O, G_N, \overline{C})$ *be an admissible input for* LM-Δ-TSP *such that* $\delta := c_O(e) - c_N(e) > 0$ *for the edge* e. *If* $\frac{\delta}{OT_{G_N}} \leq \frac{2}{5}$, *it is a* $\frac{7}{5}$*-approximation to output the feasible solution* $C := \overline{C}$ *for* LM-Δ-TSP.

Proof.

$$\frac{c_N(\overline{C})}{OT_{G_N}} \leq \frac{c_O(\overline{C})}{OT_{G_N}} = \frac{OT_{G_O}}{OT_{G_N}} \leq \frac{OT_{G_N} + \delta}{OT_{G_N}} = 1 + \frac{\delta}{OT_{G_N}} \leq 1 + \frac{2}{5} = \frac{7}{5}$$

□

Lemma 3. *Let* $(G_O, G_N, \overline{C})$ *be an admissible input for* LM-Δ-TSP *such that* $\delta := c_O(e) - c_N(e) > 0$ *for the edge* e. *If* $\frac{\delta}{OT_{G_N}} \geq \frac{2}{5}$, *there is a* $\frac{7}{5}$*-approximation for* LM-Δ-TSP.

Proof. We may assume that optimal TSP tours in G_N use the edge e. For if they did not, $\overline{C}$ would already constitute an optimal solution. Fix one such optimal tour C_{OPT} in G_N. In C_{OPT}, e is adjacent to two edges f and f'. Let v be the vertex incident with f, but not with e, and let v' be the vertex incident with f', but not with e. By P, denote the path from v to v' in C_{OPT} that does *not* involve e.

Consider the following algorithm: For every pair $\tilde{f}$, $\tilde{f}'$ of disjoint edges, both of which are adjacent to e, compute an approximate solution to the TSP path problem on the subgraph of G_N induced by the vertex set $V \setminus e$ (i. e., without *two* vertices) with start vertex $\tilde{v}$ and end vertex $\tilde{v}'$ where $\{\tilde{v}\} = \tilde{f} \setminus e$ and $\{\tilde{v}'\} = \tilde{f}' \setminus e$. It is known [13, 14] that this can be done with an approximation guarantee of $\frac{5}{3}$. Each of these paths is augmented by $\tilde{f}$, e, and $\tilde{f}'$ so as to yield a TSP tour. The algorithm concludes by outputting the least expensive of all of these tours.

Note that since *all* pairs $\tilde{f}$, $\tilde{f}'$ are taken into account, one of the considered tours uses exactly those edges $\tilde{f} = f$, $\tilde{f}' = f'$ that C_{OPT} uses. This is why the algorithm outputs a tour of cost at most

$$c(f) + c(f') + c_N(e) + \frac{5}{3}c(P) = \left(OT_{G_N} - c(P)\right) + \frac{5}{3}c(P) = OT_{G_N} + \frac{2}{3}c(P)$$

(where c is short-hand notation for c_N wherever c_O and c_N coincide) and thus achieves an approximation guarantee of

$$1 + \frac{2}{3} \cdot \frac{c(P)}{OT_{G_N}} \quad .$$

Since by Lemma 1, $\min\{c(f), c(f')\} \geq \frac{\delta}{2}$ for $i \in \{1, 2\}$, we have $OT_{G_N} - c(P) \geq \delta$ and hence:

$$\frac{c(P)}{OT_{G_N}} \leq 1 - \frac{\delta}{OT_{G_N}} \leq \frac{3}{5} \quad .$$

So, we obtain an overall approximation guarantee of $1 + \frac{2}{5} = \frac{7}{5}$. □

Lemma 2. [illegible] is an admissible input for LM-Δ-TSP such that [illegible] $\frac{2}{3}$ [illegible] approximation to [illegible] feasible solution [illegible] LM-Δ-TSP.

Proof.

$$[illegible]$$

□

Lemma 3. Let [illegible] be an admissible input for LM-Δ-TSP such that [illegible], there is a [illegible] approximation [illegible] LM-Δ-TSP.

Proof. We may assume that [illegible] edge [illegible] do not [illegible] optimal solution. Fix one such [illegible] two edges [illegible] vertex [illegible] and [illegible] be the vertex incident with [illegible] to [illegible] in G [illegible] does not involve.

Consider the following [illegible] edges. Both [illegible] adjacent to [illegible] optimal solution to the TSP path problem on the subgraph of G [illegible] without [illegible] vertex [illegible] and [illegible] approximation [illegible] all [illegible] solutions.

Note that [illegible] of the [illegible] optimal [illegible] that G [illegible] algorithm outputs [illegible] optimal solutions.

$$[illegible]$$

[illegible] optimal [illegible] approximation guarantee

$$[illegible]$$

Since by Lemma [illegible] we have [illegible] and hence,

$$[illegible]$$

So we obtain [illegible] approximation [illegible] □

with an approximation guarantee of $\frac{5}{3}$. Each of these paths is augmented by $\tilde{f}$ and $\tilde{f}'$ so as to yield a TSP tour. The algorithm concludes by outputting the least expensive of all of these tours.

Note that since *all* pairs $\tilde{f}$, $\tilde{f}'$ are taken into account, one of the considered tours uses exactly those edges $\tilde{f} = f$, $\tilde{f}' = f'$ that C_{OPT} uses. This is why the algorithm outputs a tour of cost at most

$$c(f) + c(f') + \frac{5}{3}c(P) = (OT_{G_N} - c(P)) + \frac{5}{3}c(P) = OT_{G_N} + \frac{2}{3}c(P) \quad ,$$

just as in the proof of Lemma 3. □

Using the same arguments as in the proof of Corollary 1, the preceding lemma yields the following corollary.

Corollary 2. *There is a $\frac{7}{5}$-approximation algorithm for the subproblem of* LM-Δ-TSP *where edges may only become more expensive.* □

2.3 The Near-Metric Case

The algorithm outlined in Lemma 3 can be generalized to graphs which are not necessarily metric, but only near-metric, i. e., where the metricity constraint is relaxed by a factor of β. Since it will pay off later, let us pay extra attention to the fact that input instances for all the problems from Definition 2 contain two distinct graphs, potentially obeying relaxed triangle inequalities according to different values of β.

Notice that the parameter β need not be greater for the graph with the costlier edge. Under some circumstances, it might even decrease when we modify the cost of a single edge. In the following generalization of Lemma 1, the convention is therefore that c_1 is the cost function of the less expensive graph, c_2 that of the more expensive one, and both c_i obey the Δ_{β_i}-inequality, $i \in \{1, 2\}$.

Lemma 6. *Let $G_1 = (V, E, c_1)$ and $G_2 = (V, E, c_2)$ be graphs such that c_i obeys the Δ_{β_i}-inequality for $i \in \{1, 2\}$ and some values $\beta_1, \beta_2 \geq 1$ and such that c_1 and c_2 coincide, except for one edge $e \in E$. By convention, let $c_1(e) \leq c_2(e)$. Then, every edge adjacent to e has a cost of at least $\frac{c_2(e) - \beta_1\beta_2 c_1(e)}{\beta_1\beta_2 + \beta_2}$.*

Proof. Analogous to Lemma 1. □

Note that for relatively small changes, the value $c_2(e) - \beta_1\beta_2 c_1(e)$ may well be non-positive, rendering Lemma 6 trivial in such a case.

The algorithm from Lemmas 3 and 4 should be adjusted to accommodate for the relaxation of the triangle inequality. More precisely, in order to find a Hamiltonian path between a given pair of vertices in a β-metric graph, we will employ the algorithm by Forlizzi et al. [11], a variation of the path-matching Christofides algorithm (PMCA, see [5]) for the path version of near-metric TSP, which yields an approximation guarantee of $\frac{5}{3}\beta^2$. This gives us Algorithm 1.

$$\alpha > \frac{\vartheta - 1}{\frac{5}{3}\beta_{\mathsf{L}}^2 - 1} \quad , \tag{2}$$

we are done. Let use therefore assume that (2) holds. By Lemma 6, we have

$$\min\{c(f), c(f')\} \geq \frac{c_2(e) - \beta_1\beta_2 c_1(e)}{\beta_1\beta_2 + \beta_2} \geq \frac{c_2(e) - \beta_{\mathsf{L}}\beta_{\mathsf{H}} c_1(e)}{\beta_{\mathsf{L}}\beta_{\mathsf{H}} + \beta_{\mathsf{H}}}$$

and hence

$$1 - \alpha \geq \frac{2 \cdot (c_2(e) - \beta_{\mathsf{L}}\beta_{\mathsf{H}} c_1(e))}{OT_{G_N} \cdot (\beta_{\mathsf{L}}\beta_{\mathsf{H}} + \beta_{\mathsf{H}})} \quad .$$

Putting this together with (2), we know that

$$\frac{\vartheta - 1}{\frac{5}{3}\beta_{\mathsf{L}}^2 - 1} \leq 1 - \frac{2 \cdot (c_2(e) - \beta_{\mathsf{L}}\beta_{\mathsf{H}} c_1(e))}{OT_{G_N} \cdot (\beta_{\mathsf{L}}\beta_{\mathsf{H}} + \beta_{\mathsf{H}})} \quad ,$$

which yields

$$\frac{c_2(e) - \beta_{\mathsf{L}}\beta_{\mathsf{H}} c_1(e)}{OT_{G_N}} \leq \frac{\beta_{\mathsf{L}}\beta_{\mathsf{H}} + \beta_{\mathsf{H}}}{2} - \frac{(\vartheta - 1) \cdot (\beta_{\mathsf{L}}\beta_{\mathsf{H}} + \beta_{\mathsf{H}})}{\frac{10}{3}\beta_{\mathsf{L}}^2 - 2} \quad .$$

By adding $(\beta_{\mathsf{L}}\beta_{\mathsf{H}} - 1)\frac{c_1(e)}{OT_{G_N}}$ to both sides, we are given:

$$\frac{c_2(e) - c_1(e)}{OT_{G_N}} \leq \frac{\beta_{\mathsf{L}}\beta_{\mathsf{H}} + \beta_{\mathsf{H}}}{2} - \frac{(\vartheta - 1) \cdot (\beta_{\mathsf{L}}\beta_{\mathsf{H}} + \beta_{\mathsf{H}})}{\frac{10}{3}\beta_{\mathsf{L}}^2 - 2} + (\beta_{\mathsf{L}}\beta_{\mathsf{H}} - 1) \cdot \underbrace{\frac{c_1(e)}{OT_{G_N}}}_{\leq 1}$$

and thus, substituting the value (1) for ϑ,

$$\begin{aligned}
\frac{c_2(e) - c_1(e)}{OT_{G_N}} &\leq \frac{3}{2}\beta_{\mathsf{L}}\beta_{\mathsf{H}} + \frac{1}{2}\beta_{\mathsf{H}} - 1 - \frac{(\vartheta - 1) \cdot (\beta_{\mathsf{L}}\beta_{\mathsf{H}} + \beta_{\mathsf{H}})}{\frac{10}{3}\beta_{\mathsf{L}}^2 - 2} \\
&= \frac{3}{2}\beta_{\mathsf{L}}\beta_{\mathsf{H}} + \frac{1}{2}\beta_{\mathsf{H}} - 1 - \frac{(\beta_{\mathsf{L}}\beta_{\mathsf{H}} \cdot \frac{15\beta_{\mathsf{L}}^2 + 5\beta_{\mathsf{L}} - 6}{10\beta_{\mathsf{L}}^2 + 3\beta_{\mathsf{L}}\beta_{\mathsf{H}} + 3\beta_{\mathsf{H}} - 6} - 1)(\beta_{\mathsf{L}}\beta_{\mathsf{H}} + \beta_{\mathsf{H}})}{\frac{10}{3}\beta_{\mathsf{L}}^2 - 2} \\
\text{(tedious calculations)} \quad &= \cdots = \beta_{\mathsf{L}}\beta_{\mathsf{H}} \cdot \frac{15\beta_{\mathsf{L}}^2 + 5\beta_{\mathsf{L}} - 6}{10\beta_{\mathsf{L}}^2 + 3\beta_{\mathsf{L}}\beta_{\mathsf{H}} + 3\beta_{\mathsf{H}} - 6} - 1 = \vartheta - 1 \quad .
\end{aligned}$$

Since, by the same reasoning as that of Lemmas 2 and 4, reusing the input optimal solution $\overline{C}$ inflicts a deviation from the new optimum by at most $c_2(e) - c_1(e) \leq (\vartheta - 1) \cdot OT_{G_N}$, Algorithm 1 is a ϑ-approximation algorithm. □

Hence, whenever the β values of G_O and G_N coincide, we have Theorem 4.

Theorem 4. *There is a (polynomial-time)* $\beta^2 \cdot \frac{15\beta^2 + 5\beta - 6}{13\beta^2 + 3\beta - 6}$*-approximation algorithm for* LM-Δ_β-TSP.

[illegible]

[illegible] done. [illegible] we [illegible] Lemma 6, we have [illegible]

until [illegible]

and [illegible]

[illegible] this together with [illegible]

[illegible]

which yields

[illegible]

[illegible]

[illegible] the value [illegible]

[illegible]

Since [illegible] the same [illegible] Lemmas 2 and 4, [illegible] the input [illegible] algorithm [illegible]

Theorem [illegible] approximation algorithm [illegible]

inequality, deadlines (s, D, d) for G, and a Hamiltonian cycle satisfying the deadlines[1]*, find a minimum-weight Hamiltonian cycle satisfying all deadlines.*

*If $|D|$ is a constant k, the resulting subproblem is k-Δ_β-*DLTSP. *We set* Δ-DLTSP := Δ_1-DLTSP *and* k-Δ-DLTSP := k-Δ_1-DLTSP *for all k.*

In the case of TSP with deadlines, we will regard it as a local modification to change a single deadline although the LM operation from the previous section would let us obtain exactly the same results. The connection between these two LM operations will be presented in detail in the journal version of this paper.

Definition 5. *The optimization problem* LM-DLTSP *is defined as:*
Input: *A complete weighted graph $G = (V, E, c)$, deadlines $O = (s, D, d_O)$ for G with a minimal Hamiltonian cycle satisfying the deadlines O, new deadlines $N = (s, D, d_N)$ such that d_O and d_N differ in exactly one vertex, and a Hamiltonian cycle satisfying N.*
Problem: *Find a minimum-cost Hamiltonian cycle satisfying N.*

By LM-k-DLTSP, LM-Δ-DLTSP, LM-k-Δ-DLTSP, LM-Δ_β-DLTSP, LM-k-Δ_β-DLTSP, *we denote the canonical special cases of* LM-DLTSP.

For our proofs, we will need some reductions from the following problem, which can easily be shown to be NP-hard analogously to the proof of the NP-hardness of the *restricted Hamiltonian cycle problem,* as presented, e.g., in [16].

Definition 6. *For a given graph $G = (V, E)$, s, $t \in V$ and a given Hamiltonian path P from s to t, the problem* RHP *is to decide whether G contains a Hamiltonian path starting in s, but ending in some vertex $v \neq t$.*

3.1 Bounded Number of Deadline Vertices

We start with the case where only few deadline vertices occur. Note that k-Δ-DLTSP can be approximated within a ratio of 2.5 [6, 7]. Furthermore, a lower bound of $2 - \varepsilon$ on the approximability, for every $\varepsilon > 0$, can be proved [6, 7]. We will show that this lower bound also holds for LM-k-Δ-DLTSP.

Theorem 5. *Let $\varepsilon > 0$. There is no polynomial-time $(2 - \varepsilon)$-approximation algorithm for the subproblem of* LM-k-Δ-DLTSP *where one deadline is increased by ξ time units, $\xi \geq 1$, unless $P = NP$.*

Proof. By means of a reduction, we will show that such an approximation algorithm could be used to solve RHP. Let $\varepsilon > 0$.

Let (G', P) be an input instance for RHP where $G' = (V', E')$, $|V'| = n+1$, $s', t' \in V'$, and P is a Hamiltonian path from s' to t'. Pick a $\gamma > \frac{5n+3}{2\varepsilon}$ (which implies $\frac{4\gamma+n-1}{2\gamma+3n+1} > 2 - \varepsilon$).

[1] Requiring a feasible Hamiltonian cycle as part of the input ensures that the problem is in NPO. Otherwise, it would even be a hard problem to find a feasible solution. For details, see [6, 7].

[illegible] (s, D, d) for G, and a Hamiltonian cycle satisfying the deadlines [illegible] cycle satisfying all deadlines. [illegible] constant [illegible] the resulting subproblems k-Δ_β-DLTSP. We set [illegible]-DLTSP [illegible] Δ_β [illegible] and [illegible] = $\bigcup$ Δ_β-DLTSP for all k.

In the [illegible] TSP with deadlines, we will regard it as a local modification [illegible] although [illegible] the [illegible] such [illegible]. [illegible] between these two [illegible] will [illegible] in [illegible] the [illegible] of this paper.

[illegible] is defined as [illegible]
[illegible] graph G [illegible] $D = (s, d, \ldots)$ [illegible] satisfying [illegible] deadlines [illegible] [illegible] and a Hamiltonian [illegible]
[illegible] a minimum-cost Hamiltonian cycle satisfying M.
[illegible] DLTSP [illegible] DLTSP, [illegible]-Δ_β-DLTSP, LM-[illegible] of [illegible]-DLTSP.

[illegible] problems [illegible] reduced [illegible] from the following problem, [illegible] analogously to the proof of the NP-hardness [illegible] presented [illegible].

Definition [illegible] V [illegible] d [illegible] [illegible] set [illegible] Hamiltonian [illegible].

4.1 [illegible]

We start [illegible] note that [illegible] a lower bound [illegible]. Furthermore, a lower bound [illegible] proved [illegible]. We [illegible] lower bound [illegible] TSP.

Theorem [illegible] (G, P) [illegible]

[illegible] such an approximation algorithm [illegible]
[illegible] (G', P) [illegible] where $G' = (V', E')$, $|V'| = n+1$, [illegible] V' [illegible] path [illegible] to t. [illegible] $\frac{n}{2}$ (which implies [illegible])

[1] [illegible] the problem is [illegible] feasible solution [illegible]

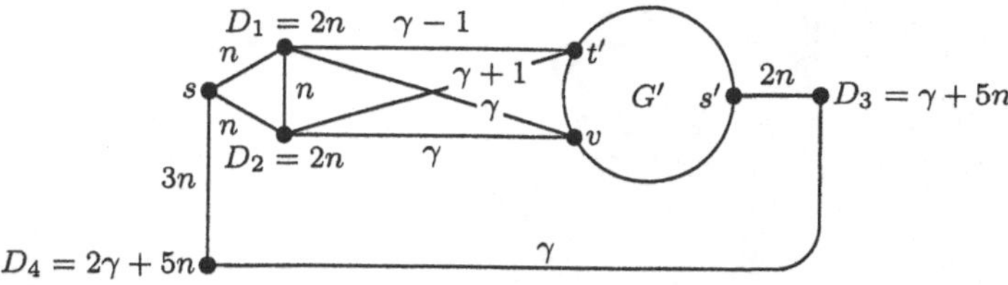

Fig. 4. Decreasing a deadline. All vertices $v' \in V' \setminus \{s', t'\}$ are connected like v.

$c(e) = 2$ otherwise. All edges depicted in Figure 4 have the indicated costs while non-depicted edges obtain maximal possible costs.

The initial deadlines are depicted in Figure 4. In this setting, an optimal solution is the cycle $s, D_2, D_1, t', \ldots, s', D_3, D_4, s$, which contains the Hamiltonian path from s' to t'. This path costs $2n + \gamma - 1$ on its way to G', spends n on the path from t' to s', and reaches s at time $2\gamma + 8n - 1$.

Now, we decrease the deadline $d(D_1)$ by ξ, whereby the old optimal solution becomes infeasible. Any new solution must visit D_1 before D_2. If we try to reuse the Hamiltonian path from t' to s', we have to spend $2n + \gamma + 1$ on the way to t'. Therefore, we cannot reach D_3 if we follow the complete Hamiltonian path. Furthermore, we cannot visit any vertex $v \in V'$ between visiting D_3 and D_4 because D_3 is not reached before $4n + \gamma$, going back to V' would cost another $2n$, and the cheapest path from V' to D_4 costs more than γ. This is why any solution using a Hamiltonian path between s' and t' violates one of the deadlines $d(D_3)$, $d(D_4)$.

If G' contains a Hamiltonian path P from s' to some $v \neq t'$, the new optimal solution contains this path in reverse on its way to D_3. The path s, D_1, D_2, P, D_3 visits all vertices in V' between v and s' and reaches D_3 at time $\gamma + 5n$. Therefore, this new optimal solution costs $2\gamma + 8n$.

If G' does not contain such a Hamiltonian path, the optimal solution cannot visit all vertices in V' before reaching D_3 or even D_4, and consequently, it is more expensive than 4γ. Thus, we could use an approximation algorithm with an approximation guarantee better than

$$\frac{4\gamma}{2\gamma + 8n} > 2 - \varepsilon$$

to solve RHP. Hence, approximating this subproblem of LM-k-Δ-DLTSP within $2 - \varepsilon$ is NP-hard. □

3.2 Unbounded Number of Deadline Vertices

When the number of deadline vertices is unbounded, we can show a linear lower bound on the approximability of LM-Δ-DLTSP. Our reduction from RHP involves two steps. A first construction will guarantee that an optimal path becomes shorter by a constant factor if a Hamiltonian path exists in the RHP

Fig. [illegible]. Reoptimizing [illegible] if [illegible] $s' \in V$ [illegible] is connected [illegible]

(c) [illegible] otherwise [illegible] is [illegible] and [illegible] above [illegible] dead [illegible] with [illegible] path [illegible] longer [illegible] possible cost.

The [illegible] are depicted in Fig. [illegible]. In this setting, an optimal solution is the [illegible] D_2 [illegible], which contains the Hamiltonian path from s to t. This path [illegible] $n+1$ on its way to C_2 [illegible] the [illegible] $D_4 + n + 1$.

Now we decrease the cost [illegible] whereby the old, [illegible] solution becomes [illegible] new [illegible] than D_2 and D_3 [illegible] to take the [illegible] from s' [illegible] have to [illegible] $2n + y + 1$ [illegible] t. [illegible] we cannot reach D_3 [illegible] complete Hamiltonian path. Furthermore, we cannot [illegible] visiting [illegible] and D_4 because D_3 [illegible] reached [illegible] would cost another $2n$ and the [illegible] path from [illegible] more than [illegible]. This is why any solution [illegible] s' and [illegible] of the deadlines of D_3, D_4 [illegible].

If [illegible] from s' to some [illegible], the new optimal solution [illegible] the path [illegible] on its way to [illegible] path [illegible] D_3 [illegible] and reaches [illegible] the $7\ell, 5n$. [illegible] the [illegible] solution [illegible].

If [illegible] such a Hamiltonian path, the optimal solution cannot visit [illegible] reaching D_3 [illegible] and consequently, it is more [illegible]. Thus, we [illegible] an approximation algorithm with [illegible] approximation [illegible].

[illegible] this [illegible] TSP [illegible].

[illegible] Unbounded Number of Deadline Vertices

When the number of deadline [illegible] we can show a linear lower bound [illegible] TSP [illegible] reduction from HHP involves two [illegible]. A first [illegible] will [illegible] that an optimal path becomes [illegible] constant factor [illegible] Hamiltonian path exists in the HHP

$$d(E_1) := X + \zeta g + \left(\frac{k-5}{2} + \zeta\right) g \quad \text{and}$$
$$d(E_{i+1}) := d(E_i) + \gamma \qquad \text{for all } i \in \{1, \ldots, k-1\} \quad .$$

If a path reaches t after $X+g$, it must proceed immediately to E_1. Note that it cannot use any other edge since it would have to use an edge of an additional cost of at least $b = g(\zeta - \frac{1}{2}) > g(\zeta - 1)$, then. Together with even the shortest path to E_1, this would violate this deadline. But then, it is forced to follow the sequence $E_2, E_3, \ldots, E_k$ to reach every deadline since even if we visited E_3 before E_2, we would incur an extra cost of b, and this would violate the deadline of E_2. Hence, the Hamiltonian cycle costs at least $X + g + (\frac{k-5}{2} + \zeta)g + k\gamma$.

A path that visits t before X can visit $E_{k-1}, E_{k-3}, \ldots, E_3$ before E_1 because this path to E_1 costs at most

$$X + b + (\frac{k}{2} - 2)g + b = X + \zeta g + \left(\frac{k-6}{2} + \zeta\right) g \leq d(E_1) \quad .$$

Closing the cycle to s, we obtain a cost of at most

$$X + \zeta g + \left(\frac{k-6}{2} + \zeta\right) g + \left(\frac{k}{2} - 1\right) g + 2\gamma = X + (k + 2\zeta - 4)g + 2\gamma \quad .$$

□

We will now employ Lemma 8 to prove the desired lower bound.

Theorem 7. *Let $\varepsilon > 0$. There is no polynomial-time $((\frac{1}{2} - \varepsilon) \cdot |V|)$-approximation algorithm for the subproblem of* LM-Δ-DLTSP *where one deadline is increased by $\xi \geq 1$, unless $P = NP$.*

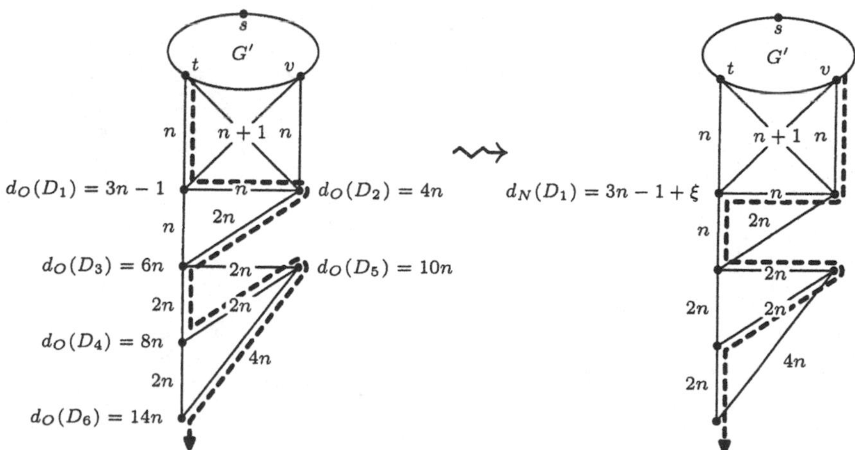

Fig. 6. Increasing a deadline: If the deadline for the vertex D_1 is increased, using a Hamiltonian path from s to v leads to a new optimal solution.

[illegible]

If [illegible] reaches [illegible] after [illegible], it [illegible] immediately to [illegible]. Note that [illegible] use an edge of an additional cost of at [illegible]. Together with [illegible] the shortest path [illegible] would [illegible]. But then [illegible] is forced to [illegible] [illegible] visited [illegible] would violate the deadline. Then [illegible] path that visits [illegible] below [illegible] costs at least

[illegible]

[illegible] of [illegible]

[illegible]

□

[illegible] Lemma 8 [illegible] desired lower bound.

Theorem [illegible]

Fig. 6. Increasing a deadline: [illegible] is increased [illegible] using a [illegible] Dark [illegible] path [illegible] to [illegible] optimal solution.

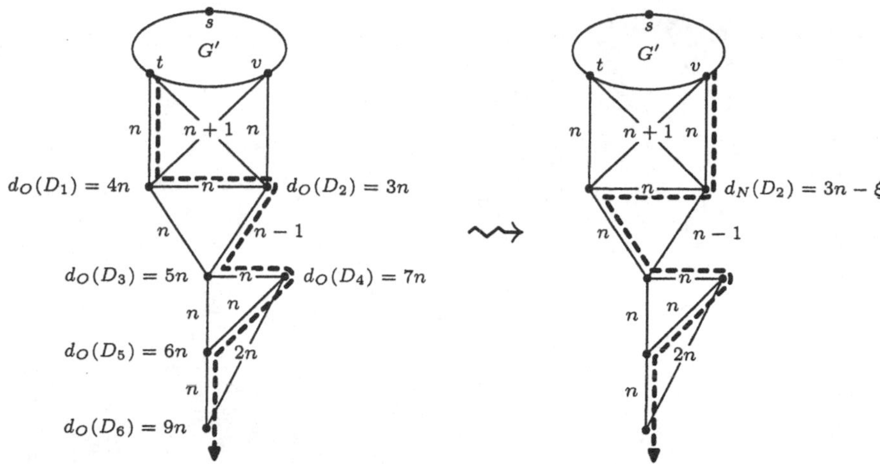

Fig. 7. Decreasing a deadline: If the deadline for the vertex D_2 is decreased, the old optimal solution (depicted on the left-hand side) becomes infeasible. If G' contains a Hamiltonian path from s to v, we obtain the depicted new optimal solution. If no such Hamiltonian path exists, the new optimal solution must follow $D_2, D_1, D_3, D_5, D_4, D_6$.

4 Conclusion

In this work, we have introduced and successfully applied the concept of reusing optimal solutions when input instances are locally modified. In the case of metric TSP, we are able to improve on the previously-known upper bound of 1.5, as achieved by Christofides' algorithm (applied to the new instance, ignoring the given optimal solution), with non-trivial extensions to the near-metric case. As for TSP with deadlines, which is remarkably hard [6], we have been able to reestablish almost all known lower bounds on the approximability of its variants in the setting of local modifications.

As an open problem, we state the question how hard it is to approximate LM-k-Δ_β-DLTSP. Another open problem is whether the NP-hard LM-Δ-TSP is also APX-hard.

References

1. T. Andreae: On the traveling salesman problem restricted to inputs satisfying a relaxed triangle inequality. *Networks* 38, 2001, pp. 59–67.
2. T. Andreae, H.-J. Bandelt: Performance guarantees for approximation algorithms depending on parameterized triangle inequalities. *SIAM Journal on Discrete Mathematics* 8, 1995, pp. 1–16.
3. M. Bender, C. Chekuri: Performance guarantees for TSP with a parameterized triangle inequality. *Information Processing Letters* 73, 2000, pp. 17–21.

Fig. 7. The means [illegible] If [illegible] for the [illegible] is decreased, the old optimal solution depicted on the [illegible] becomes infeasible. If C contains a [illegible] no such [illegible] $D_1, D_2, \ldots, D_r, D_s$.

4 Conclusion

In this work, we have [illegible] the [illegible] modified instances [illegible] TSP [illegible] on the [illegible] upper bound [illegible] as [illegible] for the new instance, ignoring the [illegible] extensions to the near-metric case. As for TSP [illegible] we have been able to establish [illegible] on the approximability of its variants [illegible] the setting [illegible] modification.

[illegible] approximate [illegible] whether the NP-hard [illegible] TSP [illegible]

References

1. T. Andreae: On the traveling salesman problem restricted to inputs satisfying a relaxed triangle inequality. *Networks* 38, 2001, pp. 59–67.
2. T. Andreae, H.-J. Bandelt: Performance guarantees for approximation algorithms depending on parametrized triangle inequalities. *SIAM Journal on Discrete Mathematics* 8, 1995, pp. 1–16.
3. M. A. Bender, C. Chekuri: Performance guarantees for the TSP with a parameterized triangle inequality. *Information Processing Letters* 73, 2000, pp. 17–21.

Spectral Partitioning of Random Graphs with Given Expected Degrees

Amin Coja-Oghlan[1], Andreas Goerdt[2], and André Lanka[2]

[1] Humboldt Universität zu Berlin, Institut für Informatik
Unter den Linden 6, 10099 Berlin, Germany
coja@informatik.hu-berlin.de

[2] Fakultät für Informatik, Technische Universität Chemnitz
Straße der Nationen 62, 09107 Chemnitz, Germany
{goerdt, lanka}@informatik.tu-chemnitz.de

Abstract. It is a well established fact, that – in the case of classical random graphs like (variants of) $G_{n,p}$ or random regular graphs – spectral methods yield efficient algorithms for clustering (e. g. colouring or bisection) problems. The theory of large networks emerging recently provides convincing evidence that such networks, albeit looking random in some sense, cannot sensibly be described by classical random graphs. A variety of new types of random graphs have been introduced. One of these types is characterized by the fact that we have a fixed expected degree sequence, that is for each vertex its expected degree is given. Recent theoretical work confirms that spectral methods can be successfully applied to clustering problems for such random graphs, too – provided that the expected degrees are not too small, in fact $\geq \log^6 n$. In this case however the degree of *each* vertex is concentrated about its expectation. We show how to remove this restriction and apply spectral methods when the expected degrees are bounded below just by a suitable constant. Our results rely on the observation that techniques developed for the classical sparse $G_{n,p}$ random graph (that is $p = c/n$) can be transferred to the present situation, when we consider a suitably normalized adjacency matrix: We divide each entry of the adjacency matrix by the product of the expected degrees of the incident vertices. Given the host of spectral techniques developed for $G_{n,p}$ this observation should be of independent interest.

1 Introduction

For definiteness we specify the model of random graphs to be considered first. This model is very similar to that considered and convincingly motivated in [9]. (In particular, we refer to Subsection 1.3 of that paper where the model is defined.)

Please use the following format when citing this chapter:

Coja-Oghlan, A., Goerdt, A., Lanka, A., 2006, in International Federation for Information Processing, Volume 209, Fourth IFIP International Conference on Theoretical Computer Science-TCS 2006, eds. Navarro, G., Bertossi, L., Kohayakwa, Y., (Boston: Springer), pp. 271–282.

Clearly it is important to obtain efficient algorithms adapted to the characteristics of these networks. One particular problem of interest is the problem of detecting some kind of clusters, that is subsets of vertices having extraordinarily many or few edges. Such clusters are supposed to mirror some kind of relationship among its members (= vertices of the network). Heuristics based on the eigenvalues and eigenvectors of the adjacency matrix of the network provide one of the most flexible approaches to clustering problems applied in practice. See for example [15] or the review [19] or [18]. Note that the eigenvalues and eigenvectors of *symmetric* real valued matrices, first are real valued and second can be approximated efficiently to arbitrary precision.

The relationship between spectral properties of the adjacency matrix of a graph on the one hand and clustering properties of the graph itself on the other hand is well established. Usually this relationship is based on some separation between the (absolute) values of the largest eigenvalues and the remaining eigenvalues. It has a long tradition of being exploited in practice, among others for numerical calculations. However, it is in general not easy to obtain convincing proofs certifying the quality of spectral methods in these cases, see [23] for a notable exception.

Theoretically convincing analyses of this phenomenon have been conducted in the area of random graphs. This leads to provably efficient algorithms for clustering problems in situations where purely combinatorial algorithms do not seem to work, just to cite some examples [2], [3], or [4], or the recent [20] and subsequent work such as [14]. In particular [3] has lead to further results [10], [11]. The reason for this may be that [3] is based on a rather flexible approach to obtain spectral information about random graphs [12]: Spectral information directly follows from clustering properties known to be typically present in a random graph by (inefficient) counting arguments. We apply this technique here, too.

In order to explain the success of spectral algorithms to detect clustering properties of large real life networks the preceding results do not seem to be readily applicable. As opposed to classical random graphs such networks are well known to have many vertices whose degree deviates considerably from the average degree, that is the degree distribution has a "heavy tail", or it seems to follow a "power law" , see for example [1] . And in fact in [21] it is shown that the largest eigenvalues of a random graph with power law degree distribution are proportional to the square root of the largest degrees, and thus do not reveal any non-local information about the graph. This result looks somehow related to the fact that the largest eigenvalue of a sparse random graph $G_{n,p}$ where $p = c/n$ is always the square root of the largest degree of the graph and that there is an unbounded number of eigenvalues of this size, see [16]. However, in the case of classical random graphs it helps to delete the vertices of highest degree as observed by [3] leaving the clustering properties of the graph essentially unchanged. However, in the case of a degree distribution with a heavy tail this trick is not useful, because significant parts of the graph may

6. Calculate the eigenvectors of R^*.
7. Let s_2, s_3 be two eigenvectors of R^* belonging to different occurrences of eigenvalues which are $\geq C_2 \cdot \overline{w}'$ in absolute value.
8. At least one of the s_1, s_2, s_3 turns out to have the property that all but $C_3 \cdot (n/\overline{w}')$ entries are close to two sufficiently different values c_1, c_2. Let V_i' be all the entries close to c_i for $i = 1, 2$. Distribute the remaining entries arbitrarily among the V_i'.

Some remarks are in order. First observe that the algorithm besides the graph needs the expected degree sequence as additional information. Note that the algorithm of [9] even gets the w_i themselves. The main idea is to use the normalized adjacency matrix R, where we divide each entry of the adjacency matrix by the expected degrees of the incident vertices (the additional factor of $\overline{w}'^2$ is only for technical convenience.) It is this choice of the matrix which makes our analysis possible.

Of course, a natural idea is to divide the entries by the *actual* degrees rather than the expected degrees, in order to remove the requirement that $w_1', \ldots, w_n'$ are given at the input. In fact, it turns out that this approach can be carried out successfully, i.e., the resulting matrix is suitable to recover the planted partition as well. Nonetheless, since the analysis is technically significantly more involved, we omit the details from the present extended abstract (the complete analysis will be given in the full paper version of this work).

In fact using R we get a situation formally rather similar to the case: classical sparse random graph with a planted partition and adjacency matrix, the situation as considered in [3] or [20]. Note that all entries r_{ij} with the same $(\psi(i), \psi(j))$ have the same expected value which makes the analogy possible. In particular we can apply [12]. The vector s_1 is necessary in order to recognize partitions which can be readily recognized just from the row sums of R. Step 5. has the analogous effect on the spectrum of R as has the deletion of high degree vertices in the case of sparse random graphs on the spectrum of the adjacency matrix. Being eigenvectors of different occurrences of eigenvalues, s_2 and s_3 are orthogonal to each other. Notions "vague" up to now, like "close" or the C_i, c_i in the algorithm are made precise through the subsequent proof of

Theorem 2. *Let D, ε, δ as defined above. There exists constants C_1, C_2, C_3 with $C_i = C_i(D, \varepsilon, \delta)$ such that the following property holds:*

Let G be some graph generated in the above model. With probability $1 - o(1)$ with respect to G Algorithm 1 produces a partition which differs from the original partition V_1, V_2 only in $O(n/\overline{w}')$ vertices.

Note that the number of vertices not classified correctly is $O(n/\overline{w}') = O(n/\overline{w})$ and thus decreases linearly in $\overline{w}$.

We present the proof of Theorem 2 in the following two sections. The proof in section 3 is based on some notions and lemmas used throughout. These are presented in section 2.

[illegible] R.
[illegible] belonging to different occurrences of eigenvalues [illegible] value.
8. At [illegible] have the property that all but [illegible] different values e.g. Let [illegible] the remaining [illegible] arbitrarily [illegible]

[illegible] No [illegible] the adjacency matrix [illegible] the expected degrees [illegible] (the additional factor [illegible] choice of the matrix which makes [illegible] as possible.

[illegible] by the actual degrees rather than the expected degrees [illegible] the requirement [illegible] approach can be [illegible] matrix is suitable [illegible] is technically significantly [illegible] the complete analysis will [illegible] version of this work.)

[illegible] we get [illegible] rather similar to the [illegible] partition and adjacency matrix, the [illegible] all entries [illegible] with the same [illegible] possible. In [illegible] vector [illegible] in order to recognize [illegible] sums of R. Step 5. [illegible] of high degree [illegible] spectrum of the adjacency matrix [illegible] different occurrences of eigenvalues [illegible] and [illegible] are [illegible]

[illegible]

Note that [illegible] vertices not classified correctly is $O(n/\sqrt{\ldots})$ [illegible]

We present [illegible] in the following two sections. The proof in section [illegible] used throughout. These are presented [illegible] 2.

Let R be some $n \times n$-matrix with random entries r_{ij} and let $V = \{1, \ldots, n\}$ be the set of indices. We assume either that all r_{ij} are independent or that the only dependence is due to symmetry. We assume that the collection of the r_{ij}'s otherwise has the same properties as the x_i's in Lemma 1, in particular $\mathbf{E}[r_{ij}] = \mu$. The subsequent Lemma 2 is as Lemma 3.6 in [3]. Its proof is analogous. A similar lemma occurs as Lemma 2.5 in [12].

Lemma 2. *With probability* $1 - o(1)$ *for any pair* (A, B) *of sets* $A, B \subseteq V$ *the following holds:*

If $m = \max\{|A|, |B|\} \leq n/2$ *then*

1. $s_R(A, B) = O(\mathbf{E}[s_R(A, B)])$ or
2. $s_R(A, B) \cdot \ln \frac{s_R(A,B)}{\mathbf{E}[s_R(A,B)]} = O(m \cdot \ln \frac{n}{m})$.

Let R be a random matrix as above and $B > 1$ be some constant. For symmetric R let $U \subseteq V$ be given by

$$u \in U \text{ if and only if } s_R(V, \{u\}) = s_R(\{u\}, V) \leq B \cdot \mu \cdot n$$

For non-symmetric R we define

$$U = \{u \in V : \max(s_R(\{u\}, V), s_R(V, \{u\})) \leq B \cdot \mu \cdot n\}.$$

The following lemma is at the heart of our results. It is a transfer of Lemma 3.3 in [3] and Theorem 2.2 in [12]. In contrast to [3] and [12] we require that only the vector y is perpendicular to $\mathbf{1}$. The proof is similar to [3] and [12]. In particular recall item 3. of the notation as introduced above.

Lemma 3. *For* R *and* U *as above with probability* $1 - o(1)$ *we have for all unit vectors* $x, y \in (\mathbb{R}^n)^*$ *with* $y \perp \mathbf{1}$ *that* $|x^t R y| = O(\sqrt{\mu \cdot n})$.

3 The analysis of the algorithm

Let $G = (V, E)$, D, V_1, V_2 and $w_1, \ldots, w_n$ as in Subsection 1.1. Let d_i be the actual degree of i in G. For $W \subseteq V$ we define $\Phi(W) = \sum_{i \in W} w_i$ and abbreviate $\Phi_i := \Phi(V_i)/\Phi(V)$. Since all $w_i \geq \varepsilon \cdot \overline{w} = \Omega(\overline{w})$ and $|V_i| = \Omega(n)$ we have

$$\Phi_i = \frac{\Phi(V_i)}{\Phi(V)} \geq \frac{\sum_{j \in V_i} w'_j}{\overline{w} n} \geq \frac{\sum_{j \in V_i} \varepsilon \overline{w}}{\overline{w} n} \geq \frac{\sum_{j \in V_i} \varepsilon}{n} = \Omega(\varepsilon)$$

and each Φ_i are bounded away from 0 by some constant. For $i \in V_1$ we have

$$\mathbf{E}[d_i] = w'_i = \sum_{j \in V_1} d_{11} \cdot \frac{w_i \cdot w_j}{\overline{w} \cdot n} + \sum_{j \in V_2} d_{12} \cdot \frac{w_i \cdot w_j}{\overline{w} \cdot n} = w_i \cdot (d_{11} \Phi_1 + d_{12} \Phi_2)$$

and for $i \in V_2$ we get

$$w'_i = w_i \cdot (d_{12} \Phi_1 + d_{22} \Phi_2).$$

[illegible] with [illegible] and let $V = \{1, \ldots, n\}$ [illegible] are independent or that [illegible] dependency [illegible] symmetry. We assume that the collection of the [illegible] has the same properties as the [illegible] in Lemma 1. In particular [illegible]. The [illegible] Lemma 2 is as Lemma [illegible] in [3], its proof is [illegible] Lemma 2.5 in [2].

Lemma [illegible]

[illegible]

[illegible]

[illegible] be some constant. For [illegible]

[illegible]

For [illegible]

[illegible]

The [illegible] of our results [illegible] [3] and [4], we require that only the [illegible] In particular [illegible]

Lemma [illegible] hold for all unit [illegible]

3 The Analysis of the Algorithm

[illegible]

[illegible]

[illegible] by some constant. For [illegible] we have

[illegible]

and for [illegible] we get

[illegible]

and all the entries of the normalized eigenvectors are $\Omega(1)$.

The expected row-sum $s_R(\{i\}, V)$ for some $i \in V_1$ is

$$\frac{\overline{w}'^2}{\overline{w} \cdot n} \cdot \left(\frac{d_{11}|V_1|}{x_{11}^2} + \frac{d_{12}|V_2|}{x_{11} \cdot x_{22}} \right) = \Theta(\overline{w}') \tag{1}$$

and for $i \in V_2$

$$\frac{\overline{w}'^2}{\overline{w} \cdot n} \cdot \left(\frac{d_{12}|V_1|}{x_{11} \cdot x_{22}} + \frac{d_{22}|V_2|}{x_{22}^2} \right) = \Theta(\overline{w}'). \tag{2}$$

The number of rows with $s_R(\{i\}, V) \geq 5 \cdot \mathbf{E}[s_R(\{i\}, V)]$ is with high probability $e^{-\Omega(\overline{w}')} \cdot n$. This can be shown as follows: Use Lemma 1 to calculate the probability that a fixed i is such a row. This probability is $c^{-\Omega(\overline{w}')}$. So, we have an expected number of such rows bounded by $e^{-\Omega(\overline{w}')} \cdot n$. Since the dependence between any two rows is small, we have a relatively small variance and Chebycheff's inequaltity gives the result.

If (1) and (2) differ by a factor of at least 25, we can simply detect large parts of V_1 and V_2 by partitioning the rows by the value of $s_R(\{i\}, V)$. This is the reason for s_1 in the algorithm. If (1) and (2) are closer, then both are relatively near to the average row-sum, which is $\Theta(\overline{w}')$. Now, let U be the set of all i, with $s_R(\{i\}, V) \leq C \cdot \overline{w}'$. The exact value of C depends on D, ε and the lower bound δ on $|V_i|/n$. A similar calculation as above shows, that $|U| \geq (1 - e^{-\Omega(\overline{w}')}) \cdot n$.

Lemma 4. *With high probability for any set $X \subseteq V$ with $|X| = e^{-\Omega(\overline{w})} \cdot n$ we have $s_R(X, V) = e^{-\Omega(\overline{w}')} \cdot n$.*

Proof. Let $X_i = X \cap V_i$. We have that

$$s_R(X, V) = \sum_{i,j=1}^{2} s_R(X_i, V_j).$$

If we can show, that with high probability for each summand the bound $e^{-\Omega(\overline{w}')} \cdot n$ holds, then the assertion follows. We give the proof for $s_R(X_1, V_1)$ explicitly. The remaining cases follow analogously.

Fix some set $X_1 \subseteq V_1$ with $|X_1| = \delta n = e^{-c_1 \cdot \overline{w}'} \cdot n$, where c_1 is some arbitrarily small constant. Then $\mathbf{E}[s_R(X_1, V_1)] = \Theta(m_{11} \cdot |X_1| \cdot |V_1|) = \Theta(\overline{w}' \cdot |X_1|) = e^{-\Omega(\overline{w}')} \cdot n$.

Let $t = |X_1| \cdot |V_1|$. We use Lemma 1. For $\{u, v\} \subseteq X_1$ we set x_i in the lemma to r_{uv} with $u < v$ and a_i to 2, because such entries are counted twice in the sum. For the other terms in $s_R(X_1, V_1)$, namely r_{uv} with $u \in X_1$ and $v \notin X_1$ we let $x_i = r_{uv}$ and $a_i = 1$. This gives for the lemma, that $a = 2$, $D \leq 2t$ and $\mu = m_{11}$. We choose $S = c \cdot e^c \cdot m_{11} \cdot t = c \cdot e^c \cdot \Theta(\overline{w}' \cdot \delta n) = e^{-\Omega(\overline{w}')} \cdot n$ for some constant c determined later. Then

$$\begin{aligned} \mathbf{Pr}\left[|s_R(X_1, V_1) - m_{11} \cdot t| \geq S\right] &\leq 2 \cdot e^{-\Omega(S^2/(m_{11} \cdot e^c \cdot t))} \\ &= 2 \cdot e^{-\Omega(c^2 \cdot e^c \cdot m_{11} \cdot t)} \\ &= 2 \cdot e^{-\Omega(c^2 \cdot e^c \cdot \overline{w}' \cdot \delta n)} \end{aligned}$$

$$\max_{\substack{u,v\\ u\perp g,h}} |v^t R^* u| = \max_{\substack{u,v\\ u\perp g,h}} \left| \sum_{i,j=1}^{2} v_i^t R^*{}_{i,j} u_j \right| \leq \max_{\substack{u,v\\ u\perp g,h}} \sum_{i,j=1}^{2} \left| v_i^t R^*{}_{i,j} u_j \right| . \qquad (3)$$

If u and v maximize the above terms, we can assume that $u = u^*$ and $v = v^*$.

Then the $u_j = u_j{}^*$ are perpendicular to $\mathbf{1}$. In addition we have $v_i^t \cdot R^*{}_{i,j} \cdot u_j = v_i{}^{*t} \cdot R_{i,j} \cdot u_j{}^*$. By the construction of R we have for all $R_{i,j}$ that the entries are bounded by some constant and the expectation of each entry is the same, namely $\Theta(d_{ij} \cdot \overline{w}'/n)$. Lemma 3 allows us to bound each term in the above sum by $O(\sqrt{\overline{w}'})$. Fact 3 can be used to bound the remaining eigenvalues of R^* by $O(\sqrt{\overline{w}'})$.

Finally we show that it is possible to obtain V_1 and V_2 by investigating the eigenvectors of R^*.

For this let v_1, v_2 be two orthonormal eigenvectors of R^* with eigenvalue $\Omega(\overline{w}')$ (in absolute value). Then v_i can be written as $v_i = c_i \cdot m_i + d_i \cdot u_i$ with $\|m_i\| = \|u_i\| = 1$ and $c_i^2 + d_i^2 = 1$. m_i comes from the space spanned by g and h, and u_i comes from the orthogonal complement. Then by the bound for (3)

$$|v^t R^* u_i| = \Omega(\overline{w}') \cdot |v_i^t \cdot u_i| = \Omega(\overline{w}') \cdot |d_i| = O(\sqrt{\overline{w}'}),$$

and $|d_i|$ must be $O(1/\sqrt{\overline{w}'})$. As $|c_i| + |d_i| \geq c_i^2 + d_i^2 = 1$, we have $|c_i| = 1 - O(1/\sqrt{\overline{w}'})$.

Since

$$0 = v_1^t v_2 = c_1 c_2 m_1^t m_2 + c_1 d_2 m_1^t u_2 + c_2 d_1 u_1^t m_2 + d_1 d_2 u_1^t u_2$$

we have

$$\begin{aligned} |c_1 c_2 m_1^t m_2| &= |c_1 d_2 m_1^t u_2 + c_2 d_1 u_1^t m_2 + d_1 d_2 u_1^t u_2| \\ &\leq |c_1 d_2 m_1^t u_2| + |c_2 d_1 u_1^t m_2| + |d_1 d_2 u_1^t u_2| \\ &= |d_1 d_2 u_1^t u_2| \leq |d_1 d_2| \\ &= O(1/\overline{w}'). \end{aligned}$$

Together with $c_i = 1 - O(1/\sqrt{\overline{w}'})$ we can follow that m_1 and m_2 must be almost perpendicular. We write $m_i = \gamma_i \cdot \chi_1/\sqrt{n} + \delta_i \cdot \chi_2/\sqrt{n}$. For at least one i we have $|\gamma_i - \delta_i| > \varepsilon$ for some small constant ε, otherwise m_1 and m_2 could not be almost perpendicular. Taking this m_i, we have that the entries belonging to V_1 differ from the other entries by at least $\varepsilon/\sqrt{n}$. This gives us the chance to identify the V_1, V_2 by the entries of m_i.

Unfortunaly, we have only v_i and not m_i. But we can assume, that in $c_i \cdot m_i$ the distance of $\varepsilon/(2\sqrt{n})$ still holds, because $c_i \geq (1 - O(1/\overline{w}')) > 1/2$. It is possible, that some entries j in u change the value of $c_i \cdot m_i(j)$, such that we put j into the wrong partition. This may happen, if the value is changed by at least $\varepsilon/(4\sqrt{n})$. But such entries are relatively rare. The entry in u_i must have an absolute value of $\Omega(\sqrt{\overline{w}'}) \cdot \varepsilon/(4\sqrt{n})$, because $|d_i| = O(1/\sqrt{\overline{w}'})$ is small. The number of such entries is bounded by $O(n/\overline{w}')$ since u has length 1. We obtain, that we are able to partition at least $(1 - O(1/\overline{w}')) \cdot n$ vertices correctly by visiting the eigenvector v_i of R^*. This finishes our proof of Theorem 2.

$$[illegible] \quad (9)$$

If [illegible] and maximize the above terms [illegible] assume that $u = [illegible]$ and [illegible]. [illegible] we have [illegible] that the entries [illegible] and each entry is the same [illegible].

[illegible] investigating the eigenvector of R'.

[illegible] eigenvector of R' with eigenvalue [illegible] with [illegible] space spanned by [illegible] and [illegible]

[illegible]

and [illegible] $= 1$, we have [illegible]

[illegible]

we have

[illegible]

[illegible] that in each [illegible] it is possible [illegible] value of [illegible] such that we [illegible] the value is changed by at least [illegible]. The entry in [illegible] must have an absolute [illegible] is small. The number [illegible] We obtain that [illegible] vertices correctly by visiting [illegible] of R'. This [illegible] proof of Theorem 2.

A Connectivity Rating for Vertices in Networks

Marco Abraham[1], Rolf Kötter[23], Antje Krumnack[1], and Egon Wanke[1]

[1] Institute of Computer Science, Heinrich-Heine-Universität Düsseldorf, D-40225 Düsseldorf, Germany
[2] C. & O. Vogt Brain Research Institute, Heinrich-Heine-Universität Düsseldorf, D-40225 Düsseldorf, Germany
[3] Institute of Anatomy II, Heinrich-Heine-Universität, Düsseldorf, D-40225 Düsseldorf, Germany

Abstract. We compute the influence of a vertex on the connectivity structure of a directed network by using Shapley value theory. In general, the computation of such ratings is highly inefficient. We show how the computation can be managed for many practically interesting instances by a decomposition of large networks into smaller parts. For undirected networks, we introduce an algorithm that computes all vertex ratings in linear time, if the graph is cycle composed or chordal.

1 Motivation and Introduction

This work is originally motivated by the analysis of networks that represent neural connections in a brain. The cerebral cortical sheet can be divided into many different areas according to several parcellation schemes [4, 9, 20]. The primate cortex forms a network of considerable complexity depending on the degree of resolution. Information forwarding is usually accompanied by the possibility to respond. Thus, the corresponding networks are generally strongly connected. From a systems point of view, it is a great challenge to analyze the influence of a single area to the connectivity structure of the hole system. Such information could be helpful to understand the functional consequences of a lesion.

We measure the influence of a vertex on the connectivity structure of a directed graph $G = (V_G, E_G)$ by a function ϕ based on the Shapley value theory, which was originally developed within game theory[1], see [16]. Our function ϕ is parameterized by a so-called *characteristic function* denoted by f_G. It counts for a set of vertices $V' \subseteq V_G$ the number of strongly connected components in the subgraph of G induced by the vertices of V'. In general, a characteristic function is a mapping from the subsets of a set of abstract objects N to the real numbers $\mathbb{R}$. The application of Shapley value computations to graphs was first done by Myerson in [10], who considered only undirected graphs. For a characteristic function $h : 2^{V_G} \to \mathbb{R}$ defined on vertex sets, Myerson analyzed

[1] In game theory literature the argument of ϕ is a game (usually denoted by letter v) over an abstract set of players N and the result is a vector of $\mathbb{R}^N$. Since we consider graphs, we prefer to use letter v for vertices rather for functions.

Please use the following format when citing this chapter:

Abraham, M., Kötter, R., Krumnack, A., Wanke, E., 2006, in International Federation for Information Processing, Volume 209, Fourth IFIP International Conference on Theoretical Computer Science-TCS 2006, eds. Navarro, G., Bertossi, L., Kohayakwa, Y., (Boston: Springer), pp. 283–298.

A Connectivity Rating for Vertices in Networks

Marco Abraham[1], Rolf Kötter[2,3], Antje Krumnack[1], and Egon Wanke[1]

[1] Institute of Computer Science, Heinrich-Heine-Universität, Düsseldorf, D-40225 Düsseldorf, Germany
[2] [illegible] Heinrich-Heine-Universität, Düsseldorf, D-40225 Düsseldorf, Germany
[3] [illegible] Heinrich-Heine-Universität, Düsseldorf, D-40225 Düsseldorf, Germany

[illegible] compute the importance of a vertex on the connectivity [illegible] and [illegible] defined accurately using Shapley value theory. In general [illegible] computation of such a rating is highly inefficient, we show how [illegible] the computation can be made [illegible] for many practically interesting in[illegible] [illegible] by a decomposition of large networks into smaller parts. For undirected networks we introduce a [illegible] that computes all vertex [illegible] in [illegible] time, if the graph is [illegible] composed or chordal.

1 Motivation and Introduction

This work is [illegible] motivated by the analysis of networks that represent neural connections in a brain. [illegible] the cortex [illegible] can be divided into many [illegible] areas according to [illegible] [illegible] [2, 9, 10] [illegible] [illegible] [illegible] network of [illegible] dependent on the [illegible] [illegible] [illegible] [illegible] [illegible] [illegible] the [illegible] [illegible] to respond. Thus the [illegible] [illegible] [illegible] [illegible] [illegible] [illegible] to [illegible] the influence [illegible] [illegible] Such information [illegible] [illegible] of a lesion.

We [illegible] [illegible] on the connectivity structure of a [illegible] based on [illegible] [illegible] theory, [illegible]

[illegible]

[illegible] values [illegible] to games was [illegible] by [illegible] [illegible] [illegible] graph [illegible] [illegible] vertex sets, Myerson analyzed

[1] [illegible] the [illegible] [illegible] (usually denoted by [illegible]) [illegible] vector of $\mathbb{R}^N$. Since we consider [illegible] [illegible] [illegible] functions.

[illegible] Wanke, E., 2006, in International Federation for Information Processing, Volume [illegible], Fourth IFIP International Conference on Theoretical Computer Science-TCS 2006, eds. [illegible] (Boston: Springer), pp. [illegible]–298.

a carrier C of f is again a carrier of f. The objects outside a carrier do not contribute anything to the computations by f.

The *sum* (*superposition*) of two characteristic functions f and g, defined by $(f+g)(S) = f(S) + g(S)$, is again a characteristic function. Let π be any permutation of N, that is, π is a one to one mapping of N to itself. For a set $S \subset N$ let $\pi(S) = \{\pi(x) \mid x \in S)$ be the image of S under π. Let f_π be the characteristic function defined by $f_\pi(S) = f(\pi^{-1}(S))$.

To rate the objects of N with respect to a characteristic function f, we use a function ϕ that associates with every characteristic function f a *rating function* $\phi_f : N \to \mathbb{R}$ such that

(Axiom 1:) for every permutation π of N and all $x \in N$,

$$\phi_{f_\pi}(\pi(x)) = \phi_f(x),$$

(Axiom 2:) for every carrier C of f,

$$\sum_{x \in C} \phi_f(x) = f(C),$$

and
(Axiom 3:) for any two characteristic functions f and g,

$$\phi_{f+g} = \phi_f + \phi_g.$$

Shapley has shown in [16] that function ϕ is uniquely defined by the three axioms above. He has also shown that the rating of an object with respect to a characteristic function f is computable by

$$\phi_f(x) = \sum_{S \subseteq N,\ x \in S} \frac{(|S|-1)!\ (|N|-|S|)!}{|N|!} (f(S) - f(S - \{x\})), \tag{1}$$

where $|S|$ and $|N|$ denote the size of S and C, respectively, or alternatively by

$$\phi_f(x) = \frac{1}{|N|!} \sum_{\pi \in \Pi_N} (f(m(\pi, x) \cup \{x\}) - f(m(\pi, x))), \tag{2}$$

where Π_N is the set of all one to one mappings (*enumerations*) $\pi : N \to \{1, \ldots, |N|\}$ and

$$m(\pi, x) = \{y \in N \mid \pi(y) < \pi(x)\}$$

is the set of all $y \in N$ arranged on the left side of x.

3 A vertex rating for directed graphs

We now define a characteristic function f_G to rate the vertices in directed graphs. The rating will measure the influence of a vertex on the connectivity

[illegible] (in a carrier [illegible]) the objects outside a carrier do not contribute anything to the computations [illegible].

[illegible] (superposition) of two characteristic functions f and g, defined by $(f+g)(S) = f(S) + g(S)$ [illegible] a characteristic function. Let π be any [illegible] of N [illegible] mapping of N to itself. For a set $S \subseteq N$ [illegible] image of S under π. Let f_π be the characteristic function [illegible] $= f(\pi^{-1}(S))$.

[illegible] of N [illegible] characteristic function f [illegible] characteristic function f [illegible]

[illegible] permutation [illegible] all $i \in N$

[illegible] $= \varphi_i(f)$.

[illegible] for every carrier C of f [illegible]

$$\sum_{i \in C} [illegible]$$

[illegible] for any two characteristic functions f and g, [illegible]

[illegible]

Shapley [illegible] is the only function [illegible] satisfying the three [illegible] the value [illegible] has the form:

$$\varphi_i(f) = \sum [illegible] \frac{[illegible]}{|N|!} [illegible] \qquad (1)$$

where $|S|$ and $|N|$ denote the size of [illegible] respectively [illegible]

[illegible]

[illegible] all [illegible]

[illegible] $|N|$ [illegible]

is the [illegible] of all [illegible] on the left side of [illegible]

3 A value rating for directed graphs

We now [illegible] function [illegible] to rate the vertices in directed graphs. [illegible] will measure the [illegible] of a vertex [illegible] on the connectivity

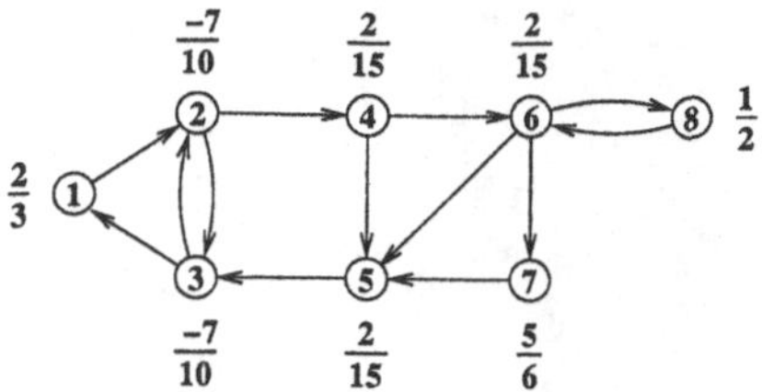

Fig. 1. The vertex rating ϕ_{f_G} for a directed graph G with 8 vertices. The smaller the rating of a vertex the greater its importance to the connectivity of the graph.

$b(V') = \{b(u) \mid u \in V'\}$ is the image of V' under b. This implies $\phi_{f_G}(v) = \phi_{f_{G'}}(b(v))$ for all vertices $v \in V$. Let $V' \subseteq V_G$ be any set of vertices of G. Graph G is called V'-*symmetric* if for every pair of vertices $v_1, v_2 \in V'$ there is an isomorphism b of G to G itself such that $b(v_1) = v_2$. In V'-symmetric graphs all vertices $v \in V'$ have the same rating. If two vertices v_1, v_2 have the same neighborhood, i.e., if $\{u \mid (u, v_1) \in E_G\} = \{u \mid (u, v_2) \in E_G\}$ and $\{u \mid (v_1, u) \in E_G\} = \{u \mid (v_2, u) \in E_G\}$, then G obviously is $\{v_1, v_2\}$-symmetric. Figure 2 shows some examples of partially symmetric graphs.

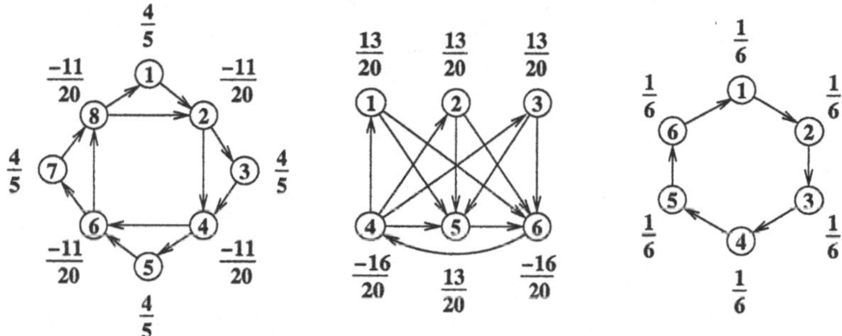

Fig. 2. The graph to the left is $\{v_1, v_3, v_5, v_7\}$-symmetric and $\{v_2, v_4, v_6, v_8\}$-symmetric, the graph in the middle is $\{v_1, v_2, v_3\}$-symmetric, and the graph to the right is $\{v_1, v_2, v_3, v_4, v_5, v_6\}$-symmetric.

The computation of a vertex rating $\phi_{f_G}(v)$ by Equation 1 or Equation 2 is highly inefficient. The number of subsets and the number of enumerations increase exponentially in the number of vertices of G. To handle the computation of ϕ_{f_G} for many practically interesting instances we will introduce a method to decompose a large graph into smaller parts. This decomposition will allow us to compute efficiently the ratings of vertices of the original graph by using the ratings of the vertices of smaller subgraphs. Our decomposition method will be introduced by the following two lemmas and Theorem 1.

The first lemma shows that the computation of a rating $\phi_{f_G}(v)$ for which the arguments of f_G are restricted to vertices of a subset $V' \subseteq V_G$ yields the computation of $\phi_{f_{G|_{V'}}}(v)$.

We will now define a property of a vertex pair u, v that allows us to compute independently the rating for two vertices u and v. That is, the rating of u in G will be equal to the rating of u in graph G without v.

Definition 1. *Let $G = (V_G, E_G)$ be a directed graph and $u, v \in V_G$ be two non-adjacent vertices, that is, neither (u, v) nor (v, u) is an edge of G. Vertex u and vertex v are* strongly separable *in G if for every strongly connected induced subgraph $H = (V_H, E_H)$ of G which contains u and v there is a strongly connected subgraph $J = (V_J, E_J)$ of H without u and v such that $H|_{V_H - V_J}$ has no path from u to v and no path from v to u.*

For the proof of the next lemma we need the notion of an undirected graph. In an *undirected graph* $G = (V_G, E_G)$ the edge set is a subset of $\{\{u, v\} \mid u, v \in V_G,\ u \neq v\}$. Analogously to the definitions for directed graphs, an *undirected path* of length k, $k \geq 1$, is a sequence $p = (v_1, \ldots, v_k)$ of k distinct vertices such that $\{v_i, v_{i+1}\} \in E_G$ for $i = 1, \ldots, k-1$. An undirected path is called an *undirected cycle* if G additionally has edge $\{v_k, v_1\}$ and the path has at least three vertices. The subgraph of G induced by a vertex set $V' \subseteq V_G$ has edge set $E_G \cap \{\{u, v\} \mid u, v \in V',\ u \neq v\}$. A graph is *connected* if there is a path between every pair of vertices, a *connected component* is a maximal connected subgraph, a *forest* is an undirected graph without cycles, and a *tree* is a connected forest.

Lemma 2. *Let $G = (V_G, E_G)$ be a directed graph and $V_H, V_J \subseteq V_G$ be two vertex sets such that $V_H \cup V_J = V_G$ and for every edge $(v_1, v_2) \in E_G$ both vertices are in V_H or in V_J, or in both sets. Let $H = G|_{V_H}$, $J = G|_{V_J}$, and $I = G|_{V_H \cap V_J}$. If every pair of vertices $u \in V_H - V_J$, $v \in V_J - V_H$ is strongly separable in G, then for every vertex set $V' \subseteq V_G$,*

$$f_G(V') = f_H(V' \cap V_H) + f_J(V' \cap V_J) - f_I(V' \cap V_I).$$

Proof. Let $V' \subseteq V_G$ be any set of vertices of G. Consider the following undirected graph $T = (V_T, E_T)$ with vertex set

$$V_T = \mathrm{SCC}(H|_{V'}) \cup \mathrm{SCC}(J|_{V'})$$

such that two vertices of V_T are connected by an undirected edge if and only if the two strongly connected components have at least one common vertex. If two distinct strongly connected components of V_T are connected by an undirected edge in T then one of them has to be from $\mathrm{SCC}(H|_{V'})$ and the other has to be from $\mathrm{SCC}(J|_{V'})$. Furthermore, for every strongly connected component C of $\mathrm{SCC}(I|_{V'})$, there is exactly one strongly connected component C_1 of $\mathrm{SCC}(H|_{V'})$ and exactly one strongly connected component C_2 of $\mathrm{SCC}(J|_{V'})$, and the common vertices of C_1 and C_2 are exactly the vertices of C.

Since every pair of vertices $u \in V_H - V_J$, $v \in V_J - V_H$ is strongly separable in G, the undirected graph T has no cycles, that is, T is a forest. The number of connected components of T (the number of trees of forest T) is equivalent to the number of strongly connected components of G. The number of connected

We will [illegible] the [illegible] property [illegible] that allows us to compute independently [illegible] rating for [illegible] and v. That [illegible] the rating of [illegible] in G will be equal to [illegible] rating of [illegible] in graph G without [illegible].

Definition [illegible] $G = (V, E)$ be a [illegible] graph and $u, v \in V$ be two [illegible] vertices [illegible] neither [illegible] is an edge of G. [illegible] strongly separable [illegible] [illegible] connected [illegible] directed [illegible] graph [illegible] [illegible] components [illegible]

[illegible] undirected [illegible] In [illegible] the edge set [illegible] set of $\{(u, v)$ [illegible] [illegible] to the definitions [illegible] graphs, an undirected path of length [illegible] is a sequence [illegible] of distinct vertices such that [illegible] An undirected path is called an [illegible] and the path has at least [illegible] edge set [illegible] there is a path between [illegible] connected subgra[illegible] [illegible] graph without cycles [illegible] is a connected forest.

Lemma 2 [illegible] $G = (V, E)$ be a [illegible] graph and [illegible] such that [illegible] for [illegible]

$$[illegible]$$

Proof. [illegible] Consider the [illegible] graph [illegible] set

[illegible]

[illegible] connected [illegible] and one [illegible] connected [illegible] common vertex [illegible] connected by an undirected edge [illegible] and the other [illegible] strongly connected compo[illegible] connected component [illegible] exactly one strongly connected component [illegible] vertices of [illegible] strongly separable in the undirected graph [illegible] is a forest. The number of connected components of [illegible] is equivalent to the number of strongly connected components [illegible] The number of connected

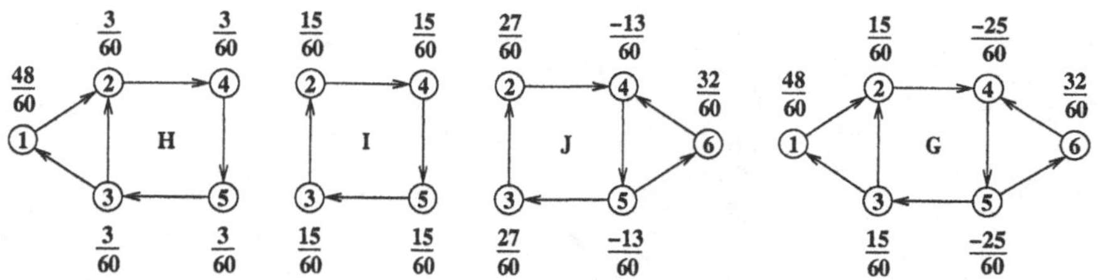

Fig. 3. Four graphs $G = (V_G, E_G)$, $H = G|_{V_H}$, $J = G|_{V_J}$, and $I = G|_{V_H \cap V_J}$ such that $V_H, V_J \subseteq V_G$, $V_H \cup V_J = V_G$, and for every edge $(v_1, v_2) \in E_G$ both vertices are in V_H or in V_G, or in both sets. Vertex pair $v_1 \in V_H - V_J$, $v_6 \in V_J - V_H$ is strongly separable in G.

polynomial time algorithms which decides whether two vertices in a directed graph are not strongly separable, unless P = NP. The NP-hardness follows by a simple reduction from the satisfiability problem. The terms we use in describing this problem are the following.

Let $X = \{x_1, \ldots, x_n\}$ be a set of *Boolean variables*. A *truth assignment* for X is a function $t : X \to \{\text{true}, \text{false}\}$. If $t(x_i) = \text{true}$ we say variable x_i is *true* under t; if $t(x_i) = \text{false}$ we say variable x_i is *false* under t. If x_i is a variable of X, then x_i and $\overline{x_i}$ are *literals* over X. Literal x_i is true under t if and only if variable x_i is true under t; literal $\overline{x_i}$ is true under t if and only if variable x_i is false under t. A *clause* over X is a set of literals over X, for example $\{x_1, \overline{x_2}, x_4\}$. It represents the disjunction of literals which is *satisfied* by a truth assignment t if and only if at least one of its literals is true under t. A collection $\mathcal{C}$ of clauses over X is satisfiable if and only if there is a truth assignment t that simultaneously satisfies all clauses of $\mathcal{C}$.

The satisfiability problem, denoted by SAT, is specified as follows. Given a set X of variables and a collection $\mathcal{C}$ of clauses over X. Is there a satisfying truth assignment for $\mathcal{C}$? This problem is NP-complete even for the case that every clause of $\mathcal{C}$ has exactly three distinct literals (3-SAT, for short).

Theorem 2. *The problem to decide whether two vertices u, v of a directed graph G are not strongly separable is NP-complete.*

Proof. Let us first illustrate that the problem belongs to NP. Two vertices u and v are not strongly separable in G if and only if G has a strongly connected induced subgraph $G' = (V_{G'}, E_{G'})$ that includes u and v such that $G'|_{V_{G'} - \{u,v\}}$ has no strongly connected subgraph $G'' = (V_{G''}, E_{G''})$ such that in $G'|_{V_{G'} - V_{G''}}$ there is no path from u to v and no path from v to u. Without loss of generality we can assume that G'' is a strongly connected component of $G'|_{V_{G'} - \{u,v\}}$. So we can non-deterministically consider every strongly connected subgraph G' of G that includes u and v. Then we can verify in polynomial time for every strongly connected component $G'' = (V_{G''}, E_{G''})$ of $G'|_{V_{G'} - \{u,v\}}$ whether $G'|_{V_{G'} - V_{G''}}$ has no path from u to v and no path from v to u. Thus, the problem to decide whether two vertices u, v are not strongly separable belongs to NP.

at least one cross edge (u', v'). In this case it is easy to destroy all paths from u to v and all path from v to u by removing a cycle that includes the edge (d, a) and the cross edge (u', v'). Thus u and v are strongly separable. □

Theorem 2 can be used to prove that deciding whether two vertices have a different rating is NP-hard. Consider again the graph $G(X, C)$ with the two vertices u and v constructed for an instance (X, C) of 3-SAT as in the proof of Theorem 2. Let $G'(X, C)$ be the graph $G(X, C)$ without the vertex v and its incident edges. Then $\phi_{f_{G(X,C)}}(u) = \phi_{f_{G'(X,C)}}(u)$ if u and v are strongly separable in G, and $\phi_{f_{G(X,C)}}(u) < \phi_{f_{G'(X,C)}}(u)$ if u and v are not strongly separable in G.

Theorem 3. *The problem to decide whether $\phi_{f_G}(u) < \phi_{f_G}(v)$ for two vertices u, v of a directed graph G is NP-hard.*

Thus, an algorithm for the computation of ϕ_{f_G} can be used to decide an NP-hard as well as a co-NP-hard decision problem.

4 A vertex rating for undirected graphs

The vertex rating ϕ_{f_G} for directed graphs can simply be extended to undirected graphs. For an undirected graph G let $\text{dir}(G)$ be the directed graph we get if we replace every undirected edge $\{u, v\}$ by two directed edges (u, v) and (v, u). Let f_G now be the function from the subsets of V_G to the real numbers $\mathbb{R}$ such that for every $V' \subseteq V_G$, $f_G(V')$ is the number of connected components in the subgraph of G induced by the vertices of V'. That is, the rating of a vertex v in an undirected graph G is equal to the rating of v in the directed graph $\text{dir}(G)$.

Figure 5 shows an example of the vertex rating ϕ_{f_G} for an undirected graph G with vertex set $V_G = \{v_1, v_2, v_3, v_4, v_5, v_6, v_7, v_8\}$.

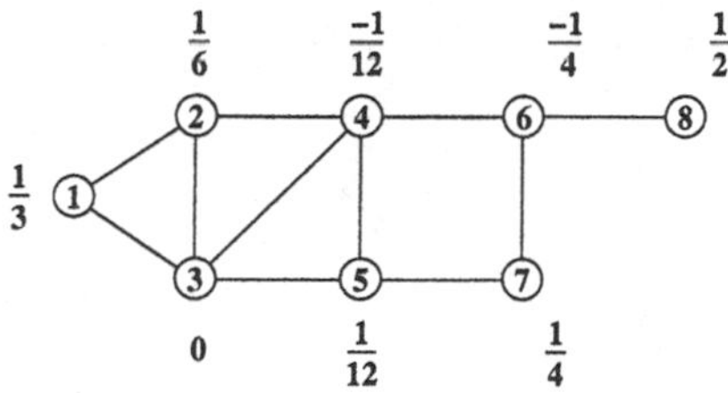

Fig. 5. The vertex rating ϕ_{f_G} for an undirected graph G with 8 vertices.

It is easy to verify that two vertices u, v of $\text{dir}(G)$ are not strongly separable if and only if G has a chordless cycle that includes u and v. A *chord* for a cycle $c = (u_1, \ldots, u_k)$ is an edge $\{u_i, u_j\}$ such that $2 \leq |i - j| \leq k - 2$. The problem of determining whether an undirected graph G contains a chordless cycle can be solved in linear time [3, 15, 17]. This is the well-known chordal

or least [illegible] is [illegible]. In this case it is easy to destroy all paths from v to [illegible] and all paths from [illegible] so that [illegible] a cycle that includes the edge (d, a) and the [illegible] edge [illegible]. Thus [illegible] are strongly separable. □

Theorem [illegible] can be used to get [illegible] that [illegible] two vertices have different [illegible] the graph $G(X, C)$ with the two vertices [illegible] of X, C of [illegible] as in the proof of Theorem [illegible] X [illegible] the graph [illegible] without the vertex [illegible] and its incident edges [illegible] and v are strongly separable in G [illegible] strongly separable in G.

Theorem [illegible] The [illegible] is decidable [illegible] of [illegible] of [illegible] graph G [illegible].

The [illegible] algorithm for [illegible] components [illegible] can be used to [illegible] in [illegible] as well as a [illegible] problem.

[illegible] vertex rating for undirected graphs

The [illegible] rating [illegible] for directed graphs can simply be extended to undirected graphs. For an undirected graph G let [illegible] be the directed graph we get if we replace every undirected edge [illegible] by two directed edges (u, v) and (v, u). [illegible] the [illegible] real numbers $\mathbb{R}$ such that [illegible] connected components in the [illegible] vertices of [illegible] rating [illegible] vertex in an undirected graph G [illegible] in the directed graph [illegible].

Figure [illegible] shows an example [illegible] vertex rating [illegible].

[illegible] The vertex rating [illegible] undirected graph G with [illegible] vertices [illegible]

It is easy to [illegible] that two vertices [illegible] of G are not strongly separable if and only if G has a [illegible] cycle that includes u and v [illegible] for a cycle [illegible] edge [illegible] that [illegible] $< k + 2$. The problem [illegible] whether [illegible] graph G contains a chordless cycle [illegible] solved in [illegible] time [illegible]. This is the well known chordal

vertex rating $\phi(u)$ for all vertices u of G is computable in linear time by the following simple procedure.

```
for every u ∈ V do {
    let φ_fG(u) := (deg(u) − 2) ∗ (−1/2); }
for every C ∈ 𝒞 do {
    for every u ∈ C do {
        let φ_fG(u) := φ_fG(u) + 1/|C|; } }
```

Since a vertex u is involved in $\text{degr}(u) - 2$ vertex identifications, the rating for u can be initialized by $(\deg(u) - 2) * (-\frac{1}{2})$. After that the algorithm adds for every cycle C the fraction $\frac{1}{|C|}$ to the ration of every vertex of C. Since the number of vertices in the sets of $\mathcal{C}$ is $\sum_{C \in \mathcal{C}} |C| = 2|E_G| - |V_G|$, the rating for all vertices in cycle composed graphs can be computed in linear time, if $\mathcal{C}$ is given.

The vertex sets of the cycles can be computed by the following algorithm. We assume that an empty vertex list is initially assigned to every edge. That is, every edge $\{u, v\}$ is initially represented as a pair $(\{u, v\}, \emptyset)$. An edge $e = (\{u, v\}, L)$ with a non-empty vertex list L represents a path between u and v passing the vertices of L. If G has a vertex u of degree 2 such that the two neighbors v, w of u are not adjacent, we remove vertex u and its two incident edges $(\{u, v\}, L_1)$, $(\{u, w\}, L_2)$ and insert a new edge $(\{v, w\}, L_1 \cup L_2 \cup \{u\})$ between u and v.

If G has a vertex u of degree 2 such that the two neighbors v, w of u are adjacent, the vertices of a cycle can be reported. Let $(\{u, v\}, L_1)$, $(\{u, w\}, L_2)$, $(\{v, w\}, L_3)$ be the three edges between the vertices u, v and w. The algorithm then reports vertex set $L_1 \cup L_2 \cup L_3 \cup \{u, v, w\}$. If graph G has no further edges than the three edges above, then all cycles are reported and the algorithm finishes. If graph G has some further edges and L_3 is non-empty, then the graph is not cycle composed. In any other case the algorithm removes the two edges $(\{u, v\}, L_1)$, $(\{u, w\}, L_2)$ and so forth. If this processing ends because there are no further vertices of degree 2, then the graph is also not cycle composed.

This algorithm computes the vertex sets of all cycles used to compose a cycle composed graph. The running time of this algorithm is $O(|V_G|^2)$ because we have to check for every vertex whether its two neighbors are adjacent. However, this problem can be eliminated by a simple trick which is also used in [19] for the recognition of outerplanar graphs. The trick is to check whether the two neighbors v, w of u are adjacent at the time when one of these two vertices v, w gets a degree of 2 or less. At that point the test can be done in a fixed number of steps and either a new edge is inserted or a cycle is reported. This modification yields a linear time algorithm for the computation of all cycles of a cycle composed graph. The following example shows a possible implementation.

The algorithm above stores in a set M all vertices of degree 2. Note that the degree of a vertex is always determined by the edges of E_G. For every vertex u adjacent with exactly two vertices v, w a new edge is inserted into a set denoted by E_{new} but not yet into edge set E_G of graph G. Whenever a vertex u of M is considered for processing it is first checked whether there are edges incident to u in set E_{new}. If E_{new} has an edge e incident to u then e will either be inserted into E_G (if the two vertices of e are not adjacent by some edge of E_G), or a cycle is reported (if the two vertices of e are adjacent by some edge of E_G). The test whether the two vertices of e are adjacent by some edge of E_G can be done in time $O(1)$ because u is one of the end vertices of e and has vertex degree 2. This proves the following theorem.

Theorem 5. *The vertex rating $\phi_{f_G}(u)$ for all vertices u of a cycle composed graph G is computable in linear time.*

The vertex rating ϕ_{f_G} is also computable in linear time for *chordal graphs*. An interesting characterization of chordal graphs is the existence of a *perfect elimination order*. Let $p = (u_1, \ldots, u_n)$ be an order of the $|V_G| = n$ vertices of $G = (V_G, E_G)$, and let $N(G, p, i)$ for $i = 1, \ldots, n$ be the set of neighbors u_j of vertex u_i with $i < j$,

$$N(G,p,i) := \{u_j \mid \{u_i, u_j\} \in E_G \ \wedge \ i < j\}.$$

The vertex order $p = (u_1, \ldots, u_n)$ is called a *perfect elimination order* (PEO) if the vertices of $N(G, p, i)$ for $i = 1, \ldots, n-1$ induce a complete subgraph of G.

Dirac [3], Fulkerson and Gross [5], and Rose [14] have shown that a graph G is chordal if and only if it has a perfect elimination order. Rose, Tarjan, and Lueker have shown in [15], that a perfect elimination order can be found in linear time if one exists. If a perfect elimination order $p = (v_1, \ldots, v_n)$ of the vertices of $G = (V_G, E_G)$ is given, then the vertex rating ϕ_{f_G} can be computed with Theorem 4 by the following algorithm. Note that, in a complete graph G with n vertices, $\phi_{f_G}(v) = \frac{1}{n}$ for every vertex of G, because G is V_G-symmetric.

1. let $\phi_{f_G}(v_n) := 1$;
2. for $i = n-1, \ldots, 1$ do {
3.   let $\phi_{f_G}(v_i) := \frac{1}{|N(G,p,i)|+1}$;
4.   for all $v \in N(G,p,i)$ do {
5.   let $\phi_{f_G}(v) := \phi_{f_G}(v) + \frac{1}{|N(G,p,i)|+1} - \frac{1}{|N(G,p,i)|}$; } }

The running time of this algorithm is linear in the size of G, because the assignment of Line 3 is done exactly $|V_G| - 1$ times and the assignment of line 5 is done exactly $|E_G|$ times. Since the perfect elimination order can be found in linear time, we get the following theorem.

Theorem 6. *The vertex rating $\phi_{f_G}(v)$ for all vertices v of a chordal graph G is computable in linear time.*

On PTAS for Planar Graph Problems

Xiuzhen Huang[1] and Jianer Chen[2]

[1] Department of Computer Science,
Arkansas State University,
State University, Arkansas 72467.
Email: xzhuang@csm.astate.edu
[2] Department of Computer Science,
Texas A&M University,
College Station, TX 77843.
Email: chen@cs.tamu.edu**

Abstract. Approximation algorithms for a class of planar graph problems, including PLANAR INDEPENDENT SET, PLANAR VERTEX COVER and PLANAR DOMINATING SET, were intensively studied. The current upper bound on the running time of the polynomial time approximation schemes (PTAS) for these planar graph problems is of $2^{O(1/\epsilon)}n^{O(1)}$. Here we study the lower bound on the running time of the PTAS for these planar graph problems. We prove that there is no PTAS of time $2^{o(\sqrt{1/\epsilon})}n^{O(1)}$ for PLANAR INDEPENDENT SET, PLANAR VERTEX COVER and PLANAR DOMINATING SET unless an unlikely collapse occurs in parameterized complexity theory. For the gap between our lower bound and the current known upper bound, we specifically show that to further improve the upper bound on the running time of the PTAS for PLANAR VERTEX COVER, we can concentrate on PLANAR VERTEX COVER on planar graphs of degree bounded by three.

1 Introduction

There is intensive research work on a class of planar graph NP-hard optimization problems, such as PLANAR INDEPENDENT SET, PLANAR VERTEX COVER and PLANAR DOMINATING SET. Approximation algorithms for these planar graph problems and related problems were studied by researchers such as Bar-Yehuda and Even [5], Lipton and Tarjan [25], Baker [4], Eppstein [16], Grohe [20], Khanna and Motiwani [24], and Cai et al. [7]. The current upper bound on the running time of the polynomial time approximation scheme (PTAS) for these planar graph problems is of $2^{O(1/\epsilon)}n^{O(1)}$ [4, 25]. In this paper, we study the lower bound on the running time of the PTAS algorithms for these planar graph problems. Our work follows some recent research progress in parameterized complexity theory [10, 11], where strong computational lower bound results on the running time of the algorithms for $W[t]$-hard problems are derived, $t \geq 1$.

** This research is supported in part by US NSF under Grants CCR-0311590 and CCF-0430683.

Please use the following format when citing this chapter:

Huang, X., Chen, J., 2006, in International Federation for Information Processing, Volume 209, Fourth IFIP International Conference on Theoretical Computer Science-TCS 2006, eds. Navarro, G., Bertossi, L., Kohayakwa, Y., (Boston: Springer), pp. 299–313.

2 Terminologies in Approximation

For a reference of the theory of approximation, the readers are referred to the book [3]. In this section, we provide some basic terminologies for studying approximability and its relationship with parameterized complexity.

An *NP optimization problem* Q is a four-tuple (I_Q, S_Q, f_Q, opt_Q), where

1. I_Q is the set of input instances. It is recognizable in polynomial time;

2. For each instance $x \in I_Q$, $S_Q(x)$ is the set of feasible solutions for x, which is defined by a polynomial p and a polynomial time computable predicate π (p and π only depend on Q) as $S_Q(x) = \{y : |y| \leq p(|x|) \text{ and } \pi(x,y)\}$;

3. $f_Q(x, y)$ is the objective function mapping a pair $x \in I_Q$ and $y \in S_Q(x)$ to a non-negative integer. The function f_Q is computable in polynomial time;

4. $opt_Q \in \{\max, \min\}$. Q is called a *maximization problem* if $opt_Q = \max$, and a *minimization problem* if $opt_Q = \min$.

An *optimal solution* y_0 for an instance $x \in I_Q$ is a feasible solution in $S_Q(x)$ such that $f_Q(x, y_0) = opt_Q\{f_Q(x, z) \mid z \in S_Q(x)\}$. We will denote by $opt_Q(x)$ the value $opt_Q\{f_Q(x, z) \mid z \in S_Q(x)\}$.

An algorithm A is an *approximation algorithm* for an NP optimization problem $Q = (I_Q, S_Q, f_Q, opt_Q)$ if, for each input instance x in I_Q, A returns a feasible solution $y_A(x)$ in $S_Q(x)$. The solution $y_A(x)$ has an *approximation ratio* $r(n)$ if it satisfies the following condition:

$$opt_Q(x)/f_Q(x, y_A(x)) \leq r(|x|) \text{ if } Q \text{ is a maximization problem}$$
$$f_Q(x, y_A(x))/opt_Q(x) \leq r(|x|) \text{ if } Q \text{ is a minimization problem}$$

The approximation algorithm A has an *approximation ratio* $r(n)$ if for any instance x in I_Q, the solution $y_A(x)$ constructed by the algorithm A has an approximation ratio bounded by $r(|x|)$.

Definition 1. *An NP optimization problem Q has a polynomial-time approximation scheme (PTAS) if there is an algorithm A_Q that takes a pair (x, ϵ) as input, where x is an instance of Q and $\epsilon > 0$ is a real number, and returns a feasible solution y for x such that the approximation ratio of the solution y is bounded by $1 + \epsilon$, and for each fixed $\epsilon > 0$, the running time of the algorithm A_Q is bounded by a polynomial of $|x|$.*[4]

An NP optimization problem Q has a *fully polynomial-time approximation scheme* (FPTAS) if it has a PTAS A_Q such that the running time of A_Q is bounded by a polynomial of $|x|$ and $1/\epsilon$.

[4] There is an alternative definition for PTAS in which each $\epsilon > 0$ may correspond to a different approximation algorithm A_ϵ for Q [19]. The definition we adopt here may be called the *uniform PTAS*, by which a single approximation algorithm takes care of all values of ϵ. Note that most PTAS developed in the literature are uniform PTAS.

algorithm of time $O(2^{O(1/\epsilon)}n^{O(1)})$ for PLANAR INDEPENDENT SET, as an application of a separator theorem on planar graphs. Based on the outer-planarity of planar graphs, Baker [4] designed EPTAS algorithms of time $O(2^{O(1/\epsilon)}n)$ for several famous NP-hard optimization problems on planar graphs, such as PLANAR VERTEX COVER, PLANAR INDEPENDENT SET, and PLANAR DOMINATING SET.

In [6], Cai and Chen proved that if an optimization problem has a fully polynomial-time approximation scheme (FPTAS), then the corresponding parameterized problem is fixed-parameter tractable (in FPT). Later this result was extended in [9] by Cesati and Trevisan: All optimization problems that have efficient polynomial time approximation schemes (EPTAS) have their parameterized problems in FPT. Therefore, the parameterized versions of these aforementioned optimization problems, PLANAR VERTEX COVER, PLANAR INDEPENDENT SET, and PLANAR DOMINATING SET, are in FPT.

Alber et. al [2] designed parameterized algorithms of time $2^{O(\sqrt{k})}n^{O(1)}$ for the parameterized versions of the above NP-hard optimization problems. A lot of research has been done on these problems to try to further improve the time complexity of the parameterized algorithms. Interested readers are referred to [1, 23, 17, 18].

Cai et. al [8] proved the following lower bound result for the parameterized algorithms of these problems:

Lemma 1. *(Lemma 5.1 in [8])* PLANAR VERTEX COVER, PLANAR INDEPENDENT SET, *and* PLANAR DOMINATING SET *do not have parameterized algorithms of time* $2^{o(\sqrt{k})}n^{O(1)}$, *unless* VERTEX COVER-3 *has* $2^{o(k)}n^{O(1)}$*-time parameterized algorithms.*

The class SNP introduced by Papadimitriou and Yannakakis [26] contains many well-known NP-hard problems including, for any fixed $q \geq 3$, CNF q-SAT, q-COLORABILITY, q-SET COVER, and VERTEX COVER, CLIQUE, and INDEPENDENT SET [22]. It is commonly believed that it is unlikely that all problems in SNP are solvable in subexponential time. Impagliazzo, Paturi and Zane [22] studied the class SNP and identified a group of SNP-complete problems under the serf-reduction, such that if any of these SNP-complete problems is solvable in subexponential time, then all problems in SNP are solvable in subexponential time. This group of SNP-complete problems under the serf-reduction includes the problems CNF q-SAT, q-COLORABILITY, q-SET COVER, and VERTEX COVER, CLIQUE, and INDEPENDENT SET.

We have:

Lemma 2. *(Theorem 3.3 in [13]) The* VERTEX COVER-3 *problem can be solved in* $2^{o(k)}n^{O(1)}$ *time if and only if the* VERTEX COVER *problem can be solved in* $2^{o(k)}n^{O(1)}$ *time.*

Therefore Lemma 1 could be restate as:

VERTEX COVER problem Q. The running time of the algorithm $A_{\leq}$ is dominated by that of the algorithm A_Q, which is bounded by $2^{o(\sqrt{1/\epsilon})}n^{O(1)} = 2^{o(\sqrt{k})}n^{O(1)}$. Thus, the parameterized version $Q_{\leq}$ of the PLANAR VERTEX COVER problem is solvable in time $2^{o(\sqrt{k})}n^{O(1)}$. Therefore, the result in the theorem follows from Lemma 3.

The proofs for PLANAR INDEPENDENT SET and PLANAR DOMINATING SET are similar and hence are omitted.

Corollary 1. PLANAR VERTEX COVER, PLANAR INDEPENDENT SET, *and* PLANAR DOMINATING SET *have no PTAS of running time* $2^{o(\sqrt{1/\epsilon})}n^{O(1)}$, *where* $\epsilon > 0$ *is the given error bound, unless all SNP problems are solvable in subexponential time.*

By a comparison with the upper bound on the running time of the EPTAS algorithms for these planar graph problems in Baker [4], which is $2^{O(1/\epsilon)}n^{O(1)}$ (also in Lipton and Tarjan [25]), we can see that there is a gap between the upper bound result and our lower bound result in Theorem 1. To come up with new approaches to improve the upper bound on the running time of the EPTAS algorithms in [4] will be interesting research. To study this issue, we concentrate on the PLANAR VERTEX COVER problem in the next section.

4 Upper Bound on Running Time of PTAS for Planar Vertex Cover

In this section, we study the PTAS algorithms for the VERTEX COVER problem on planar graphs of degree bounded by 3, abbreviated as P-VC-3. The VERTEX COVER problem on general planar graphs is abbreviated as P-VC.

From the proof of Theorem 1, we get the following lemma:

Lemma 4. *The* P-VC-3 *problem has no EPTAS of running time* $2^{o(\sqrt{1/\epsilon})}n^{O(1)}$, *where* $\epsilon > 0$ *is the given error bound, unless the* P-VC-3 *problem has a parameterized algorithm of time* $2^{o(\sqrt{k})}n^{O(1)}$.

It is well known that a planar embedding of a planar graph can be constructed in linear time [21]. We define an operation, called the *unfolding operation*, based on a planar embedding of a planar graph.

Definition 5. *Suppose that* G *is a planar graph with a planar embedding* $\pi(G)$, *and that* v *is a degree-*d *vertex in* G, *where* $d > 3$, *with neighbors* $v_1, v_2, \ldots, v_d$, *such that when one traverses around the vertex* v *on the embedding* $\pi(G)$, *the edges incident to* v *are in the cyclic order* $[v, v_1], [v, v_2], \ldots, [v, v_d]$. *The unfolding operation on the vertex* v *will do the following: remove the vertex* v *from* $\pi(G)$, *and add a path of length* $2d - 5$:

$$P_v = \{y_1, x_1, y_2, x_2, \ldots, y_{d-3}, x_{d-3}, y_{d-2}\}$$

VERTEX COVER [illegible] Q [illegible] is dominated [illegible] that of [illegible] algorithm [illegible] bounded by [illegible] $\varepsilon^{O(1)} = 2^{o(\sqrt{k})} n^{O(1)}$. Thus, [illegible] PLANAR VERTEX COVER problem is solvable in time $2^{o(\sqrt{k})} n^{O(1)}$. Therefore, the result in the theorem follows from [illegible].

The proofs for PLANAR INDEPENDENT SET and PLANAR DOMINATING SET [illegible].

Theorem [illegible]. [illegible] VERTEX COVER, PLANAR INDEPENDENT SET, PLANAR DOMINATING SET [illegible] time $2^{o(\sqrt{1/\varepsilon})} n^{O(1)}$, where [illegible] is the given [illegible] problems [illegible] polynomial time.

By a comparison with the [illegible] time of the EPTAS [illegible] for these planar graph problems in Baker [4], which is [illegible] (also [illegible] and Tarjan [illegible]), we can see that there is a gap between the upper bound results and the lower bound result [illegible] Theorem [illegible] with [illegible] the running time of the EPTAS [illegible] [4] [illegible]. To study this issue, we concentrate on [illegible] VERTEX COVER problem in the next section.

4 [illegible] Bound on Running Time of PTAS for Planar [illegible] Cover

In this section [illegible] the PTAS algorithm [illegible] VERTEX COVER problem on planar [illegible] as [illegible] VERTEX COVER [illegible] planar graphs [illegible].

From the [illegible] the following lemma.

Lemma [illegible]. [illegible] problem [illegible] running time [illegible] where [illegible] problem [illegible] $O(n)$.

It is well known that [illegible] planar graph [illegible] can be constructed in [illegible] [illegible] called the unfolding operations based on [illegible] planar embedding [illegible] graphs.

Definition [illegible]. [illegible] planar embedding $\pi(G)$ [illegible] v with neighbors [illegible] embedding $\pi(G)$ [illegible] The [illegible] operation [illegible] remove the vertex [illegible] $\pi(G)$ [illegible]

In the following discussion, *cleaning* a vertex cover C_2 means that we apply the processing of clean-one and clean-two on C_2. After the cleaning process, we say that the vertex cover C_2 is *clean*. By the above discussion, in a clean vertex cover C_2 of the graph G_2, we have

Claim. Either all $d-3$ vertices x_i, $1 \le i \le d-3$, are in C_2 and none of the $d-2$ vertices y_j, $1 \le j \le d-2$, is in C_2; or all $d-2$ vertices y_j, $1 \le j \le d-2$, are in C_2 and none of the $d-3$ vertices x_i, $1 \le i \le d-3$, is in C_2.

Let C_1 be any vertex cover of the graph G_1 such that C_1 has k_1 vertices. If $v \in C_1$ (so v covers the d edges $[v, v_1]$, ..., $[v, v_d]$ in G), then by replacing v in C_1 by the $d-2$ vertices $y_1, y_2, \ldots, y_{d-2}$ in G_2, we obviously get a clean vertex cover C_2 for the graph G_2. The vertex cover C_2 has $k_1 + (d-3)$ vertices. On the other hand, if v is not in C_1 (so the edges $[v, v_1]$, ..., $[v, v_d]$ must be covered by the vertices v_1, ..., v_d in C_1), then by adding the $d-3$ vertices $x_1, x_2, \ldots, x_{d-3}$ to C_1, we get a clean vertex cover C_2 for the graph G_2 and C_2 contains $k_1 + (d-3)$ vertices. In conclusion, from a vertex cover of k_1 vertices for the graph G_1, we can always construct a (clean) vertex cover of $k_1 + (d-3)$ vertices for the graph G_2.

Conversely, suppose that we are given a clean vertex cover C_2 of the graph G_2, where C_2 has k_2 vertices. If C_2 contains the $d-2$ vertices $y_1, y_2, \ldots, y_{d-2}$, then replacing the $d-2$ vertices $y_1, y_2, \ldots, y_{d-2}$ in C_2 by a single vertex v gives a vertex cover of $k_2 - (d-3)$ vertices for the graph G_1. On the other hand, if C_2 contains the $d-3$ vertices $x_1, x_2, \ldots, x_{d-3}$, then removing these $d-3$ vertices from C_2 gives a vertex cover of $k_2 - (d-3)$ vertices for the graph G_1. In conclusion, from a vertex cover of k_2 vertices for the graph G_2, we can always construct a vertex cover of $k_2 - (d-3)$ vertices for the graph G_1.

Now suppose that the set of vertices of degree larger than 3 in the graph G_1 is $V_{>3} = \{u_1, u_2, \ldots, u_r\}$. Denote by $deg(u)$ the degree of the vertex u. Inductively, suppose that the graph G_{i+1} is obtained from the graph G_i by unfolding the vertex u_i, for $1 \le i \le r$. Note that the graph G_r has its degree bounded by 3, and we say that the graph G_r is obtained from the graph G_1 by *unfolding all vertices of degree larger than 3.* Let C_1 be a vertex cover for the graph G_1 with $|C_1| = k_1$. By the above discussion, we can construct from C_1 a vertex cover C_2 of $k_1 + (deg(u_1) - 3)$ vertices for the graph G_2; then from C_2, we can construct a vertex cover C_3 of $k_1 + (deg(u_1) - 3) + (deg(u_2) - 3)$ vertices for the graph G_3, ..., and finally we construct a vertex cover C_r of $k_1 + \sum_{i=1}^{r}(deg(u_i) - 3)$ vertices for the graph G_r.

On the other hand, let C_r be a vertex cover of k_r vertices for the graph G_r. First we clean C_r to get a clean vertex cover C_r' for G_r. Since cleaning does not increase the size of the vertex cover, we have $|C_r'| \le |C_r| = k_r$. Now by the above discussion, we can get a vertex cover C_{r-1} of $|C_r'| - (deg(u_r) - 3) \le k_r - (deg(u_r) - 3)$ vertices for the graph G_{r-1}. Cleaning the vertex cover C_{r-1} gives us a clean vertex cover C_{r-1}' for the graph G_{r-1}, and by the above processing we can get a vertex cover C_{r-2} of $|C_{r-1}'| - (deg(u_{r-1}) - 3) \le k_r - (deg(u_r) - 3) -$

$(deg(u_{r-1}) - 3)$ vertices for the graph G_{r-2}, ..., finally, we will construct a vertex cover of at most $k_r - \sum_{i=1}^{r}(deg(u_i) - 3)$ vertices for the graph G_1.

In particular, the above discussion enables us to derive a relation between the minimum vertex covers for the graphs G_1 and G_r. Let k_1 and k_r be the sizes of minimum vertex covers of the graph G_1 and G_r, respectively. By the above discussion, from a minimum vertex cover for the graph G_1, we can construct a vertex cover of $k_1 + \sum_{i=1}^{r}(deg(u_i) - 3)$ vertices for the graph G_r. Therefore, $k_1 + \sum_{i=1}^{r}(deg(u_i) - 3) \geq k_r$. On the other hand, from a minimum vertex cover of the graph G_r, we can construct a vertex cover of no more than $k_r - \sum_{i=1}^{r}(deg(u_i) - 3)$ vertices for the graph G_1, thus $k_r - \sum_{i=1}^{r}(deg(u_i) - 3) \geq k_1$. Combining these two relations, we get $k_1 + \sum_{i=1}^{r}(deg(u_i) - 3) = k_r$.

Summarizing the above discussion, we get the following:

Claim. Let G_1 be a graph in which the set of vertices of degree larger than 3 is $V_{>3}$. Let G_r be a graph obtained by unfolding all vertices of degree larger than 3 in G_1. Then from a vertex cover C_1 for the graph G_1, we can construct in polynomial time a vertex cover of $|C_1| + \sum_{u \in V_{>3}}(deg(u) - 3)$ vertices for the graph G_r; and from a vertex cover C_r for the graph G_r, we can construct in polynomial time a vertex cover of at most $|C_r| - \sum_{u \in V_{>3}}(deg(u) - 3)$ vertices for the graph G_1. Moreover, the size of a minimum vertex cover of the graph G_r is equal to the size of a minimum vertex cover of the graph G_1 plus $\sum_{u \in V_{>3}}(deg(u) - 3)$.

Using the unfolding operations, we can prove

Lemma 5. *The* P-VC-3 *problem has no parameterized algorithm of time* $2^{o(\sqrt{k})}n^{O(1)}$, *unless the* P-VC *problem has a parameterized algorithm of time* $2^{o(\sqrt{k})}n^{O(1)}$.

Proof. Suppose the P-VC-3 problem has a parameterized algorithm A of time $2^{o(\sqrt{k})}n^{O(1)}$. We have the following algorithm A' shown in Fig 3 for the P-VC problem.

We prove the algorithm A' is correct. By Claim 4, OPT_1 is a vertex cover for the graph G_1 with $|OPT_2| - \sum_{u \in V_{>3}}(deg(u) - 3)$ vertices and OPT_1 is computable in time $n^{O(1)}$. Since OPT_2 is a minimum vertex cover for the graph G_2, by Claim 4 again, a minimum vertex cover for the graph G_1 contains $|OPT_2| - \sum_{u \in V_{>3}}(deg(u) - 3)$ vertices. In conclusion, OPT_1 is a minimum vertex cover for the graph G_1.

We analysis the running time of A' in the following.

For the graph $G_1 = (V_1, E_1)$, $V_1 = V_{\leq 3} \cup V_{>3}$, where $|V_1| = n$ and $|E_1| = m$, we can always assume $|OPT_1| \geq n/2$ by applying the NT-theorem [12]. That is, the parameter $k \geq n/2$. After applying the unfolding operation on each $v \in V_{>3}$, we get the new planar graph $G_2 = (V_2, E_2)$ with degree bounded by 3. The construction of G_2 can be done in polynomial time.

For a planar graph with n vertices and m edges, we have [14]:

$$m \leq 3n - 6. \tag{1}$$

Algorithm A'

Input: A planar graph $G_1 = (V_1, E_1)$, $V_1 = V_{\leq 3} \cup V_{>3}$, and an integer $k > 0$.

Output: Output "Yes", if the size of the minimum vertex cover OPT_1 of G_1 satisfies $|OPT_1| \leq k$. Otherwise, output "No".

1. Let $V_{>3}$ be the set of all vertices of degree larger than 3 in the graph G_1. Construct a planar graph G_2 by unfolding all vertices of degree larger than 3 in G_1.

2. Run the algorithm A on the graph G_2 with the parameter $k_2 = 1, 2, ..., |V_2|$. We get a minimum vertex cover OPT_2 for the graph G_2.

3. Construct a vertex cover OPT_1 for the graph G_1 from OPT_2 such that $|OPT_1| = |OPT_2| - \sum_{u \in V_{>3}} (deg(u) - 3)$.

5. If $|OPT_1| \leq k$, **Return** "Yes"; Otherwise, **Return** "No".

Fig. 3. Parameterized algorithm for PLANAR VERTEX COVER.

By Equation 1, for the graph G_1, the total degree of all its vertices satisfies:

$$\sum_{v \in V_1} deg(v) = 2m \leq 2(3n - 6) < 6n, \tag{2}$$

We have

$$\begin{aligned} |V_2| = |V_{\leq 3}| + \sum_{v \in V_{>3}} ((deg(v) - 3) + (deg(v) - 2)) \\ < |V_{\leq 3}| + 2 \sum_{v \in V_{>3}} deg(v) \\ \leq |V_1| + 2 \sum_{v \in V_1} deg(v) \\ \leq n + 12n = 13n = O(n). \end{aligned}$$

Therefore, the calls to the algorithm A on the graph G_2 takes time $2^{o(\sqrt{|V_2|})}|V_2|^{O(1)} = 2^{o(\sqrt{n})}n^{O(1)} = 2^{o(\sqrt{k})}n^{O(1)}$. All the other steps of the algorithm A' takes polynomial time $n^{O(1)}$. Therefore the algorithm A' has running time $2^{o(\sqrt{k})}n^{O(1)}$.

Therefore, from Lemma 4, Lemma 5 and Theorem 1, we have

Theorem 2. *The* P-VC-3 *problem has no EPTAS of running time* $2^{o(\sqrt{1/\epsilon})}n^{O(1)}$, *where* $\epsilon > 0$ *is the given error bound, unless all SNP problems are solvable in subexponential time.*

$\mathcal{A}$-point [illegible]

Input: A planar [illegible] $k = \lceil \log_2 1/\epsilon \rceil$, and an integer $k > 0$.

Output: Output [illegible] the size of the minimum vertex cover OPT_1 of G_1 [illegible] satisfies [illegible] Otherwise, output [illegible]

[illegible] of all vertices of degree larger than 3 in the graph G_1 [illegible] construct [illegible] vertices of [illegible] larger than [illegible]

2. [illegible] We get a [illegible]

3. [illegible] vertex cover OPT_1 [illegible] such that [illegible]

4. [illegible] Return [illegible]

Fig. 3 [illegible] algorithm [illegible] PLANAR VERTEX COVER

[illegible] for the [illegible] all the vertices [illegible]

[illegible] (2)

We have

[illegible]

[illegible] calls the algorithm [illegible] graph [illegible] takes time $2^{O(\sqrt{k})}$ [illegible] Therefore [illegible] has running time $2^{O(\sqrt{k})} n^{O(1)}$.

Thus [illegible] from Lemma [illegible] Theorem 1, we have

Theorem [illegible] PTAS of running time $2^{O(\sqrt{1/\epsilon})} n^{O(1)}$, [illegible] unless [illegible] SNP problems are solvable in subexponential time.

$$\leq |OPT_1| + 6n$$
$$\leq |OPT_1| + 12|OPT_1|$$
$$\leq 13|OPT_1|.$$

Therefore,

$$|OPT_2| \leq 13|OPT_1|. \tag{3}$$

By Claim 4, we have

$$|OPT_1| = |OPT_2| - \sum_{u \in V_{>3}} (deg(u) - 3)$$

and

$$|C_1| \leq |C_2| - \sum_{u \in V_{>3}} (deg(u) - 3)$$

Therefore, we have

$$|C_2| - |C_1| \geq |OPT_2| - |OPT_1|$$

or equivalently

$$|C_2| - |OPT_2| \geq |C_1| - |OPT_1|$$

From this, we derive immediately

$$\begin{aligned} & |C_1|/|OPT_1| - 1 \\ = & (|C_1| - |OPT_1|)/|OPT_1| \\ \leq & (|C_2| - |OPT_2|)/|OPT_1| \\ \leq & 13(|C_2| - |OPT_2|)/|OPT_2| \\ = & 13(|C_2|/|OPT_2| - 1) \\ \leq & 13 * (\epsilon/13) \\ = & \epsilon. \end{aligned}$$

Here we have used the assumption that $C_2|/|OPT_2| \leq 1 + \epsilon' = 1 + \epsilon/13$, and the fact $|OPT_2| \geq 13|OPT_1|$.

The call of the algorithm A on the graph G_2 takes time $f(1/\epsilon')n^{O(1)}$. All the other steps of the algorithm B take polynomial time $n^{O(1)}$. Therefore, the running time of the algorithm B is $f(13/\epsilon)n^{O(1)}$, and the approximation ratio for the algorithm B is $1 + \epsilon$.

5 Summary

In this paper, we have proved lower bound results on the running time of the PTAS algorithms for a class of planar graph problems including PLANAR INDEPENDENT SET, PLANAR VERTEX COVER and PLANAR DOMINATING SET. We pointed out that there is a gap between our lower bound result and the current

16. Eppstein D (2000) Diameter and treewidth in minor-closed graph families, Algorithmica 27:275-291
17. Fomin FV and Thilikos DM (2003) Dominating sets in planar graphs: branch-width and exponential speed-up. Proc. of the Fourteenth Annual ACM-SIAM Symposium on Discrete Algorithms, pp. 168-177
18. Fomin FV and Thilikos DM (2004) A simple and fast approach for solving problems on planar graphs. Lecture Notes in Computer Science 2996:56-67
19. Garey M and Johnson D (1979) Computers and intractability: a guide to the theory of NP-Completeness. W. H. Freeman, New York
20. Grohe M (2003) Local tree-width, excluded minors, and approximation algorithms, Combinatorica 23:613-632
21. Hopcroft JE and Tarjan RE (1974) Efficient planarity testing. Journal of the ACM 21:549-568
22. Impagliazzo R, Paturi R, Zane F (2001) Which problems have strongly exponential complexity? Journal of Computer and System Sciences 63: 512-530
23. Kanj I, Perkovic L (2002) Improved parameterized algorithms for planar dominating set, Lecture Notes in Computer Science 2420:399-410
24. Khanna S, Motwani R (1996) Towards a Syntactic Characterization of PTAS, STOC 1996: 329-337
25. Lipton RJ, Tarjan RE (1980) Applications of a planar separator theorem. SIAM J. Comput. 9:615-627
26. Papadimitriou CH, Yannakakis M (1991) Optimization, approximation, and complexity classes. Journal of Computer and System Sciences 43: 425-440
27. Papadimitriou CH and Yannakakis M (1999) On the complexity of database queries. Journal of Computer and System Sciences 58:407-427

Index